Adapted City

MAXINE GOODMAN LEVIN
COLLEGE OF URBAN AFFAIRS

Cleveland State University

iety

. Ledebur,

Maxine Goodman Levin College of Urban Affairs
Cleveland State University

This new series focuses on key topics and emerging trends in urban
policy. Each volume is specially prepared for academic use, as well as for
specialists in the field.

THE ADAPTED CITY
Institutional Dynamics
and Structural Change
H. George Frederickson,
Gary A. Johnson, and
Curtis H. Wood

SUBURBAN SPRAWL
Private Decisions and Public Policy
Wim Wiewel and Joseph J. Persky, Editors

THE INFRASTRUCTURE OF PLAY
Building the Tourist City
Dennis R. Judd, Editor

The Adapted City

Institutional Dynamics and Structural Change

H. George Frederickson,
Gary A. Johnson, and
Curtis H. Wood

CITIES AND
CONTEMPORARY
SOCIETY

M.E.Sharpe
Armonk, New York
London, England

Library of Congress Cataloging-in-Publication Data

Frederickson, H. George.
  The adapted city : institutional dynamics and structural change / by
H. George Frederickson, Gary A. Johnson, and Curtis H. Wood.
     p. cm. — (Cities and contemporary society)
Includes bibliographical references and index.
ISBN 0-7656-1264-X (cloth: alk. paper) — ISBN 0-7656-1265-8 (pbk.: alk. paper)
  1. Municipal government—United States. I. Johnson, Gary A. (Gary Alan)
II. Wood, Curtis H. III. Title. IV. Series.

JS331.F74 2003
320.8'5'0973—dc21   2003000338

Printed in the United States of America

The paper used in this publication meets the minimum requirements of
American National Standard for Information Sciences
Permanence of Paper for Printed Library Materials,
ANSI Z 39.48-1984.

BM (c)   10   9   8   7   6   5   4   3   2   1
BM (p)   10   9   8   7   6   5   4   3   2   1

For the mayors, council members, managers,
and administrators who make American cities work

Contents

Tables and Figures

Tables

Figures

Preface

That we get to choose those who govern us is one of the elemental civics lessons in American democratic self-government. We regularly exercise this precious right through the elections of mayors, city council members, county commission, and school board members, as well as state and federal political leaders. All of those elections and the offices filled by them are based on an equally elemental civics concept—the jurisdiction. In American federalism, the jurisdiction indicates a dizzying range of greater and lesser units of government, ranging from the United States of America to the smallest city. Large jurisdictions such as the national government and the fifty state governments have fixed and settled boundaries and mostly fixed and settled arrangements for governing. Through the electoral process we regularly change those who hold office in the federal and state governments, but we almost never change the fixed and the settled arrangements for governing. Furthermore, the arrangements for governing the federal and state governments are essentially the same: a separately elected executive—the president or governor exercising executive powers; a legislature made up of two chambers (except in Nebraska) exercising legislative and budgeting powers; and a free standing judiciary. This separation of powers traces to the founders and to a Constitution designed to provide government, on one hand, while pitting the branches of government against each other so as to check and balance the abuse of governmental power, on the other hand.

These elemental lessons in American civics are generally well known and understood. Much less well known and understood is the very big exception to these lessons—American cities. Unlike the national and state government with fixed and settled arrangements for democratic self-government, the arrangements for government in American cities are anything but fixed and settled. This book is about how and why cities change their governing arrangements.

As in many matters associated with systems of democratic self-government, the subject of variations and differences in the structures of American cities can be controversial. The beauty of democracy is that all citizens can (and should) hold and express their beliefs and preferences not only about who should be elected to represent them but also about what the nature of those elections should be. And citizens can and should have views and opinions regarding the organization and day-to-day functioning of their cities and should exercise those opinions in the public arena. For example, many people who now prefer directly elected mayors with extensive executive powers have strong feelings on that subject. Many others prefer mayors to be chosen by city councils from among their members. Some prefer mayors with only ceremonial powers, while others prefer strong mayors with extensive political and executive powers. Cities are the places in which we live, and we rightly take seriously how our cities are governed and exercise our democratic prerogatives in the pursuit of our preferences.

Among those with opinions on how city government should be organized are those who have dedicated their careers and professions to serving the people of the city. City managers and chief executive officers, police and fire chiefs, public works directors, librarians, directors of parks and recreation, and all of the other professional city leaders have an important stake in the effectiveness of the city. They, probably more than anyone else, know the details of how cities operate. And they rightly have opinions, and often strong opinions, regarding how cities should be organized, governed, and managed.

It is not unusual to confuse scholarly research and academic findings with advocacy or preference on the part of the scholars. As we establish political, administrative, and adapted cities as useful conceptual and empirical categories, and as we describe them, some readers might assume that we are advocating or favoring particular city forms or institutional structures. This is particularly the case with respect to conciliated cities. The conciliated city is merely a way to describe cities that have fused the logic of the separation of powers with the logic of unity of powers. We insist that to have established the conciliated city as a category is not to advocate it, to favor it, or to be thought to be recommending it. Our findings indicate that this category is growing, but we also insist that this is an empirical finding and nor merely an artifact of our biases as scholars. Throughout the book, we have been as objective and as candid as we can be about the strengths and weaknesses of each type of city. At several points we describe the trade-offs associated with moving from one city structural category to another.

We are unashamedly biased in one important respect. All of the research reported here serves to indicate that American cities are remarkably vibrant, adaptable, responsive, interesting, and effective systems of local democratic self-government.

We thank our colleagues in the Department of Public Administration at the University of Kansas. The study of American cities is deeply embedded in the ethos and culture of the department, and we could not have asked for a more informative and stimulating place to work. We especially thank our colleague John Nalbandian for guidance and direction. Diana Koslowsky and Sabine Jones were extremely patient with endless drafts of the manuscript and were cheerful advocates of the project. Our friend James Svara of North Carolina State University read the entire manuscript and provided especially useful suggestions for improvement. William Hansell, the just retiring executive of the International City/County Management Association, was a valuable supporter of the project and an even more valuable critic. While thanking them all, we take full responsibility for the final project and leave it to those who read it for the most important evaluation of all.

The
Adapted City

MAXINE GOODMAN LEVIN
COLLEGE OF URBAN AFFAIRS

Cleveland State University

Introduction

This book is about where most Americans live—cities. Americans have become an increasingly urban people, 80 percent of us now living in metropolitan areas with populations of more than 100,000, and 75 percent of us living in incorporated cities of 10,000 or more (U.S. Department of Commerce 1998). American cities and those of us who live in them are the subject of a vast and varied literature of which this book is just a small part, dealing as it does with three particular subjects. First, American cities are political institutions with formal structures that determine the patterns of democratic self-government practiced in each city. This book is about those structures. Second, American cities are the democratic political institutions nearest the citizens; cities are the government at hand. Americans count on cities to provide order, safety, reliability, convenience, mobility, and favorable settings for the pursuit of our economic, social, artistic, and political interests. To achieve what we expect, it is essential that our cities be both politically responsive and well managed. This book is about variations in the political organization and administrative management of American cities. Third, it is conventional wisdom that government is rigid, static, and deeply resistant to change. In virtually all respects, including how they are democratically structured and how they are organized and managed, American cities are in fact malleable, plastic, changeable, and responsive. This book is about how cities have changed and are changing.

Work on this book began in the early 1990s, generally informed by our direct observations of and experiences with local government. We engage in research and writing on American local government, and we teach those who aspire to careers in local government, particularly careers in city administration. Like others who study American cities, we presumed to understand city structures in terms of the two primary categories or types of cities—those with the mayor-council or strong-mayor form, and those with the council-manager form. Based on our observation of cities over many years, it seemed to us that, while these two forms were once useful descriptions of the political and administrative arrangement in American cities, over the past forty years mayor-council and council-manager cities are becoming less and less distinct from each other. It is our empirical observation that categorizing cities as mayor-council or council-manager had little real capacity to explain how cities were actually democratically structured, organized, and managed.

In the United States there are approximately 7,500 cities. The original structure of American city government, the mayor-council model, is essentially a separation-of-powers structure based on the design of the federal government and the state governments. Sometimes called the presidential model, the mayor-council model now includes fewer than half of all American cities. A contrasting model of local government, the council-manager model, was a significant part of Progressive Era government reforms. Council-manager cities are unity-of-powers structures modeled on business corporations. This model also resembles the parliamentary form of national government. Just over half of all American cities use the council-manager model. For reasons explained later in this chapter, we use the term "political cities" to describe mayor-council cities and their common separation-of-powers and checks-and-balances structural characteristics. We use the designation "administrative cities" to describe council-manager cities and their unity-of-powers characteristics.

The availability, in one nation-state, of 7,500 cases of democratic local government with contrasting presidential and parliamentary forms provides an extraordinary laboratory for the study of democratic institutional structures. This laboratory is greatly aided by the availability of extensive data on American cities.[1] The size of this database facilitates the testing of hypotheses and the replication of findings essential to good social science. More important than the abstractions of social science, there are possible applications to other democratic governments of generalizations based on the findings of such research, applications that hold potential for improving the quality of government. With such data, one can construct generalizations about the architecture of the institutions of democracy that have explanatory power.

As part of the Progressive Era and the Reform Movement, which began late in the nineteenth century, the coming of council-manager government, or administrative cities, more than any other idea (with the possible exception of jurisdictional suburbanization) influenced the character and quality of American local government (Stillman 1974). For much of the twentieth century, the council-manager form of city government was thought to be the new idea, the reform model. As we approach the hundredth anniversary of council-manager government, it is no longer a new idea. The municipal reform movement, of which council-manager government was such an important part, is over. The rapid increase in the number of council-manager cities is also over. Council-manager government was designed to solve corruption, inefficiency, and management problems, and it did. Now that corruption, inefficiency, and poor management are no longer compelling problems, most reform cities with council-manager structures have turned their attention to issues of economic development, political responsiveness, and equity. Council-manager government, some argue, is a large and influential idea whose time has passed.

The two ordinary categories of cities are in fact legal distinctions. In the statutes of all fifty states, the residents of a particular area may, under certain rules and procedures, incorporate a city. In most states, these statutes provide for at least two city types, the mayor-council form and the council-manager form. Within these legal forms, however, city residents may adopt extensive variations. Therefore, within a particular state, two cities may be legally established as, say, mayor-council cities, yet be very different structurally. In addition, most states provide for the creation of charter cities, a legal process by which the residents of a city may custom-design the particular details of a democratic structure into a draft charter and then vote to accept or reject that charter. For the first fifty years of the twentieth century, the two statutory categories of American cities were relatively good descriptions of distinctly different structures, structures based on distinctly different kinds of democratic logic. Beginning in the 1950s, cities using both structures began a steady process of structural adaptation: the adapted cities reform was under way. But these cities continued to be legally categorized as either mayor-council or council-manager structures, categories that often masked actual structural details. Chapter 3 is a reconsideration of the reform movement from the perspective of new reform, which began in the middle of the twentieth century.

The two dominant forms of American local government, the council-manager system and the mayor-council system, are also institutional concepts. As we describe in Chapter 2, it is rightly assumed that institutions matter, that different institutions, ceteris paribus, produce different results (Weaver and Rockman 1993). Between the early years of this century and the 1950s, the structural differences between council-manager and mayor-council government were rightly judged to be important. For example, in the first half of the twentieth century, the municipal reform movement used changed structures to largely eliminate city graft and corruption. We believe that the city structural changes of the second half of the twentieth century are equally important. The purpose of this book is to describe those changes and the likely result of those changes.

In our initial approach to the subject, we thought of these two structures as clearly distinct, a bimodal distribution of structural characteristics. We used Figure 1.1 to graphically represent a bimodal distribution of political cities and administrative American cities.[2] In this bimodal distribution, most

Figure 1.1   **The Structural Characteristics of American Local Government, 1910–60**

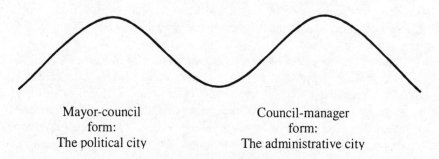

Mayor-council
form:
The political city

Council-manager
form:
The administrative city

political cities resting on mayor-council legal platforms exhibited relatively similar characteristics, such as directly elected mayors, mayoral veto power, partisan elections, and council members elected by party and by district, essentially the same separation-of-powers and checks-and-balances model of government one finds in the fifty American states as well as in our national government. At the time, most administrative cities had different characteristics. City council members were elected at large and without partisan references; a manager was appointed by the council on the basis of professional competence. If there was a mayor, he or she was chosen by the council, from among the council, rather than directly elected by the people; the mayor's duties were only ceremonial.

Much of the study of structural change in American cities is preoccupied with overall reforms and pays little attention to incremental structural adaptations. Studies of this sort have used the two legal statutory categories of cities—mayor-council and council-manager—and assumed that these two categories captured and summarized a wide range of variation between and within each of the two types. Because replacing mayor-council government with council-manager government, or vice versa, is very rare, it would seem that there has been little change in municipal structures (Protasel 1988). Debate over the strengths and weaknesses of each model, while important, has tended to obscure a profound pattern of change that has been under way in local government. While many scholars and informed observers have been discussing the merits of political and administrative cities, in fact most jurisdictions over 50,000 in population have quietly and steadily become something different.

Beginning in the 1950s, the most prominent features of council-manager government, such as a professional executive and a merit civil service, were being widely adopted in mayor-council cities (Renner and De Santis 1998).

The most prominent features of mayor-council government, such as a directly elected mayor and some council elected by districts, were being widely adopted in council-manager government. By the 1990s, the fusion of these two models had resulted in the dominant modern form of American local government, the adapted city. Almost all cities are still formally or legally labeled either mayor-council or council-manager cities, according to the state statutes under which they are organized or based on their charter from the state. But there are many details in the two categories and, as in most things, the details matter. This book focuses on the details of changes in city government because these details are the key to understanding cities as dynamic institutions.

Our research finds that the detailed features of these traditional models have been so mingled as to all but eliminate the importance of the formal designation of a city as either a mayor-council or council-manager city (Ebdon and Brucato 2000). This is not to suggest there are not some "pure" mayor-council and council-manager cities, because there are. It is to suggest, however, that there are fewer of them as time passes and that the adapted city is now the mode, especially for cities over 50,000 people. Nor do we suggest that the different values upon which mayor-council and council-manager forms of government are based are now less important. In fact, values such as professional administration, on the one hand, and democratically elected political leadership, on the other, are so important that they are no longer exclusively associated with one or the other model of local government. The emergence of the adapted city is a splendid example of the innovation, creativity, and malleability of American local government.

If the adapted city is increasingly the norm, how can it be best described and understood? As indicated earlier in this introduction, we initially thought to use the logic of statistical central tendency and the concept of the normal distribution. In the normal distribution, cases (cities) tend to cluster around the center, defined as the mean, median, or mode. In the normal distribution, standard deviation would indicate that 67 percent of the cases (cities) fall within plus or minus one standard deviation from the mean and 95 percent of the cases fall within 1.96 or essentially two standard deviations from the mean. Following this logic, Figure 1.2 represents the emergence of the adapted city is the modal structure of American cities.

Using the logic of the normal curve, we consider here the political, administrative, demographic, and value characteristics of adapted cities.

Change in the political details of city government in the past thirty years has been incremental. Figure 1.3 sets out our initial hypothesized assumptions regarding the direction of changes in administrative council-manager cities as indicated by the arrows. Cities with council-manager platforms are increasingly turning to directly elected mayors, usually for a full four-year

Figure 1.2 **The Adapted City as the Mean in a Normal Distribution**

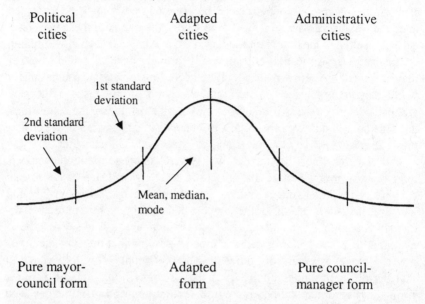

term. These mayors are now more often full-time paid political leaders. As the arrows indicate, these cities have adapted from the pure logic of unity of powers in the direction of the logic of separation of powers.

Conversely, we hypothesize that political cities on mayor-council legal platforms have not, as a general rule, changed the structural characteristics of the office of the mayor. The point is clear—administrative cities have adopted many of the *political* characteristics of political cities, while retaining their statutory designation as council-manager cities, becoming in fact adapted cities. In adapted cities, we argue, the dynamics of mayor-city manager relations have been profoundly changed. The manager in such a setting often becomes a partner with the mayor in matters of policy development (Nalbandian 1991). In addition, in adapted cities, the mayor is often directly involved in the day-to-day administrative affairs of the city (Svara 1989).

The structures of city council elections in administrative council-manager cities have also changed incrementally over the past thirty years. The movement has been in the direction of both larger councils and council members elected by district.

The logic of the unity of powers associated with the original administrative council-manager city has, as a result of these adaptations, been significantly altered. The city manager in an adapted city will experience a relationship with members of the city council and with the mayor that is rather different than a city manager would experience in an administrative

Figure 1.3 **The Political Characteristics of Adapted Cities**

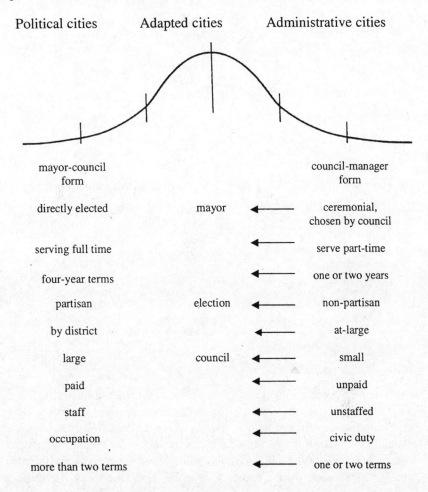

nonadapted council-manager city. Council members elected from districts act as advocates, ombudsmen, and communication channels for their constituents. Competition between council members and between council members and the mayor is no longer a matter of a weekly council meeting; it can be continuous and pervasive (Bledsoe 1993). The successful manager in such a setting must have a keen understanding of local politics yet not be seen as a politician. The manager of an adapted city may no longer merely manage the daily operations of the city; instead, the manager is likely to be part of a political leadership group. As a result of all these changes, adapted cities

Figure 1.4 **The Administrative Characteristics of Adapted Cities**

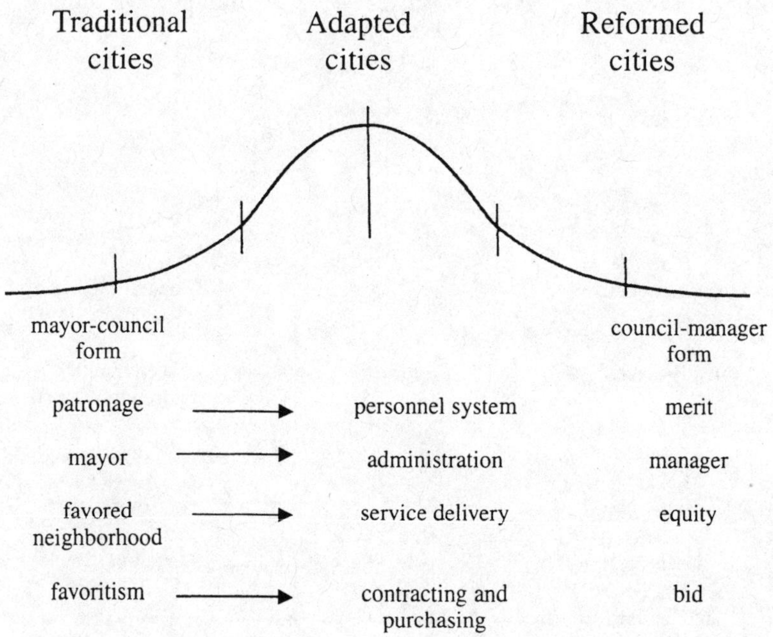

Traditional cities	Adapted cities	Reformed cities
mayor-council form		council-manager form
patronage ⟶	personnel system	merit
mayor ⟶	administration	manager
favored neighborhood ⟶	service delivery	equity
favoritism ⟶	contracting and purchasing	bid

have become more political and more responsive than administrative cities. And, at least in the opinion of most city managers, adapted cities are less administratively efficient and harder to manage. As administrative cities change the structure of their political characteristics in the direction of adapted cities, they trade some efficiency for political responsiveness and identifiable political leadership. Chapter 4 describes the patterns of transition in American cities from political separation of powers to administrative unity of powers—what came to be described as municipal reform—and then the gradual movement of administrative cities back toward separation of powers, moving in the direction of the adapted city. Chapters 7, 8, and 9 describe these structural changes in detail.

Most of the change in the past thirty years in the administrative architecture of cities has been made by political cities with mayor-council charters. As the arrows in Figure 1.4 hypothesize, we argue that most political cities have adopted administrative features of city government previously associated primarily with administrative cities.

For example, civil service systems are now at least as common in political as in administrative cities. Most larger cities (over 50,000 population) now have appointed professional chief administrative officers (CAOs), usually selected by the mayor. The CAOs of these cities have educational and experiential qualifications that are equivalent to those of city managers in administrative cities with council-manager charters of comparable size.

The original council-manager administrative cities emphasized efficiency, economy, and fairness in service delivery. The "decision rules" of professional local government service delivery, such as the greater deployment of police at high crime periods and in high crime areas, are now standard practices in administrative cities. Purchasing and bidding controls and other good management practices are also now standard in political cities.

In most administrative respects, mayor-council cities, particularly those over 50,000 in population, have become adapted political cities. As the era of municipal reform has passed, so too has the era of local bosses, patronage, and endemic corruption. Cities with mayor-council statutory platforms have become more efficient, honest, and equitable, and cities with council-manager statutory platforms have become more politically responsive. Both have become adapted cities. Chapter 3 describes American cities in their political, prereform separation-of-powers context. Chapter 4 sets out in detail the processes of the administrative changes that have resulted in the transition of political cities to adapted political cities.

Changes in city government structure appear to be responses to changes in city demographics. Figure 1.5 describes changes in city demographics in America, with the arrows representing our hypothesized direction of change.

As cities grow older, especially the early inner-ring suburbs built between the 1930s through the 1950s, they increasingly resemble demographically the center cities and are likely to become adapted cities. The gradual outward diaspora of racial and social classes to the suburban cities of metropolitan areas increases the likelihood that cities affected by that diaspora will take on adapted city characteristics. Conversely, more homogeneous outer-ring suburbs, exurbs, and smaller rural cities are less inclined toward the features of the adapted city. Finally, size matters; we hypothesize that as city populations increase they are more likely to take on the structural features of adapted cities.

The rapid adoption of the council-manager model of city government from the 1920s through the 1960s reflected changing values and circumstances, as the arrows in Figure 1.6 indicate. The rapid movement of both mayor-council political cities and council-manager administrative cities toward the fused adapted model also reflects changing values and circumstances. As political cities face increasingly serious social problems and fiscal crises, we hypothesize that the importance of good management and efficiency increases,

Figure 1.5 **The Demographics of Cities**

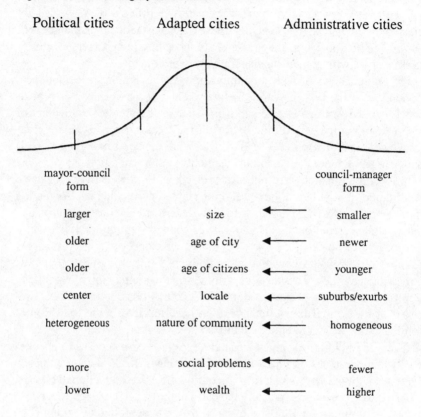

Political cities   Adapted cities   Administrative cities

mayor-council form		council-manager form
larger	size ←	smaller
older	age of city ←	newer
older	age of citizens ←	younger
center	locale ←	suburbs/exurbs
heterogeneous	nature of community ←	homogeneous
more	social problems ←	fewer
lower	wealth ←	higher

enhancing the probability that they will adopt administrative changes. For example, in most larger mayor-council cities there is now a professional CAO as well as other professional managers. Civil service systems were adopted for the same reasons. These cities clearly wished to retain the responsiveness, inclusiveness, and competitiveness of mayor-council government while adding the efficiency and equity previously associated mostly with council-manager cities.

In council-manager administrative cities there has been a widespread adoption of features such as directly elected mayors, full-time paid mayors, district-based council elections, and full-time paid city council members, all steps that reflect the increased importance of the values of political competition, leadership, inclusiveness, and representation in these cities.

The value preferences of citizens and leaders are one thing; the governmental concepts designed to put these values into effect are another. It has

Figure 1.6 **The Guiding Governmental Concepts and Values of Adapted Cities**

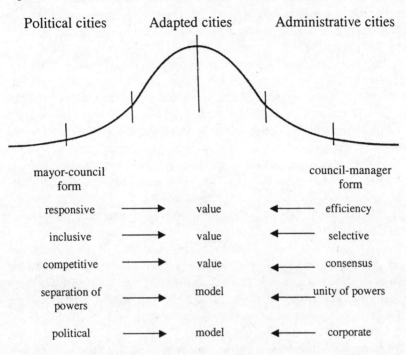

been assumed, on one hand, that an institutional design based on the logic of the separation of powers and political competition will cause inclusiveness; that is, neighborhoods and interest groups will have a voice. It is also assumed that this model favors the development of political leadership. Much of the logic of political cities is based upon these assumptions.

On the other hand, following the logic of the unity of powers, the city council appoints a city manager on the basis of merit and all aspects of the city administration are directly supervised by the manager. This is the corporate model in which it is rightly assumed that the values of efficiency and good management are sovereign.

Citizens now appear to want, simultaneously, both political responsiveness and administrative efficiency. Citizens assume that these are or can be compatible values and appear to favor the modification of city institutional structure to further these values. In Chapter 10 we consider in detail the compatibility of these competing assumptions.

While there has been some abandonment of council-manager governments in favor of the mayor-council form, the much more common pattern of structural change has been incremental, step by step toward the adapted city model. Greg Protasel's research indicates that administrative cities have moved to the adapted administrative model, to close what he describes as the political leadership gap (1988).

Are the adapted administrative cities resting on council-manager charters or platforms still fundamentally different from adapted political cities resting on mayor-council charter platforms or law? The "formalists" and the stronger advocates of either mayor-council or council-manager government would likely answer this affirmatively. To them, the fusion of features found in the adapted city does not fundamentally alter the essential character of the jurisdiction as either political or administrative. The "behavioralist," on the other hand, would likely answer no. The fusion of institutional features characteristic of adapted cities so alters the behavior of city councils, mayors, city managers, and CAOs as to render the original charter or legal standing of the cities of marginal importance.

Both the formalists and the behavioralists are right. Some adapted cities do not alter the separation-of-powers or the unity-of-powers principles found in political and administrative cities. However, in some adapted cities there is a fusion or unification of the political logic of separation of powers and the administrative logic of unity of powers that creates what we will call the conciliated city.

We have found the language and vocabulary used in the study of city structures and the reform or change of those structures to be woefully inadequate. This vocabulary, based on the formal and legal designation of cities as either mayor-council or council-manager, does not capture variations between them or help in describing patterns of structural change. As our research progressed, it became increasingly clear that we could not describe our findings using only these categories, so we created our own vocabulary and set up additional categories, designed to accurately reflect our findings. We have used the flexibility of the English language to describe the concepts and categories in different ways. Like much of the English language, this vocabulary has more than one way to speak about the same thing.

We use the phrase "political city" to describe cities with separation-of-power structures and presume to use that phrase to comprehend not only cities but also states and nations with separation-of-powers structures. We use the word "political" to suggest that the structural arrangements were originally designed to address these questions: Who is to have power? How can their power be controlled? Obviously, the characteristics of political cities refers to the original form of American cities, the mayor-council model. Our research will show that political cities are increasingly rare.

The administrative city, as we have mentioned, grew out of the Progressive Era and replaced the separation of powers with a set of structural arrangements designed to address administrative questions: How can the city be efficient? How can the city control corruption? The administrative city is the reform of the political city. We will show that the classic administrative city with a pure council-manager charter is increasingly rare.

Most American cities are now adapted. Because this is such a large group of cities, we found it necessary to create three different categories or variants of adapted cities.

First are the adapted political cities, which are cities that have retained the basic elements of separation of powers but have also adopted important administrative features that have buffered the political nature of these cities and increased their management capacities. Most adapted political cities rest on the mayor-council statutory or legal platform (a few are on council-manager legal platforms) but are clearly distinguishable from their political city cousins.

The second variety is the adapted administrative cities, which have retained the basic elements of the unity-of-powers model but have so modified that model as to be clearly distinguishable from administrative cities. Most of these cities are on council-manager statutory platforms.

The third category is the conciliated cities. "Conciliated" means "assembled," "united," or "made compatible" and is used here to describe those cities that are no longer obviously based solely on a separation-of-powers model or a unity-of-powers model.

Based on this vocabulary, a five-part schema categorizing American cities according to the details of their structures is set out in Chapter 7, Table 7.4, Types and Categories of American Cities. One can certainly quarrel with the details in terms of where cities are situated on the schema. For example, is City A, with a council-appointed city manager, at-large election of city council members, and a mayor chosen from among the city council (an administrative city), significantly different from City B, with a council-appointed city administrator, a council elected by district, and a directly elected mayor (an administrative adapted city)? Although both cities appear to retain the unity-of-powers principle, we are convinced that these structural differences are important and influence the allocation of political and administrative power among the mayor, the council, and the city administrator as well as the day-to-day functioning of city government. Therefore, we would describe City B as an adapted administrative city.

The development of the concept of the adapted city is a response to the theoretical and empirical challenges of understanding American local government. "Because cities have adopted a myriad of structural arrangements that cannot easily be considered part of one model or the other, researchers must reflect this situation in order to be more useful from both a theoretical and practical standpoint" (Renner 1988b, 8). The purpose of this book is the development of a theory and a vocabulary by which we can better understand how American local government really works.

This is a study of change in the structures of American local governments. A central thesis of the study is that the formal structures of American cities are highly dynamic, reflecting changing circumstances and public preferences. The municipal reform era was notably successful in professionalizing and cleaning up American cities, using the logic of charter structures. In the last forty years there has been an equally important, but less well understood reform of municipal structures. The purpose of this book is to describe and analyze the adapted city, the primary pattern of municipal reform in the last half of the twentieth century.

Our findings indicate that cities are much more structurally dynamic than the literature suggests. In fact, American cities are remarkably fluid and adaptable. Structural changes, however, are frequently punctuated, sporadic, and, above all, incremental; they do not flow in a steady current. The pace and direction of structural change in American cities are important; taken in the aggregate, these incremental structural changes add up to a great deal of structural innovation.

To defend the proposition that American city structures are highly dynamic and that the contemporary reflection of that dynamism is the emergence of adapted cities, we use a mixture of methodologies. Because of the sweep of time covered in this study, history is important and is used throughout. Quantitative data are also important and several parts of the study use descriptive statistics to explain patterns of change in the structures of American cities. To bring some of the details of history and statistics to life, there are several city case studies. Finally, as in all scholarly research, we explain our findings through definitions, assumptions, and deductive reasoning.

In Chapter 2, we develop a theory of institutional dynamics, which accounts for or explains patterns of reform, change, and adaptation. Institutional dynamics is built on concepts of the diffusion of innovation taken primarily from sociology (Rogers 1995; DiMaggio and Powell 1991) and the theories of changing eras or epochs (Kaufman 1991; Hirschman 1982).

In Chapter 3, we begin with a study of the prereform era and the influence of industrialization, immigration, and urbanization on city government. We describe the rise and fall of city bosses and their political machines and the war on graft and corruption. In Chapter 3 we describe the municipal reform movement and particularly the rise of the council-manager form of city government and its effect on American cities. While this era in American history is well known and understood, our review lays the groundwork for our later claims about changing city government structures. We also describe the impact of suburbanization on city government structure and the distribution of wealth and resources among units of government. Jurisdictional suburbanization resulted in homogeneous communities that overwhelmingly adopted the administrative structure, the council-manager form of government. By the 1970s, however, the process of establishing new suburban cities had slowed considerably. In the 1990s, inner suburbs became more heterogeneous as minority populations emigrated from central cities. Over time, inner-ring suburban cities changed their structural arrangements to enhance political representation and responsiveness, and most of them are now adapted administrative cities.

Chapter 4 charts, in detail, the evolution and adoption of political cities resting on mayor-council platforms. During the course of the twentieth century, the majority of them have changed to become adapted political cities. The story of how profoundly political cities were affected by the Progressive Era and the municipal reform movement has been a well-kept secret.

Chapter 5 describes the evolution of the administrative cities resting on council-manager platforms. Over time, most of these cities have adopted a directly elected mayor, district-based city council elections, and other political changes. Here we tell the story of the evolution of the council-manager model of city government to the adapted administrative model.

One very good way to understand how cities have changed is to examine the evolution of the Model City Charter, the subject of Chapter 6. There have been seven Model City Charters developed by the National Civic League. The first model in 1900 endorsed mayor-council city government. From 1915 to 1933, the Model City Charter endorsed the council-manager form. Beginning in 1941, however, the model offered the mayor-council form as an acceptable alternative. This model change occurred, we suggest, because mayor-council cities were becoming more like council-manager cities as they hired CAOs and adopted merit systems, purchasing standards, and bidding standards. Following the logic of the institutional theory of innovation, these seven versions of the Model City Charter influenced how cities structured themselves and how they changed these structures. At this writing, a committee of the National Civic League is developing the eighth Model City Charter.

In Chapter 7, we turn to quantitative empirical evidence using the five-part schema presented in Table 7.4. We present findings from the 1992 and 1996 International City/County Management Association (ICMA) surveys and a 1998 survey we conducted of 116 American cities. These three bodies of data describe in detail the patterns that define the adapted city. In Chapter 8 we present further evidence confirming our hypothesis and operationalize adapted logic by comparing the structures and practices of the 19 political

cities, 19 adapted political cities, 15 conciliated cities, 17 administrative cities, and 46 adapted administrative cities included in our survey.

In Chapter 9 we describe the conciliated city variant of adapted cities. The
conciliated city is a merging of the mayor-council and council-manager forms
of government that is so complete that it is impossible to use legal categories
such as the council-manager form or mayor-council form to describe it. Likewise, conceptual categories such as unity of powers or separation of powers
fail to describe conciliated cities. So, we developed a new category and describe it in detail in Chapter 9, including case studies of two conciliated
cities, Cincinnati, Ohio, and Oakland, California.

We finish this introduction with our boldest claim. Our research indicates
that the remaining political and administrative cities are still quite distinct,
continuing to exhibit the important differences between separation-of-powers
and unity-of-powers structure. There are, however, fewer and fewer political
and administrative cities. Most American cities are now best described as
adapted. Our research indicates that cities we classify as adapted are more like
each other than they are like either political or administrative cities. In Chapter
10 we summarize and conclude our study and present data in support of our
claim that adapted cities are now the clearest and most empirically accurate
representation of how Americans govern themselves at the local level.

Notes

1. The primary data sources are the computer tapes and documents of the U.S.
Census of Governments, the ICMA *Municipal Year Books*, the *City-County Data Books*,
and data and documents from the U.S. Advisory Commission on Intergovernmental
Relations.

2. We recognize that dichotomous categories do not constitute the basis for bimodal
distribution in nonparametric statistics. We simply use Figure 1.1 to visually represent
our initial and rather simplistic comparisons of political and administrative cities.

Theories of Institutional Dynamics

To understand the changing structures of American cities, it is important to set out the assumptions and theories that guide this study. We follow the Kurt Lewin (1936) dictum that, "from a practical point of view the mere gathering of facts has very limited value. It cannot give an answer to the question that is most important for practical purposes—namely, what must one do to obtain a desired effect in given concrete cases? To answer this question it is necessary to have a theory, but a theory which is empirical and not speculative. This means that theory and facts must be closely related to each other." As we tell our graduate students preparing for careers in local government leadership, there is nothing more practical than a good theory. Students tend to roll their eyes at this statement and swallow the theory like medicine. Only later, after experience in the field, do they develop a respect for theory. This chapter will put the adapted American city into theoretical perspective, with trust that both understanding and explaining the adapted American city will be made easier with this theory. Finally, theories of institutional dynamics used here should make our study more easily comparative both to other studies of cities and to the processes of change in other formal institutions.

We begin with two assumptions. First, we hold to the positivist assumption that there are discernible patterns in collective human behavior and that our objective is to find those patterns. Second, cities are the collective institutions that people build for themselves, both in physical and social terms. Just as they build their physical houses, and adapt and remodel them, and build their roads and water systems, they also build their cities as organizations and as governmental jurisdictions. The processes of building, adapting, and remodeling the institutions of local government are dynamic, responding to changing needs, circumstances, and values.

Our study of the changing structural characteristics of American cities is part of a broader body of social science theory generally described as institutionalism or the new institutionalism (March and Olsen 1989; DiMaggio and Powell 1991; Lynn 1996; Rogers 1995). Individuals, families, neighborhoods, interest groups, and businesses function in the context of the city as an institution. How we function in relationship to the institutional city is determined in part by the particular structure of that city. In its formal manifestations, the city sets the rules of participation, exercises authority by lawmaking (statutes, ordinances, and regulations) and by carrying out the law, selects persons to politically represent all residents or some subset of residents, operates a permanent bureaucracy, provides services, and determines who will pay what in taxes. How the city does each of these things is determined by its structure. These structures, as a general rule, tend to conform to societal expectations of how cities should look and function (Lynn 1996, 125). The extent to which societal expectations are matched by the function of the city is the measure of its legitimacy (Stone 1987). Some institutions are highly resistant to change while others are dynamic. We chose to describe the findings of our research on changes in American cities as a form of institutional dynamics.

Theories of institutional dynamics are used here to capture the processes of institutional change in cities. Institutional dynamics, as used here, will combine two rather well-known conceptual approaches to institutional study. The first is theories of the diffusion of innovation taken from sociology and political science. The second is the application of theories of eras or epochs, which account for long-term shifts from one to another dominant ideology.

The Diffusion of Innovation

The progressive movement in the first fifty years of the twentieth century spread many important organizational and policy innovations, including the council-manager form of city government, the short ballot, the secret ballot, merit systems in government, workers' compensation laws, aid to the blind and deaf, and minimum-wage laws. Edgar McCoy (1940) measured state policy innovations between 1869 and 1931, including old-age pensions, women's suffrage, and workers' compensation, and ranked the states according to whether they were early or late adopters. Using maps, he found the centers of these innovations to be in New York, California, Wisconsin, and Michigan and traced the paths of diffusion in concentric circles from those centers. Paths of diffusion were influenced by state variations in transportation and communication capacities, wealth, and urbanization. From this study grew the McCoy Innovation Index, which even now explains regional patterns of innovation diffusion.

Long before the federal government took on widespread regulatory and social responsibility roles, the states were busy with the diffusion of innovation, including the regulation of railroads, health, and labor. Laws found their way verbatim from one neighboring state to another. New York, Michigan, Ohio, Minnesota, Wisconsin, and Illinois are identified by the historian William Brock (1970) as the taproots of the expansion of state social responsibility.

Herbert Jacob's *Silent Revolution* (1988) explains the rapid diffusion of no-fault divorce laws. New York and California adopted this concept in 1966 and 1970, respectively; by 1974, forty-nine states had no-fault divorce laws; and in 1985 the lone holdout (South Dakota) joined in. Jacob found no evidence that the idea was propagated by the usual sources—social movements or interest groups, policy networks, bureaucrats, governors, or legislators. Because no-fault divorce was noncontroversial, cost-free, and had been successfully implemented by other states, it spread rather easily. Moving beyond his case study, Jacob argues that many other laws spread in a similar fashion.

Evidence suggests a contagion process. Peter Eisinger (1988), in the most extensive study to date, reports that the number of business location incentive programs (mostly tax abatements) increased from 840 in 1966 to 1,213 in 1985. The average number of programs per state doubled during those years. Surely this rapid spread of location incentives did not happen because state governments independently reached the same conclusion about their desirability.

Competition to lure automobile manufacturers to a particular state serves as another example. In the early 1980s, bidding wars broke out among states that sought plants to be built by General Motors, Toyota, Nissan, and other car companies. State officials promised all sorts of inducements, such as land purchases, site renovations, transportation improvements, worker training subsidies, and Saturday school for the children of Japanese workers. The winners were geographically contiguous states under a lot of economic pressure. States that lost the first competition redoubled their efforts in the next round. The cost per worker escalated each time, rising from $11,000 per worker in 1980 to $50,580 by 1986. Surely this escalation of costs is a product of a diffusion process (Feiock 1989).

At the same time that interstate competition stimulates states to spend more on economic development, it also pressures them to do less in other areas, most notably welfare. Competition exerts a downward pressure on a state to stay in line lest it become a "welfare magnet"—a haven for undesirable citizens.

Peterson and Rom in *Welfare Magnets* (1990) illuminated this debate by a careful statistical analysis of welfare benefit levels, poverty rates, and state-level explanatory variables. They found that the poor move in response to benefit levels (and to employment opportunities). They also found that state policymakers are sensitive to the size of the poor population and to the possibility of welfare migration, and they reduce benefits accordingly. This action produced a convergence effect that pushed benefit levels downward.

Richard Nathan (1993) observed that states have often undertaken liberal initiatives when the national government is captured by conservatives;

later, when liberals capture Washington, they bring along policies that already have been tested. Noting that state initiatives in the 1920s were the models for federal New Deal programs in the 1930s, Nathan finds it unsurprising that the opposite situation obtained in the 1980s: conservatives controlled Washington while liberals turned to the states. This is part of an equilibrating tendency in our federal system wherein interests not satisfied at one level turn to another. This tendency counters the centralizing trend most observers see in American federalism and lends credence to James Madison's (1788) claim that "opposite and rival" interests could be accommodated in a federal system.

It is a safe estimate that at least half of American cities with populations between 25,000 and 200,000 have exactly the same dog leash law. This is not because Ann Arbor and Beverly Hills have the same dog problems; it is because dog leash laws and most other laws were taken from model laws— in the case of cities, model laws put together and distributed by the National League of Cities and the National Civic League. Indeed, there is a possibility that Beverly Hills and Frankfort, Germany, have the same dog leash laws due to the handiwork of the International Union of Local Officials and their model laws publications.

Doubtless, the ultimate study is Everett M. Rogers' *Diffusion of Innovations* (1995). Rogers, in a synthesis of thousands of studies of change, found that innovations or reforms spread in diffusions, which exhibit a common pattern—the S-curve. At first, the adoption of change or reform is slow, with experimentation, trial and error, and the challenges of being the guinea pig. Once a few others adopt reform successfully, there tends to be a steep climb in adoption, followed by a leveling off. When institutional change reaches the leveling-off stage (it may include most other similar institutions, as graphed in Figure 2.1, or fewer, but innovations are seldom judged to have been successfully spread if they involve fewer than half of the cases), further investments in seeking additional adopters are usually wasted. "Diffusion refers to the spread of something within a social system" (Strang and Soule 1998, 266) This spread is from a source to one or more adopters and can include the spread of types of behavior, technology, beliefs, and, most important for our purposes, structure. Diffusions in social systems happen in surprisingly predictable ways, and the spread of structural changes among American cities are a very good example of that.

Although Rogers and others who have studied the processes of diffusion tend to focus their interests on what they describe as innovation, the patterns of change and reform in the structures of American cities exhibit virtually all of the features of the theory of the diffusion of innovation. Most prominent of these features is the S-curve. As we describe in detail in Chapter 4,

Figure 2.1 **The Diffusion of Innovation S-Curve**

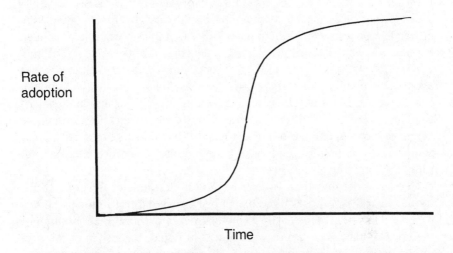

Rate of
adoption

Time

the municipal reform movement began slowly late in the nineteenth and early in the twentieth centuries. By the 1920s, municipal reform was a well-known set of ideas and a widely shared ideology, particularly among opinion leaders. From the mid-1920s through the 1940s it spread steadily, resulting in the almost universal adoption of municipal civil service personnel systems, bid and contract controls, the short ballot, the secret ballot, and the systematic elimination of political party designations for those standing for city office. And, of course, the council-manager form of government grew steadily during this period, particularly in the midwest, the south, and the west. The new cities in the great American suburban diaspora almost all adopted the council-manager form. By the mid-1960s, the municipal reform movement was running out of gas and a new set of ideas was steadily emerging, the so-called reform of the reform or the postreform movement. This movement too can be seen as an S-curve and it appears, as we demonstrate in Chapter 10, our conclusion, to be in the midst of a steep climb, a climb that will no doubt level off in the years to come.

Patterns of diffusion (some people are more comfortable calling diffusion simply "change," while those who favor a particular diffusion tend to call it a reform or an innovation) are explained by a series of attendant hypotheses.

First is the association between the presence of a perceived crisis and the propensity to adopt a change (Rogers 1995; Strang and Soule 1998). As we illustrate in Chapter 4, in the early history of the transition from political cities to administrative cities, there was a ten- to fifteen-year period of the adoption of the "commission" form of American local government (most

American counties use a version of the commission form of local government). This diffusion can be traced to a hurricane in Galveston, Texas, in
1900. Galveston adopted a commission form of city government, due to the
crisis. The governor initially appointed the commissioners; the appointed
commission was subsequently elected by the citizens of Galveston (McComb
1986). Moreover, as a result of the Galveston experience, several other cities
adopted the commission form of government. This particular reform did not
last, however. The problems associated with graft and corruption in American cities were described or characterized as crises or disasters, during the
height of the municipal reform era (Flentje 1993). The fat boss mayor characterized in the political cartoons of the day had a surprising capacity to
further the interests of reformers.

Second, diffusion theory describes the importance of the compatibility between the purposes of a change or reform and the dominant values
of a social system. This easily explains the almost universal adoption of
the council-manager form of government in homogeneous American suburbs. The logic of the administrative city, with its professional manager, a
merit-based civil service, and a part-time city council made up of members
all elected at large, fits comfortably with the dominant values of middle-
class families able to commute by car to their jobs and to escape the problems of the inner city. We argue in Chapters 6 through 10 that, starting in the
1960s, the demographics of many American cities changed and with those
changing demographics came different values and concerns on the part of
those now living in those cities. In political cities, the dominant values appeared to promote more effective and efficient local governments, so political cities adapted accordingly. In administrative cities, the residents became
increasingly concerned with identifiable political leadership, with some form
of direct political accountability, so administrative cities adapted accordingly.

Third, spatial proximity is important in diffusion theory. Midwestern and
western cities, for example, were early adopters of many of the features of
municipal reform, and the spatial proximity of these cities helps explain why.
In the northeast, by comparison, there were fewer examples of "reformed
cities" and there has been somewhat less diffusion of municipal reform there.
In Chapters 8 and 9 we describe the diffusion of municipal structural adaptations from Cincinnati, which greatly strengthened the powers of the mayor
while retaining a city manager, to Kansas City, Missouri, with evidence that
the proximity of the two cities was a factor.

Fourth, "the mass media play a crucial role in amplifying and editing the
diffusion of collective action" (Strang and Soule 1998, 270). The press tends
to focus on problems and things going wrong, and such a relentless focus
influences broadly based public opinion, lending itself to a general view that

something needs to be done or that things need to be fixed. Crime and drugs are associated with getting tough on crime, which results in sentencing guidelines—three strikes and you're out—and the currently popular "broken windows" concept. When the city is slow to plow the streets after a snowstorm, the press reports and amplifies the matter and elected officials are held responsible. Logically these officials will look for ways to "solve the problems" and often the solutions are structural, these days in the direction of changing the city structure to give the mayor more power. The contemporary media tend to be as enthusiastic about strengthening the role of the mayor as they were about weakening the role of the mayor seventy-five years ago. The most widely read publication in American local government is *Governing* magazine. *Governing* has run several major stories on the growing popularity of the so-called strong mayor and on the importance of mayoral leadership in modern American cities (Gurwitt 1993). In both the reforms of seventy-five years ago and in contemporary reforms, the media have played a central role.

Fifth, change agents are often the carriers of change, the agents of diffusion. "The professions and occupational communities form an allied source of new practice" (Strang and Soule 1998, 271). These communities of experts provide the venues for discussions, conferences, e-mail correspondence, newsletters, and magazines. Many mayors are active in the National Municipal League (NML) and are influenced by opinion leaders active in NML and by the literature and other services of NML. City managers are active in the International City/County Management Association (ICMA) and are likewise influenced by ICMA opinion leaders and read the ICMA publications. Many top consulting firms, such as the Innovations Group, are change agents influential in suggesting changes. It would be unusual in the extreme for a consulting firm to review a city and to conclude that everything is fine and that nothing needs to be changed.

Sixth, closely associated with the media and with diffusion change agents is the matter of setting fashions. "Today, the management fashion industry is very big business. While the theorization and hyping of organization action has always been fundamental in managing, a strong trend toward the externalization or organizational analysis is apparent. The consultant, the guru, the management scholar populations are on the rise, as are the output of the business press and the sales of business books" (Strang and Soule 1998, 278). In a thorough review of the movement of social policy, Hood and Jackson found that it was not analysis or rational reasoning that moved policy. Instead, just as Aristotle argued, individuals and the institutions they inhabit are moved by rhetoric, by the power of narratives, stories, examples, and by arguments that win in the context of circumstances that people understand

(Hood and Jackson 1991). Like fashion, preferred "doctrines" change over time and tend to move in S-curve patterns. Doctrines can and do move across institutions by contagion, mimicking, and the bandwagon effect, often with little connection to data, analysis, or informed historical understanding (Strang and Soule 1998).

The seventh factor influencing patterns of the diffusion of change is perhaps the most interesting and unique. It turns out that both individuals and institutions tend to change so as to accrue prestige, status, and social standing. "Models of management diffuse from central firms to the larger business community as they prove their utility in responding to new politico-economic conditions. Haverman shows that deregulation led thrifts to follow large, financially profitable thrifts into new markets" (Strang and Soule 1998, 275). This process led to disastrous investments in Mexico. Midsized companies use the accounting firms used by large well-known companies, seeking the legitimacy that those firms might carry. Universities mimic Ivy League and other prestige schools, justifying changes on the basis of similar changes at prestige universities. In the era of prizes, report cards, and rankings, the pressure to mimic prestige institutions is increased. Cities prepare for years to apply to receive an All-American City designation given by the National Civic League. Cities likewise conform to a set of established criteria to receive a favorable report card grade in the *Governing* magazine evaluations of city effectiveness. Cities compete for the Harvard Innovation Awards, each claiming that the change it made was especially significant, productive, or equitable. Both corporations and public agencies compete for the government-sponsored Baldrige Awards, which are based on highly questionable criteria such as benchmarking (benchmarking is actually copying the innovations of others rather than being innovative yourself).

In our research on how cities change and adapt their formal structures, we found evidence of the S-curve of the diffusion of innovation and further evidence of the influence of all of these factors. Crisis was more important in some cities, proximity more important in others, fashion and prestige more important in others.

Here is a selection of Rogers's hypotheses verified by a synthesis of over 3,000 studies (1995).

1. A crisis emphasizes the relative advantage of an innovation and affects its rate of adoption.
2. The compatibility of a new idea, as perceived by members of a social system, affects its rate of adoption.
3. The communicability of an innovation, as perceived by members of a social system, affects its rate of adoption.

4. Earlier adopters are younger in age than later adopters.
5. Earlier adopters have higher social status than later adopters.
6. Earlier adopters have a more favorable financial position than later adopters.

Based on these findings of diffusion of institutional innovation research and the theory derived from it, it would be expected that the pattern of changes in the structures of cities would exhibit the same properties. The findings derived from our research on the structural dynamics of American cities do approximate diffusion of innovation theory.

Theories of Eras and Epochs

The theory of structural dynamics is also based on the logic of eras or epochs. In his research, the eminent political scientist Albert O. Hirschman found long-term cycles of change in values, attitudes, and ideology (1982). In very broad terms, he describes these cycles as eras or epochs of shifting involvement between the collective pursuit of the public interest and the individual or small-group pursuit of private interests. In the United States, at this point, for example, we have low voter turnout; institutions generally and public institutions particularly are held in low regard in studies of public opinion; and there is generally little trust in either public officials or public institutions. We are in an era of private interests, following a fifty-year era of public action—World War I and II, the New Deal, and a long period of positive government. In the era of public action and positive government, there were trade-offs and costs in the form of big government, higher taxes, regulations, restrictions on individual uses of property, and very high complexity. And we learned that there were certain intractable problems that even positive government could not entirely solve, such as poverty, drug abuse, and terrorism. As the most recent era of positive government matured, in the 1950s and early 1960s, people could easily see the benefits, costs, and trade-offs of public policy choices that were made. And, to use Hirschman's term, the people were disappointed. We also saw the limitations and failures of public institutions, such as Watergate and the war in Vietnam. In this context there gradually developed a new acceptance of private interests that has probably been the dominant ideology in the last thirty years. As a consequence, public and other institutions have downsized, contracted out, privatized, and deregulated. This is a dynamic process of institutional change, broadly reflecting social change and changed contextual circumstances.

Herbert Kaufman (1963) developed a very similar theory to explain how the public shifts from support for "representativeness" to support for bureaucratic, neutral competence and executive leadership (1963). He also found similar cycles with respect to the preference for centralization versus decentralization and regulation versus deregulation. All are, he claims, a form of natural selection, evolution, or what is called structural dynamics.

Our study demonstrates that patterns of structural change in American cities very much resemble both Hirschman's and Kaufman's arguments about the longer-term eras or epochs of public preferences and changed circumstances. And this study finds that cities tend to change incrementally more often than changing dramatically from one to another institutional structure. This pattern of incremental structural change is the S-curve found in virtually all studies of the diffusion of innovation.

The key concepts in the theory of structural dynamics as applied to the structure of American cities are these:

1. Cities will tend to change their structures in a piecemeal fashion; radical wholesale change in structure is rare.
2. This change will tend to follow an S-curve of diffusion of innovation.
3. When aggregated, incremental changes in city structures will tend to move in cycles or epochs of reform, usually over periods of thirty to fifty years.

These concepts will be used throughout the study to describe structural change in American cities and to defend the proposition that most cities have now adapted essentially new standard arrangements for their government.

To describe the fluidity in structural arrangements, we will use the term "structural dynamics." This term has several theoretical underpinnings. First, it borrows some logic and terminology from the natural sciences, particularly biology and geology. For example, population ecology originally described the sustainable population level of a given species within an environmental niche. By extension, the population ecology theory of organizations postulates that there is an inherent tension or struggle between organizations and their environment. One would not develop an explanation of the overall population of any animal species without taking into consideration such factors as the amount of food available, the climate, or the presence of competitors (Gray and Lowery 1993, 1996). American cities provide an excellent laboratory for testing population ecology theories of organizational change because they are the governments closest to the people and because they include a wide range of institutional structural choices democratically made by citizens and their representatives.

In the population ecologists' view, the ability to obtain a resource niche and outperform one's competitors is all-important. In population ecology, it is assumed that there are resource limitations that influence the growth, development, and decline of organizations and the role of successful innovations in shaping new forms of organizations.

Organizations adapt through the dissemination of innovations—in the case of American cities, by borrowing structural adoptions from other cities. This diffusion of innovation does much to explain the fluidity of American local governments.

In nature, collaboration is just as common as competition, and so it is in government organizations. Given the turbulence and complexity of local politics, it is not surprising that American cities have a multitude of ways in which they collaborate. Formal and informal professional organizations are just one way in which elected officials and administrators develop horizontal and vertical integration (Frederickson 1999). An ecological perspective, which emphasizes collaboration as well as competition, contributes to our understanding of how to organize and manage American cities.

Contrary to one of the dominant theoretical approaches in urban politics, this study does not support the view that cities are unable to engage in redistributive policies because citizens and officials pursue self-evident interests through an objectively determined environment. We propose a more active view of the relationship between the citizens in a community and their interests—one in which political actors are seen as aggressively and continually reinterpreting and redefining their interests in an uncertain and undetermined world. The data presented here support this approach.

3

Political and Administrative Cities

The story of the American city begins with the separation of powers. At the national level, the notion of separated powers was a remedy for one of the most formidable problems the framers of the United States Constitution faced—despotic, authoritarian, nondemocratic government. The remedy was limited government brought about by designing a government structurally to check the powers of one branch by the powers of the others. The founders understood the necessity of creating a central government while minimizing the possibility that the authority of the central government would be abused. Only power, they believed, could check the abuse of power. The Constitution established the system of checks as well as the multiple-level, federal relationship between local governments, the states, and the national government. "In order to lay a due foundation for that separate and distinct exercise of the different powers of government, which to a certain extent is admitted on all hands to be essential to the preservation of liberty, it is evident that each department should have a will of its own; and consequently should be so constituted that the members of each should have as little agency as possible in the appointment of the members of the others" (*Federalist* #51, reprinted in *The Federalist* 1961, 348). Despite Alexander Hamilton's concerns that the national government would be weak or inefficient, his Federalists embraced separation of powers and limited government. Only later did the national government strengthen the presidency, elect senators directly, expand the franchise, establish a civil service, and create the independent regulatory commissions (which have executive, legislative, and judicial powers), all done, at least in part, to make government more efficient.

The separation-of-powers structure adopted for the federal government became the template for the states and the cities. For over a century, from the ratification of the Constitution through the early twentieth century, virtually all cities of any size governed themselves using this model. Because it was the first model, and because there was little variation in its features from city to city, we chose to call them political cities.

We describe political cities as based on a mayor-council legal platform, including all or almost all of the structural characteristics of the mayor form of government, particularly a directly elected mayor, the separation of powers between the mayor and the city council, district elections for the council, and no professional chief administrative officer. In the prereform and early municipal reform period, this is, although somewhat simplified, an accurate description of the structure of almost all American cities. In the municipal reform era, mayor-council cities adapted, and that is the subject we consider in Chapter 4.

Administrative cities rest on council-manager platforms, have councils elected at large, a symbolic mayor selected from the council, and unity of powers. The administrative city is operated by a city manager, chosen on the basis of merit, at the head of a merit-based civil service system all reporting to the manager. By the 1920s, this was the city structure recommended in the Model City Charter, a subject we consider in Chapter 6. All but a few of the cities adopting the council-manager statutory platform between 1920 and 1960 adopted the pure or orthodox reformed administrative city model, with little variation from city to city. Although this administrative city construct is somewhat simplified, it is an accurate representation of the common characteristics of these cities between 1912 and the mid-1960s. There were a few outliers with, for example, a directly elected mayor, but these were the exception. The later wholesale modification of structural details of administrative cities, which began in the 1960s, is the subject of Chapter 5.

Political Cities: The Prereform Era

At about the same time as the framing of the Constitution, the charter of the city of Baltimore (1799) provided for the separation of powers and checks and balances between the mayor and city council (Adrian 1988). The structure of Baltimore's city government was obviously modeled on what became the state of Maryland. In essence, the mayor-council city had been born, and in time it came to be the universal political structure of American cities. Jeffersonian and Jacksonian traditions expressed at the city level insured that the powers of the mayor and council would be relatively weak because of checks and balances. At the time, the political and executive authority of the mayor and council was further diluted because department heads in many cities were directly elected. Because of checks and balances between the mayor and the council and the direct election of other administrative officers, this form of city government came to be called the weak mayor model.

At the federal level, the checks-and-balances form also came to be known as the presidential model, particularly as a way to distinguish it from the British parliamentary model. At the level of the American states, we could rightly refer to it as the governor's model, because it is essentially the same as the federal presidential model. The endurance of the American constitutional model not only in our national government but also in all fifty states is remarkable. Over the past two centuries there have been some structural adaptations, such as the Nebraska unicameral model, but all of the key elements of constitutional checks and balances are still in place. In stark comparison, over the past two centuries many American cities have changed their political structure remarkably.

At the city level, the presidential model came to be called the mayor-council form, not the mayor form, which would have made the nomenclature parallel to the presidential and gubernatorial model. Because many American cities would later adopt an entirely different model of local government, it is useful to describe the original mayor-council structure as a political city.

After the Civil War, the boss and party machine system grew rapidly. Patronage began in Jefferson's administration, flourished during the Jacksonian era, and was commonplace in American cities in the 1850s. Local political bosses, who controlled the party and the nomination processes, also influenced election and public policy outcomes. City political bosses, usually mayors, had substantial patronage at their disposal in the form of jobs, contracts, and favors for loyalists. Newly arrived, lower-income ethnic immigrants often formed the political base of boss mayors, particularly in coastal cities such as New York, Boston, and Baltimore.

Political cities were embedded in an economic, social, and political context that was powerfully important, particularly in terms of eventual reform and the eventual emergence of administrative cities.

As growth and industrialization came, people's expectations of the city changed. Between the 1840s and the 1920s, the number of cities with a population over 100,000 increased more than five times and smaller cities with populations of 10,000 to 25,000 persons increased more than six times (Glaab and Brown 1967). Metropolitan growth was accompanied by the diffusion of urban populations. New York tripled its population with the annexation of Brooklyn in 1898. Other metropolitan areas such as Chicago, Cleveland, Pittsburgh, Detroit, Los Angeles, Seattle, Atlanta, and Birmingham more than doubled (Kantor 1988, 87). The main sources of increased population in urban areas were migrants from rural areas and immigrants from foreign countries. The increased productivity of farm labor in the late nineteenth century and commercial and industrial demand for labor contributed to the massive movement of rural labor to urban areas. By 1910, about one-third of the urban population was estimated to be in-migration rural-born Americans (Glaab and Brown 1967), and until the 1920s, when federal laws restricted the influx of foreigners, there was a flood of foreign immigrants, primarily from Europe. By 1920, almost half of the urban population was the foreign born and their descendants (Miller 1973).

As cities industrialized and their populations increased, several distinct characteristics of American urban areas emerged. First, the economically uneven pattern of urban development between core and peripheral cities began. Core cities earned a dominant position in the market, as distant towns became economically subordinate to core cities. Though suburban areas were potential threats to core cities, it was not until the 1920s that the automobile started to make long-distance commuting possible. Other factors helped give dominant market positions to core cities. The reduced cost of long-distance freight by railroads, lower production costs caused by capital-intensive technological innovations, the growth of trusts and big corporations, and the concentration of labor and capital markets in core cities resulted in the siting of industry and commerce in places where they could be most profitable—the center cities.

Politically important changes were also in motion. At the national and state level, the idea of the direct popular election of the president and of governors became increasingly popular. Printed secret ballots also reinforced popular control. These changes had several important ramifications in cities. Population growth provided new incentives for citizens to see their voting power as leading to job and business opportunities through patronage and constituent services. Commercial and business groups saw public services as necessary conditions for the success of their businesses, which resulted in an increase in the number of services provided to business by local governments. The diversification of the urban population along ethnic, religious, and cultural lines intensified political and social cleavages. New patterns of urban land use divided the central business area in many American cities into "segregated zones" along ethnic, religious, and racial class lines. The growing immigrant population and its ghettoization aroused new political conflicts related to differences in lifestyle, religion, and culture (Katznelson 1981).

In the era of political cities, the federal government generally took a laissez-faire stance regarding city development, while concentrating on national growth (Kantor 1988, 97). Though railroads stimulated the industrialization of American cities, no new federal grants to railroads were added after 1872 (Poulson 1981). Federal intervention in city development was rare, except for two major programs: assistance in harbor construction and flood control, and, much later, grants-in-aid for state highway construction (Poulson 1981). Contrary to the nonintervention policy of the federal government in city affairs, state governments had different interests and incentives. Until the 1950s, state governments had judicial and constitutional supremacy over cities. This was confirmed in 1868 by "Dillon's Rule" named after Judge Dillon's ruling in the case of *City of Clinton v. Cedar Rapids and Missouri Railroad Company*, which restricted the proprietary power of municipal corporations and protected private property rights from municipal control (Elkin 1987, 19–21). Dillon's Rule also balanced urban and rural political power as represented in state governments. Dillon's Rule was upheld by the U.S. Supreme Court in 1903 and 1923 (Krane, Rigos, Hill 2001). However, the growing political power and market position of cities in the national economy led these conflicting relationships between state and local governments to converge. State prosperity depended on city growth and the states knew it. As a result, city governments were given wide autonomy when making urban policy.

In time, city political machines began to have problems. First, the distributional politics of the political machine seemed unstable and inefficient to the middle-class and urban business community (even to immigrants, because certain groups were favored over others). The public sector under machine politics grew largely because machine leaders tried to maintain the governing system by providing jobs and services to voters who supported them. In response, machine leaders expanded public services, such as police and fire, and built better streets and new civic centers. However, the hidden incentives of jobs and contracts for select individuals meant that these public services were administered inequitably and inefficiently. "Political marketing" through which jobs and contracts were informally distributed in return for payments to political leaders is one example.

In response, the interests of the middle class and the business community united to oppose political machines. Further, immigrant assimilation was of little interest to business leaders, and the lack of business capacity to influence city affairs resulted in the embrace of the ideals of the "good government movement"—efficiency, political neutrality, centralized authority.

In the initial stages of machine politics, the interests of political leaders and business elites generally converged into a tacit agreement. Instead of intervening in developmental decisions, political leaders pursued personal advancement by distributing jobs or contracts and manipulating racial and ethnic conflicts. Political machines were viewed by business groups as a defense against the demands of the disadvantaged. Machine politicians responded to the demands from the disadvantaged as individuals—not as a social class. In essence, the machines became a social control mechanism for the masses. On the other hand, business considered city political machines necessary to a stable and reliable market climate. In return for bribes and support for political machines, businesses would be left alone. Acquisition of monopolistic positions by public utilities and annexation of territory to central cities were examples of business influence in developmental politics.

As the concerns of cities turned to industrial growth, urban policy started to emphasize the physical reconstruction of city centers to accommodate commercial and production activities. However, there were internal conflicts between democratic systems that produced community decisions through consensus, on the one hand, and the power of business that tried to subordinate city decision-making processes to market mechanisms, on the other hand.

The hottest issue for local governments in developmental policy during the machine era is well described in the following:

> The politics of urban economic development were thrown into an "uneasy relationship" between the calculus of democracy and the calculus of the market. The liberal-democratic characteristics of the regime ensured that the division of labor (and control) between public vs. private power over community development was an issue throughout the period. The issue constantly before city governments was this: *How much economic autonomy could private economic enterprise permit in a political order that enabled other interests to voice political demands regarding urban development?* [italics in original] (Kantor 1988, 102)

As mass democracy emerged in the industrial era, the power of business groups weakened and the power of machine political leaders grew. One important reason for the weakened power of business in developmental decision making was its divided interests. Speculative entrepreneurs were best served by fragmented, decentralized, and corrupted city governments such as the Tweed Ring in New York City. Centralized, bureaucratic, corrupted political machines, however, protected big corporate interests. Under the Tweed Ring in New York City, wealthy, speculative enterprises (e.g., utility investors, real estate speculators, and contractors) could get large benefits from disorganized politics because they could easily find opportunities to expand their business by exchanging cash payments with subsets of the permeable and corrupt political structure. Corporate lawyers and managers, by contrast, managed big corporations, and their interests were thought to be enhanced by the orderly operation of a community economy or market.

The kind of politics exemplified by the Tweed Ring was based on a patronage system under which political leaders had to sustain their governmental powers by paying money to legislators, offering jobs to partisans, or sponsoring a large number of projects for credit markets. The efforts of politicians to maintain a disorganized regime made them pursue inflationary policies by issuing municipal bonds. The increased indebtedness of cities eventually threatened their financial and business institutions by depreciating the value of the bonds. Disorganized city politics could not in the long run effectively deal with increasing social problems, such as the tensions between workers and employers, confrontations between native-born Americans and immigrants, and immigrants' complaints of poor health care, poverty, poor housing, and crime. These social problems made business leaders anxious about the declining business climate.

By the late nineteenth century, political, social, and economic forces in American cities combined to make a fertile seedbed for municipal reform. There was, as Hirschman noted, widespread disappointment with the functioning of political cities. The era of political representativeness in America was drawing to a close, and to use Kaufman's concept, the increasing power of the values of neutral professional competence and executive leadership was at hand. The story of the administrative city was beginning.

Early Municipal Reform

On January 25, 1894, 147 citizens gathered in Philadelphia to attend the first National Conference for Good City Government. The purpose of the conference was to consider ways to rid cities of graft, corruption, patronage, and the spoils associated with city bosses and political machines. In 1897, a committee of reformers established the National Civic League, still a lively organization dedicated to good local government, which developed the first Model City Charter. The charter they adopted recommended the mayor-council form of government and an independent civil service commission whose commissioners "shall prescribe, amend and enforce regulations for appointments to, and promotion in, and for examinations in the administrative service of the city . . ." (Model City Charter 1900, 23). So the early forces of municipal reform tended to favor strengthened executive leadership in the hands of what came to be called the "strong mayor."

"By the late nineteenth and early twentieth century, decentralized and fragmented municipal governments became prime targets for domination by centralized political party machines. From the perspective of the reformers, machines would fill in any existing power vacuum and create order out of chaos" (Renner and DeSantis 1993, 57). As a result, reformers turned to the executive (mayor) for leadership. In 1880, the strong mayor-council plan was enacted in Brooklyn. Under the new charter in Brooklyn, the comptroller and auditor were the only two elected department heads. The nonelected department heads were responsible to the mayor (Schiesl 1977). In 1885, the strong mayor-council system went into effect in Boston and Philadelphia, and the Los Angeles voters approved expanded mayoral powers in 1888 (Schiesl 1977). In 1891, Indianapolis gave the mayor full powers of appointment of department heads. The 1898 San Francisco charter included provisions for a strong mayor. In the early 1900s, Boston and New York City gave the mayor power of appointment and removal of administrative officers. Gradually, the idea spread to other cities. By the 1890s, the mayor was the dominant figure in prestige and power. By 1900, twelve of the twenty-three biggest cities had strong mayor charters in place. The nineteenth century ended with the hope that strong mayors would balance the powers between the mayor and the city council and somehow lessen the power of party-based bosses and political machines (Griffith 1974). It didn't work.

Primary opposition to political machines came from middle- and upper-class white Anglo-Saxon Protestants (WASPs) who had dominated the local political process before the period of immigration (Renner and DeSantis 1993). Convinced they were disadvantaged by the status quo, WASPs became the core of the municipal reform movement. Their agenda included civil service (merit) systems for hiring public employees, competitive bidding among firms for government contracts, the secret ballot, fair election practices, nonpartisan elections, short ballots, at-large elections, initiative and referendum measures, and the council-manager form of government (Renner and DeSantis 1993). Beginning in the 1890s, the progressive movement mobilized by businesses, professionals, and WASPs was challenging the existing machine politics system in many American cities. Hofstader (1955, 5–6) describes "progressivism" from the 1890s to the 1920s as "an effort to restore economic individualism and political democracy that was widely believed to have existed earlier in America and to have been destroyed by giant corporations and corrupt political machines." Progressives hoped to bring back a kind of morality and civic purity that was believed to have been lost.

Hofstader (1955) explained the cause of the progressive movement by distinguishing the political ethics of Yankee Protestants on one hand and European immigrants on the other. Yankee Protestant political ethics emphasized disinterest on the part of citizens in public affairs, the pervasiveness of general principles and abstract laws, and institutional support for individual development through economic means. The ethical system of immigrants was based on their social and cultural backgrounds: lack of independence in political activities, dependence on authority and hierarchy, priority of family over individual life, and personal obligation and loyalty in political relationships. The power of business leaders with Yankee Protestant political ethics was gradually overcome by the political power of immigrants and their patrimonial political ethics.

The struggle between political machines and reformers during the Progressive Era was essentially a fight over control of jobs and ways of distributing local government services, not their *re*distribution between different social classes. The structural characteristics of the reform project made it more difficult for disadvantaged groups to participate in local politics. Reformed local government would prove to be an inferior means of social control because it relied on some disenfranchisement of the poor, rather than on providing a political reward structure to contain mass influence. The reform project shifted fights over distributive policies to a new set of actors (professional bureaucrats) who played according to a new set of rules.

The Development of Administrative Cities

Council-manager government was a response to the separated-powers structural logic of the political city. Reformers advocating council-manager government wished not simply to replace bad leaders with good or to strengthen the powers of the mayor; they proposed to change the structure of government to combat what they believed to be the pathologies associated with city politics. They associated those pathologies directly with the separation of powers. Better cities could be achieved, they believed, by changing the formal machinery of government. For a guide, they looked to the corporate model, with a board setting general policy and all of the day-to-day work under the direct control of a corporation president.

This model, applied to city government, replaced the strong mayor with a professional city manager appointed by the council. Mayors in administrative cities were chosen not by the people but by the other members of the city council and had only symbolic powers—that is, no more power than other council members. In administrative cities, council-manager government included a formal civil service system and a professionally managed bidding and purchasing system. Checks and balances were replaced by the neutral professional competence represented by an appointed city manager who appointed all city department heads on the basis of merit. City policy-making powers were unified in a council elected at large, thus depriving precincts and neighborhoods of particularized forms of representation. Administrative powers were unified under the city manager. One sphere of power was not to meddle in the affairs of the other.

Before cities could adopt such a model, either they had to secure a charter from the state spelling out the allocation of political powers or, as later developed, states established statutes providing for council-manager cities as an alternative to the mayor-council format depending on the votes of city residents. In the early twentieth century, the concept of unity of powers as embodied in council-manager government and the logic of the unity of powers applied to cities was novel. When Staunton, Virginia, hired a manager in 1908 there was a glimpse of what was to come. However, Staunton did not adopt a full, legal, council-manager platform until 1920. The first city to adopt the full council-manager statutory platform was Sumter, South Caro-

Figure 3.1 **Number of Council-Manager Cities**

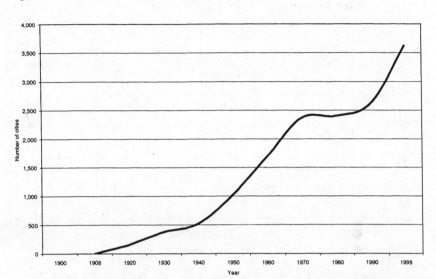

lina, in 1912. Gradually states approved council-manager home rule charters for particular cities or adapted general statutes authorizing council-manager government, always, of course, dependent on the vote of city residents. In the 1920s, due to a generalized diffusion of innovation, dozens of cities adopted council-manager government and that momentum increased through the 1930s, slowed somewhat in the late Depression and World War II years, and then increased sharply in the 1960s and 1970s. Not until the early 1980s did the adoption of council-manager government slow to a trickle. Although not as steep as some innovation S-curves, the adoption of council-manager government nevertheless follows the S-curve, as Figure 3.1 illustrates.

By 1934, when the International City and County Management Association (ICMA) first began surveying cities, 22 percent of American cities had adopted the council-manager form of government and 52 percent were mayor-council governments (ICMA *Municipal Year Book 1934*). As Figure 3.2 illustrates, the gap between the two forms gradually diminished until 1972, when, for the first time, the number of council-manager cities exceeded the number of mayor-council cities. The biggest changes occur between 1945 and 1975, a period of rapid suburbanization and the incorporation of many new suburban cities.

For the past twenty years, the ratio of mayor-council to council-manager cities has stabilized, with council-manager cities increasing slightly as a percentage of all cities. This stability is, however, misleading. While almost all

Figure 3.2   **Percentage of Mayor-Council and Council-Manager Cities from ICMA Surveys**

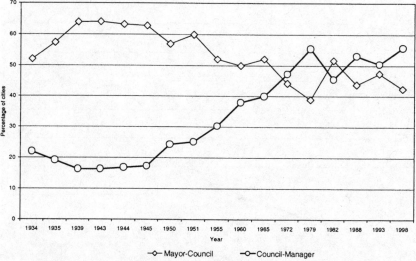

cities have retained their statutory platform as either council-manager or mayor-council, many of them have made important changes in the detailed features of their structure, the subject of the remaining chapters of this book.

The Moral Force in Municipal Reform

Often overlooked in the emergence of administrative cities is the remarkable moral tone of their advocates. As theories of the diffusion of innovation predict, changing values are often at the center of institutional reform. This moral tone was particularly evident in the political battles over reform in those political cities that changed to the administrative form. One of the best examples is the story of Wichita, Kansas. In 1907, Henry J. Allen bought the *Wichita Beacon*, entered politics, and almost immediately began a media campaign to clean up Wichita physically and morally. In 1911, he secured the city's printing contract but lost it in 1915 when his supporters on the commission were not reelected. In 1914, Allen ran for governor but lost. So Allen had more than just moral outrage to explain his newspaper's campaign for moral reform.

In order to reverse his own sagging political fortunes and clean up Wichita, Allen became an outspoken proponent of the council-manager plan. Allen and the city manager plan were good for each other because the city manager plan was "good government, as it promoted professional, business-like government in line with Allen's progressive reform image and ideals." With support from the *Beacon*'s rival newspaper, the *Eagle,* Allen began a civic campaign promoting the city manager plan of government. Both papers used the news and editorial columns to generate support, focusing initially on state legislative action, next on a local petition drive to place on the ballot a proposed change from the political mayor-council form to the administrative council-manager government. "Stories of how the manager plan was working in other U.S. cities formed a large part of the civic campaign" (Flentje 1993, 23). Dominating these stories, however, was Dayton, Ohio. Allen visited Dayton in 1915 and wrote an enthusiastic story, called "Running a Modern Town," in support of the city manager plan (Flentje 1993). A delegation of Wichita Rotarians made a trip to Dayton in 1916. City officials and civic reformers from Dayton also visited Wichita on several occasions. The repeated use of Dayton as the model of the city manager form of government led an opponent of the city manager cause in Wichita to remark, "Aren't you tired—sick and tired of having Dayton flaunted in your face by a crowd of reformers" (Flentje 1993, 20, 23, 24).

The campaign for council-manager government in Wichita was supported by a constituency of mostly middle- and upper-class businessmen, professionals, and active women—who were at the forefront of Progressive Era changes nationally. However, the civic campaign was ultimately aided by a moral campaign. "In Wichita, the objective was not only good government but moral government" (Flentje 1993, 25).

Moralism has permeated Kansas's political culture from the very beginning. In the 1850s, Kansas led the nation against slavery. In 1880, Kansas became the first state in the nation to adopt constitutional prohibition and one of the last states to rescind prohibition. Moralism also shaped Wichita politics. Conflicts over moral issues such as liquor, prostitution, and gambling had roots in the early years of Wichita. In 1916, Henry J. Allen was closely associated with these moral issues and linked them directly to the politically based mayor-council form of government. In order to sell the council-manager plan to the people, civic reformers needed to convince them that there was a crisis, and the police became the perfect target. The largest and most visible of the city departments, the police department was highly politicized, filled with patronage, and not very well managed. By 1916, many people were convinced that "moral codes were being violated and that enforcement of these codes was selective. Violators without standing . . . were being harassed, while prominent perpetrators were not interfered with." Allen's *Beacon* unleashed an emotional attack against the mayor and the city police department, charging ineffective law enforcement against gambling houses and joints. Evangelist E.J. Bulgin lambasted city hall for permitting bootlegging in Wichita. A crowd of five hundred citizens listened to Andrew Brodie, a local pastor, say that "the best plan of all is the city manager plan." By that time, " civic and moral forces had joined arms for the city manager cause" (Flentje 1993, 26, 28, 29). In Albert Hirschman's terms, the people of Wichita were disappointed with the structure of city government.

"With the chief defender of the status quo [the mayor] emasculated, the proponents of the city manager plan were not seriously challenged in clearing the legislative hurdles necessary to securing a city manager state law." In the final days of the campaign, a number of Protestant ministers urged adoption of the city manager plan from their pulpits. On March 9, 1917, the citizens voted overwhelmingly for the city manager plan. "The coalition for good and moral government which was guided by Henry Allen, supported by the Governor of Kansas, publicized by the *Beacon* and the *Eagle,* assisted by Rotarians both in and out of Wichita, and bolstered by Wichita churchmen, made the final act of placing a city manager law on the books in Kansas a relatively peaceful affair" (Flentje 1993, 29, 31).

On June 15, 1917, a new city council appointed Louis Ash as the first city manager of Wichita. Ash's statement to the local press summarized the long fight for reform in Wichita and Kansas: "I believe in a clean city. . . . I will insist on an absolutely clean city. . . . I am a member of the Presbyterian Church and believe in the highest moral standards. . . . I will not let politics enter the city affairs in any way" (Flentje 1993, 36).

The moral and civic campaign to bring good and moral government to Kansas and Wichita is representative of what happened in many states and American cities during the Progressive Era. The spread of the city manager plan throughout the nation was a process of the diffusion of innovation. The adoption of the administrative council-manager plan in Wichita and in many other cities in the years to come verifies several of the explanations of the diffusion of innovation found in the research of others (DiMaggio and Powell 1991; Strang and Soule 1998; Rogers 1995). First, the corruption of city government in Wichita allowed the advocates of change to foster a growing sense of crisis and thereby increase the prospects for change. Second, the dominant moral standards of the community demanded a compatible structure of government. Wichita is on the midwestern plains and its people strongly reflect an individualistic, moralistic political culture. Third, it is probably not coincidental that Dayton, Ohio, was used as the primary government model for Wichita to follow. Dayton is a midwestern city, like Wichita, and relatively close geographically. Fourth, as theories of innovation predict, the mass media played a very important role in bringing governmental reform to Wichita. Fifth, change agents like the local church leaders, Rotarians, business leaders, and women's groups were carriers of change, the agents of

Figure 3.3   **Council-Manager Cities by City Size**

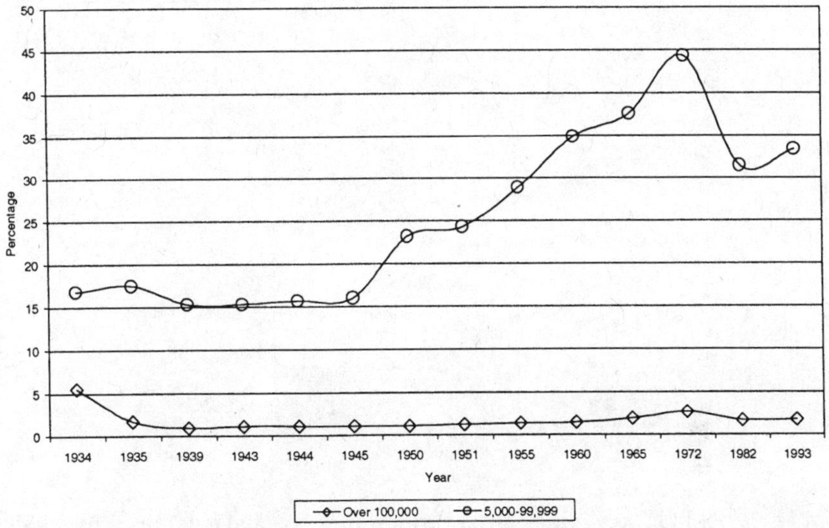

diffusion. Sixth, it is clear that the reformers of Wichita wanted to "mimic" Dayton and the other cities that had successfully implemented the city manager plan. Seventh, Allen's motives were not solely civic-minded or moralistic. His crusade to bring the city manager plan to Wichita was a way to acquire prestige, status, and social standing, and possibly the city's printing contract. The civic campaign helped him to reverse his political misfortunes and to sell his newspapers.

Variations in the Diffusion of Administrative Cities

Hidden in this general S-curve of the adoption of administrative city structures are several important variations. The first and probably the most important variation is by city size. As Figure 3.3 shows, cities over 100,000 population have been less inclined to adopt council-manager government than cities under 100,000 population. In larger cities, the combined forces of population, heterogeneity, and age account for their tendency to retain the political mayor-council structure. But we demonstrate in Chapter 4 that, over the years, larger cities, while retaining the formal mayor-council nomenclature, modified their structures incrementally to take on many of the features of administrative cities.

Second, because smaller and medium-size cities were more likely to be of the council-manager form, logic suggests that suburban and independent (not

Figure 3.4   **Council-Manager Cities By City Location**

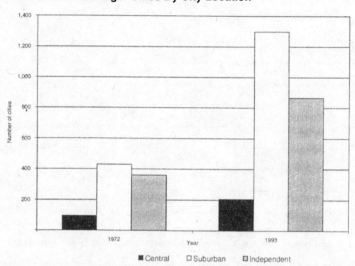

in a metropolitan area) cities, because they are small and medium-size, would tend in the direction of the administrative model. Data for 1992 and 1993, shown in Figure 3.4, dramatically make this point. By a very wide margin, larger and often central in metropolitan areas tend to retain the mayor-council form and its political arrangements while their suburbs and exurbs tend strongly to the council-manager form and its administrative emphasis. As suburban cities have grown in population, they have become more heterogeneous and more like the central cities they surround. They have almost all retained the council-manager statutory platform, but, as we describe in Chapter 5, most have significantly adapted their structures, taking on many of the features of political cities.

The nation's metropolitan areas grew dramatically between 1950 and 1960, increasing their populations by about 23 million people. In the same period, however, the major core cities lost population. Richard Stillman (1974) reports that

> St. Louis's population dropped by 100,000, Detroit's by 180,000, Cleveland's by 30,000, and Washington, D.C.'s by 38,000 in this period. Yet the population for these metropolitan areas showed striking gains, most largely on account of suburban growth: the St. Louis area increased by 19.8 percent; the Detroit area by 24.7 percent; the Cleveland area by 22.6 percent; the Washington area by 36.7 percent. . . . The expanding suburban populations created sudden new demands for public services—sewers, water, roads, schools, housing—as well as for more sorts of local governments. . . . The shocks of suburbanization in the 1950s caused council

Figure 3.5   **Percentage of Council-Manager Cities by Region**

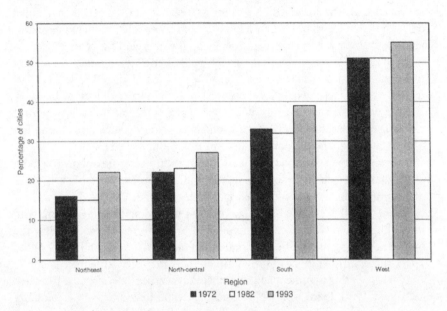

members to turn to managers for help. . . . Councilmen were eager to turn
these intricate problems over to a technician and relieve themselves of many
of the administrative difficulties. . . . Hence, a spurt in growth of manager
government appeared after World War II, particularly in new suburban settle-
ments. (22–23)

In the best early study of this subject, Robert Wood (1958) connected the
values of those who moved to the suburbs and their propensity to embrace
council-manager government: "defined as an ideology, a faith in communities of limited size and a belief in the condition of intimacy is quite real. The
dominance of the old values explains more about the people and the politics
of the suburbs than any other interpretation" (266).

There is wide variation by region in the form of local government, as
Figure 3.5 indicates. There are more political cities in the Northeast, North
Central and South and more administrative cities in the West.[1] These trends
reflect the general patterns of population migration to the south and west.
This expansion coincides in time with the popularity of manager government, as can be seen in the comparative growth of manager government in
1972, 1982, and 1993.

These trends may also reflect the long-standing contention of Daniel Elazar
(1994) that there are variations in political culture by region. He describes

three dominant political cultures—individualistic, moralistic, and traditional-istic (120–21). The administrative values associated with council-management cities are close to Elazar's individualistic and moralistic political cultures—tending to favor expertise, professionalism, government as a commonwealth, merit systems, bureaucracy, and "clean" or "healthy" government. In tracing the migration of these ideologies over time across the United States, he particularly found these two political cultures in the midwest, the mountain states, and the west, the same regions with the highest percentage of administrative cities. The border states and the south tend to be traditional, favoring the values of the status quo and the political legitimacy of established elites.

Patterns of the adoption of council-manager city government involve both cities that *changed* their form of government and newly established cities that simply adopted the model as they incorporated. One could argue, for example, that the S-curve of the adoption of the council-manager form with its administrative values can be explained primarily by the increase in the number of cities, and particularly suburban cities in the period from 1930 to 1970, the era of the greatest growth in council-manager city government.

Our test of this argument suggests that this is essentially correct. Between 1910 and 1930, there were approximately 1,000 new cities almost equally divided between the two types. But, between 1930 and 1970, the forty-year period covering most of the S-curve of the adoption of council-manager gov-ernment, the total number of American cities more than doubled, from about 3,200 to about 6,700. During this same period, the percentage of cities with council-manager platforms grew from 12 percent to 35 percent of all cities. We estimate that 57 percent of the new cities that incorporated during this period, many of them in the suburbs and in the southwest and west, adopted the council manager platform and embraced its administrative values. The rate of increase in the number of new cities is now much lower and the ratio of new cities choosing the political or the administrative manager systems is once again about equal.

This finding is evidence of the logic of long eras (thirty to fifty years), or epochs of changing values. The widespread adoption of administrative city government in the maturing stages of the Progressive Era is a reflection of the hegemony of values associated with that era. While the local government application of progressive thinking was called municipal reform, and many cities actually reformed by changing from political to administrative struc-tures, more were new cities choosing the administrative model at the outset. Much of the attention in the literature on this subject has focused on cities that changed—Cincinnati, Kansas City, Dayton, and many others. These are dramatic stories of stamping out corruption, tossing out boss mayors, and bringing clean, honest government to the city. Our treatment of Wichita,

Kansas, earlier in this chapter is illustrative. Because of the power of these stories, it is easy to forget that most cities adopting council-manager government and its administrative values were new, fully formed, without need of reform. As we describe in Chapter 5, beginning in the 1970s these administrative cities began their own process of reform.

The municipal reform period between the 1930s and the 1950s can be characterized as a time of ripened reform. Stone and Saunders (1987, 110) summarized three basic principles of good government during this time period:

1. There is an overriding public interest that is superior to the particular interests of the various segments of the urban community.
2. This general interest is more easily discovered through cooperation than through political conflict and competition.
3. Solving technical problems is the central task of local government; "politics" is therefore to be minimized.

During the New Deal era (1933–40), programs like the Federal Emergency Relief Administration were designed to give money to the unemployed; the Works Progress Administration was structured to enhance the working conditions of Americans. The Public Works Administration was created to construct public works, and public housing programs were established to provide low-priced residences for the poor. By enlarging federal programs for the development and the stability of cities, Democrats appealed to a broad range of city constituents and became the dominant political party in America.

During the 1940s and 1950s, there were significant changes in federal urban policies. While the New Deal provided social relief in the central cities, national urban policy in the next two decades provided powerful subsidies and mortgage inducements for home ownership. This policy drove, and to some extent still drives, the forces of suburbanization, and, as we have found, almost all of the new suburban cities adopted the administrative model. Investment decisions made by the War Production Board during World War II, the federal interstate highway programs, and the Federal Housing Administration mortgage insurance program were highly development-oriented federal urban policies. These programs encouraged suburban development by inducing the middle class to move out of older, inner cities and facilitating low-cost housing ownership by new immigrants from rural areas. An important reason why urban policies were oriented toward development both in the suburbs and downtown areas of American cities was that the federal government and both political parties were chasing the increased voting power of the new suburban middle class, which was not particularly interested in redistributive policies for the urban poor. These federal policies had the effect of essentially requiring cities to have qualified bureaucracies (Stone and Saunders 1987, 285).

The bureaucratization of administration resulting from the reform movement brought several consequences. Because department officials were appointed on the basis of merit, skill, and expertise and were protected by civil service laws, they came to possess self-directing power in community affairs. Administrative officials did not want outside interference and generally had discretionary power to carry out their agency's mission. As Lowi (1964, 207) described this situation, "The department bureaucracies are not neutral, they are only independent." The high professionalization of city bureaucracies tended to block the upward mobility of less educated, ethnic, and minority groups.

Suburban growth imposed severe social costs on virtually everybody in metropolitan areas (Kantor 1995). The transformation of suburbia into a sprawling network of preponderantly low-density, white, prosperous communities has meant the creation of a veritable wall of separation between city and suburb based on class and race, locking urban America into a segregated society. Most central cities now disproportionately include those who have been left behind—the poor, minorities, unemployed, and others unable to take advantage of the suburban dream. This has, in turn, created a mismatch of need and resources between city and suburb; hard-pressed central cities must cope with the greatest demands for public service even as the government revenues for meeting them increasingly lie in the suburban rings (Cox 1973; U.S. Department of Housing and Urban Development 1980; Johnson and Leland 2000).

By the mid- to late 1960s, it was thought that reform was over. It is common to assume that the great period of structural change in American cities was also over. In fact, in the rest of this book we demonstrate that the pace of structural adaptation by American cities did not stop—it did not even slow down. But it did change. Both political and administrative cities moved steadily toward another alternative, the adapted city. Before we turn to that subject, this chapter closes with a consideration of the big questions.

Were the Municipal Reformers Right?

Did the unity-of-powers model applied to American cities achieve the purpose of the reformers? Does governmental structure matter? At the end of the reform era, were political and administrative cities really that different? To answer these questions, we turn to the findings and opinions of the leading urban scholars in the 1960s and 1970s.

One purpose of reform was to eliminate city political machines, boss mayors, job patronage, and contract graft. Virtually all those who study cities agree that by the 1960s corruption in American cities had been sharply reduced. As Banfield and Wilson (1963) reported,

> If honesty, impartiality, and efficiency—efficiency "in the small"—are the criteria, council-manager cities have with few exceptions been conspicuously well governed. To be sure, they would probably have been well governed under a mayor-council plan; it is because the city wants good government that it gets the council-manager plan in the first place. Nevertheless, although there is no way of proving it, we suspect that the council-manager plan has been a cause as well as an effect of "good government," and that most of the cities that have it are, by these criteria, better governed than they otherwise would have been. (185)

By the 1960s, incidents of political corruption in administrative cities were rare and, when they happened, usually involved rather small matters. But political cities were also influenced by the reform movement and adopted civil service systems, bid and contract controls, and other technical processes to reduce corruption. Chapter 4 treats this subject in greater detail.

By the 1960s there were virtually no political machines or party bosses in administrative cities. The definitive study of the time, Lineberry and Fowler's "Reformism and Public Policies in American Cities" (1967), found that

> the goal of the reformers has been substantially fulfilled, for nonpartisan elections, at-large constituencies, and manager governments are associated with a lessened responsiveness of cities to the enduring conflicts of political life. Or, as Stone, Price, and Stone (1940) argued in their study of changes produced by the adoption of manager governments, the council after the reform "tended to think more of the community as a whole and less of factional interests in making their decisions. If one of the components of the middle class reformers' ideal was "to seek the good of the community as a whole" and to minimize the impact of social cleavages on political decision making, then their institutional reforms have served, by and large, to advance that goal." (121–22)

A review of mayor-council cities in the early 1960s argues:

> The old-style politician got his power in part by deliberately sacrificing the efficiency and integrity of city services. He could ignore intensely moved minorities because he used jobs, favors, and protection to maintain his organization and get the vote. This, of course, made for bad administration. The new-style politician, whose power—such as it is—arises from

other sources, is not under the necessity to interfere with the processes of administration. On the contrary, he wants the approval of the middle class voters who regard good government and good administration as practically synonymous, and therefore he has the strongest incentive to search out and eliminate inefficiency and corruption. (Banfield and Wilson 1963, 186)

This was particularly true in larger political cities.

One of the purposes of reform was to bring businesslike practices, efficiency, and economy to the city. A 1967 study found that council-manager cities over 50,000 population tended to tax and spend less than mayor-council cities over 50,000 population. Obviously, spending less is an administrative value. Since that time, however, the results of research on the subject have been ambiguous. David Morgan and John Pelissero (1980), using time-series analysis, matched eleven cities of each type and found that taxing and spending differences were slight. Banfield and Wilson (1963) argued the opposite and added a note of despair about ever really knowing whether reformed cities are more efficient.

The expectation that the plan would reduce the cost of local government has been sadly disappointed. Generally, taxes have gone up, not down, after its adoption. The reasons for this, its supporters assert, are twofold: (1) citizens now have greater confidence in the integrity of their government and are therefore willing to entrust more money to it, and (2) the centralization of authority now permits the government to undertake larger tasks. (186)

Virtually all of the studies of comparative efficiency make the point that efficiency in the abstract may have been achieved by municipal reform, but reform was more efficient in some cities than in others.

Reformed cities (cities with manager governments, at-large constituencies, and nonpartisan elections) appeared to be unresponsive in tax and spending policies to differences in income, educational, occupational, religious, and ethnic characteristics of their populations. In contrast, unreformed cities (cities with mayor-council governments, ward constituencies, and partisan elections) reflected class, racial, and religious composition in their taxing and spending decisions. (Dye 1973)

Nevertheless, as a result of reform, city government was "much more honest, efficient and democratic than it was a generation ago," according to William

Anderson, a leading authority on American local government at the time (quoted in Wood 1958, 53).

There is virtually no disagreement that the forces of structural change had a powerful effect on many city governments. By the 1960s, the distinctive characteristics of political and administrative cities—separation of powers versus unity of powers, partisan versus nonpartisan elections, district versus at-large elections, patronage versus merit, and, most of all, the mayor-council versus the council-manager models—resulted in two very distinct kinds of American cities. The reformers were generally right that changing structural characteristics resulted in efficient, better-managed, and less corrupt local government. At the same time, most of the scholars of the day argued that reform came at a price:

> With the passing of political machines, the governance of cities increasingly has been influenced by bureaucratic independence and expertise. So the merit system and the professionalized civil service have been faulted for depersonalizing city government and isolating it from the individual. Middle class city dwellers do not suffer unduly from this situation; they have fewer needs for public services and are reasonably well positioned to make the system respond. . . . Municipal reform may contribute to more businesslike management of a city, but it does so at a price—less responsiveness to disadvantaged groups within the community and more control by autonomous bureaucrats. (Morgan 1989, 48)

After the 1970s, changing values and disappointment with the status quo would change both political and administrative cities just as the reform movement had driven earlier change. New S-curves of innovation would change city structures in the coming decades. The era of adapted cities was under way.

Note

1. Northeast (Connecticut, Maine, Massachusetts, New Hampshire, Rhode Island, Vermont), mid-Atlantic (New Jersey, New York, and Pennsylvania), North Central (Illinois, Indiana, Michigan, Ohio, Wisconsin, Iowa, Kansas, Minnesota, Missouri, Nebraska, North Dakota, and South Dakota), South (Delaware, Florida, Georgia, Maryland, North Carolina, South Carolina, Virginia, West Virginia, Alabama, Kentucky, Mississippi, Tennessee, Arkansas, Louisiana, Oklahoma, and Texas), West (Arizona, Colorado, Idaho, Montana, Nevada, New Mexico, Utah, and Wyoming, Alaska, California, Hawaii, Oregon, and Washington).

The Evolution of Political Cities

Modern municipal reform is all around us, not in the language of early reform but in a new language. Because earlier reforms were mostly successful, modern reforms deal with new and different problems. These reforms take essentially two forms. The first is the reform of administrative cities, usually cities with council-manager legal or charter platforms; this subject is a favorite of research scholars and is written about often (Svara 1989; Protasel 1989; Newland 1989). These reforms have mostly to do with structural adaptations designed to make administrative cities more politically responsive, adaptations such as directly elected mayors, full-time paid mayors, staff for mayors, council members elected by district, full-time paid council members, staff for council members, and even, in some cases, mayoral involvement in budget preparation and department head selection and direction. How many administrative cities became adapted administrative cities is the subject of the next chapter.

Much less well known is the story of both the early and present-day reform of political cities, usually cities with mayor-council legal or charter platforms. This is the story told here. We begin the story with a review of the distinctions between political cities and adapted political cities. We then present empirical evidence of these adaptations and account for the approximate patterns of change and the forces behind them. Finally, to illustrate a modern adapted political city, we present a case study of Topeka, Kansas.

The primary differences between political cities and adapted political cities are these. Political cities have a directly elected mayor with full executive powers in a separation-of-powers context, always on a mayor-council platform. Political cities may or may not have a merit civil service, routinized auditing requirements, or bid and purchase controls. Political cities elect their council members by district. The mayor has full executive power, including the veto over actions of the city council. In larger political cities, both the mayor and council members have staff. Adapted political cities resemble their political parents because they retain many of the basic elements of the separation of powers with a directly elected mayor with full executive powers and a city council with all legislative powers. But adapted political cities have all made primary administrative adaptations, including adoption of a top position for a professional chief administrative officer, an established civil service, and auditing and bid and purchase controls. In addition, we categorize cities in which the council members are elected at large as adapted political cities.

The point is that many local jurisdictions that would formerly have been labeled political cities have adopted many key elements of the municipal reform agenda and have, thereby, significantly adapted in the direction of less corrupt government and more management efficiency and effectiveness. When these adaptations are fully evident, these cities are distinct enough from political cities to constitute a different empirical category of cities, the adapted political city. In this chapter, we trace the nature of these changes and find that, while incremental and nondramatic, the sum of these changes makes the few remaining political cities distinct from the much more common adapted political cities.

Adapted political cities almost always rest on mayor-council legal platforms, like their political city cousins. Because of their long-time designation as either mayor-council or council-manager cities, it is very common for both scholars and practitioners to assume that these two categories are viable empirical distinctions. But genuine, orthodox political and administrative cities, while clearly very different, are increasingly rare, the outliers or the exceptions. In this chapter we describe how political cities became adapted political cities. Once this description is complete, we set the stage for the bolder claim that adapted political cities and adapted administrative cities are now more like each other than like their political city or administrative city parents.

Management Adaptations

Consistent with the view that government should be run on business principles, municipal reformers sought to reorganize public employment into a system based on merit and efficiency rather than family relationships, friendship, or political party affiliation (Schiesl 1977). "As a personnel policy, the merit system is characterized by emphasis on competence in the selection and subsequent treatment of government employees. A person's ability to render satisfactory service and the qualities of his performance on the job take precedence over other considerations such as party affiliation. . . . Examinations are competitive and the names of those who pass are placed on eligible lists in the order of their rating" (Schultz 1949, 536). "The most acrimonious debates over civil service procedures occurred before 1900; after 1910 the procedures were generally discussed without much conflict, and by 1920 civil service procedures were accepted as the proper way to conduct city business" (Tolbert and Zucher 1983, 24).

In 1883, the Pendleton Act put appointment, promotions, and removals on a merit basis using a system of competitive examinations. The Pendleton Act was a federal government response to President Garfield's assassination by a disgruntled job seeker. But it was also a response to rampant political corruption and dissatisfaction with the performance of government (Tolbert and Zucher 1983). In 1883, a bill passed in the state of New York that was similar to the Pendleton Act (Schiesl 1977; Gottfried 1988). The bill authorized cities over 50,000 in population to establish a civil service board to supervise a system of competitive examinations. In 1884, Massachusetts created a state civil service commission to administer city civil service systems (Gottfried 1988). This law brought the selection of laborers in the city of Boston under civil service regulations. In 1895, Milwaukee adopted civil service reform by placing the power of public appointment in the hands of a civil service commission. A year later, civil service reform came to Chicago. By the middle 1890s, the electorate in Philadelphia, Toledo, New Orleans, and Seattle had approved charter amendments establishing civil service regulations in their governments (Schiesl 1977). In 1898, San Francisco approved a reform charter that provided for a merit-based civil service system. In 1903, Los Angeles adopted a civil service system (Lockard 1969). Fairlie (1908) mentions that by 1908 a number of cities had established civil service examinations. In some cities, however, only the police and fire departments were protected against political appointments. In 1924 the Los Angeles civil service code was expanded to give department heads more security and tenure, thereby enhancing administrative stability and continuity (Lockard 1969). It was clear that the logic of a merit-based civil service would eventually come to dominate hiring and promotion in almost all cities regardless of structure or form.

"The beginnings of state and local civil service based on the merit system appeared in 1884, but the principle did not become widely accepted until the 1930s" (Adrian 1967, 320–21). "By 1935, over 450 cities across the United States had enacted some type of civil service legislation. Thus, by 1935 the transformation of city government from a politically based system to a bureaucratically based system was well under way" (Tolbert and Zucker 1983, 23). In the 1930s and beyond, states began to implement laws requiring cities to use merit-based civil service. By 1938, 674 cities operated under merit systems (Belsley 1938). According to Harold Zinc (1939), 80 percent of cities over 100,000 people operated under at least a partial civil service plan. Of the 682 cities that had a civil service system, 447, or two-thirds, administered their own program, and 235, or one-third, had state-administered systems (Zinc 1939). Zinc was impressed, in 1939, with the progress cities were making in civil service reform, and he indicated that whether a city did or did not have civil service provisions had more to do with size than form of government. He found that small cities were less apt to have civil service provisions in place (Zinc 1939).

In 1939, amendments to the Social Security Act required every state to establish a merit system. Also during this year, a poll conducted by the National Institute of Public Opinion showed that 75 percent of voters favored a civil service system for government employees (Belsley 1939).

In 1940, an amended version of the Hatch Act laid down rules prohibiting local employees from making contributions to political parties and participating in politics (Belsley 1943). By 1963, the states of Iowa, New York, and Ohio required all cities to adopt a civil service system. At the same time, 51 percent of cities in other states had implemented civil service requirements (Wolfinger 1984). By 1978, twenty-four states (see Figure 4.1 below) required all cities to have civil service systems based on merit (ACIR 1993).

Today, most state constitutions have provisions patterned after the Fifth and Fourteenth Amendments of the U.S. Constitution, that prohibit discrimination in employment in all state and local governments. Most cities have enacted employment antidiscrimination legislation patterned after Title VII of the Equal Employment Opportunity Act of 1972 (Gottfried 1988).

Civil service reform has profoundly affected all cities, regardless of form or structure. The move away from the spoils system and toward a merit-based civil service during the twentieth century are a clear sign that mayor-council cities are becoming more professional and administrative.

Because merit-based civil service systems are all but universal (there are a few exceptions), all cities, even those that pioneered separation-of-powers features in city government, have adapted in the direction of administrative effectiveness and professional administration. But in many political cities, merit systems could be described as "soft" or "porous," allowing some political patronage by the mayor, either alone or in cooperation with allies on the city council (Ehrenhalt 1996). Therefore, we concluded that the presence of either a soft or firm merit-based civil service system, while a significant adaptation, is not sufficient to recategorize a city from the political to the adapted political category.

Accounting and Auditing, Budgeting, Purchasing, Bidding

In the last fifty years, many states have adopted laws requiring cities to establish accounting and auditing standards, budgeting and finance rules, purchasing procedures, and bidding requirements. In addition, the General Accounting Standards Board (GASB) has promulgated generally accepted accounting principles that are followed by most cities. The Government Finance Officers Association (GFOA) recognizes cities for following recognized budgeting, financial, and accounting principles and standards. In fiscal 1999, 564 cities were awarded the Distinguished Budget Presentation Awards Program, and 70 percent of all cities over 50,000 population participate in the Certificate of Achievement for Excellence in Financial Reporting (CAFR) program offered by GFOA (GFOA 2001). State laws, the GASB mandates, and the budgeting and financial reporting programs offered by GFOA have made cities more professional and accountable regardless of government form or structure.

By 1978, thirty-one states required cities to follow uniform accounting procedures under state law, and between 1978 and 1990 another four states mandated such accounting procedures. By 1978, thirty-one states set purchasing standards for cities, and by 1990, thirty-nine states required such purchasing standards—an increase of eight states in twelve years. By 1978, nineteen states required cities to perform competitive bidding on all purchases over a specified amount, and by 1990, twenty-six states had such a requirement, an increase of seven states. By 1978, twenty-seven states required cities to conduct an independent post-audit, and by 1990, thirty-eight states required cities to perform an independent post-audit, an increase of eleven states (ACIR 1993). The changes in state laws pertaining to uniform accounting procedures, purchasing standards, competitive bidding for cities, and audits between 1978 and 1990 show that diffusion of innovation is still occurring, but at a much less rapid pace than during the reform era, demonstrating the predictable S-curve pattern of the diffusion of innovation.

Figure 4.1 graphically represents the standards that states have imposed on cities as of 1990.

Like city merit-based civil service systems, we found that uniform accounting, budgeting, purchasing, and bidding standards are common. This is another very significant group of structural and procedural adaptations in the direction of clean government and greater administrative effectiveness, particularly for political cities. However, because these changes are so universal, we decided not to include such changes as criteria by which a political city would be recategorized as an adapted political city.

The Movement to Chief Administrative Officers

As cities became more urban and heterogeneous, as the scope of local government services expanded, and as organizations became more complex and technical, mayor-council cities recognized the need for more professional executive leadership to manage the day-to-day operations of the city. "Heavy

Figure 4.1   **State Requirements as of 1990**

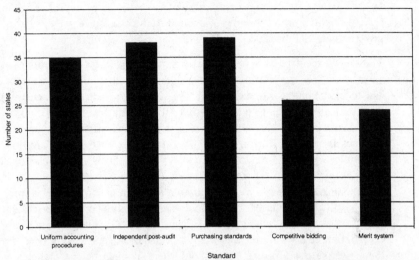

Source: ICMA, *Municipal Year Book*, 1934, 1950, 1960, 1968, and 1988.

demands on the time and effort of the mayors of large cities, especially because of their dual role as administrative heads and political leaders," led to
the creation of an administrative officer (Schultz 1949).[1] An appointed chief
administrator also makes it possible for the mayor to concentrate on political
leadership and policy development. In 1931, San Francisco was the first
mayor-council city to hire a professional chief administrative officer (CAO)
(Adrian 1988). The San Francisco charter included provisions against interference by the mayor in appointments, contracts, and requisitions under the
direct control of the CAO. The CAO was also given direct control over public works, health, hospitals, purchasing, and the budget. The CAO in San
Francisco could only be removed by popular recall or by a two-thirds vote of
the council (Bromage 1957). With the success and continuing expansion of
the office of chief administrator in mayor-council cities, the differences in
professionalism between mayor-council and council-manager cities began
to diminish (Adrian 1988).

> The establishment of a top personal aide to the mayor who serves as the
> CAO is a postwar [World War II] development. . . . We find that the CAO
> post seems to have been established largely for two reasons—as a compro-
> mise between the manager plan and the strong mayor government, and as
> a means of providing for professional administration without eliminating
> the mayor as the symbolic head and chief policy maker of the city. (Adrian
> 1961, 446)

Appointment of such an assistant on a professional basis is recommended by the Model City Charter Committee of the National Municipal League for cities which prefer the mayor-council to the council-manager plan of government. (Schultz 1949, 345)

The chief executive in a strong-mayor city may well recognize his own shortcomings as an administrator and attempt to do something about it. The most common method of buttressing his position is to appoint an able, professionally experienced administrator to the position of chief fiscal officer, usually called the controller. The chief fiscal officer or controller may act as a deputy mayor and attend to many details of administration. The typical politician-mayor is not always willing to choose professional deputies, however. In order to provide some legal incentive for the mayor to do so, there has been a trend toward the establishment of a chief administrative officer by charter or ordinance. The CAO's powers vary considerably from one city to another, and sometimes the CAO position can scarcely be differentiated from the chief budget or fiscal officer. According to the theory of the position, the CAO should be appointed by the mayor and should perform, in general, such functions as the supervision of heads of various departments, preparation of the budget (or supervision of the budget director), and personnel direction. (Adrian 1955, 210)

Los Angeles and Philadelphia added CAOs by charter in 1951, New Orleans in 1952, the cities of New York, Boston, and Newark in 1953, and gradually thereafter most large and many smaller cities did so too (Adrian 1988). The Los Angeles CAO served the mayor and council and was given extensive executive authority (Lockard 1969). In New Orleans, the charter called for the chief administrator to appoint department heads, with the approval of the mayor, and supervise them.

By 1960, some mayor-council cities were granting CAOs similar powers enjoyed by city managers in council-manager cities.

According to Wallace S. Sayre and Herbert Kaufman, "the CAO and his office staff had become the most fully realized assets of the mayor's office . . . the mayor's most active problem-solvers, especially in matters requiring interdepartmental agreements or departmental reorganizations." The office of Managing Director, in Philadelphia, had "contributed both to strong, productive political leadership in the office of mayor and to high-quality professional administration in most departments of Philadelphia's city government." (Adrian 1961, 451)

Surveys conducted by the International City/County Management Association (ICMA) between 1972 and 1998 show that the number of mayor-council cities that have added the position of CAO has increased dramatically

Figure 4.2 **Mayor-Council Cities with Chief Administrative Officer**

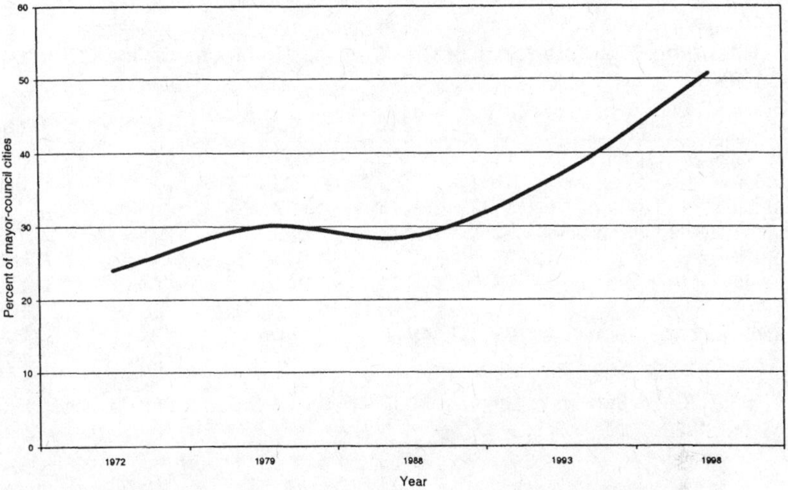

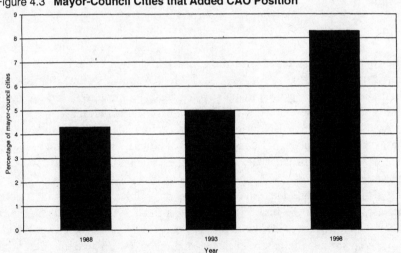

Source: ICMA, *Municipal Year Book*, 1972, 1988, 1993, and 1988.

Figure 4.3 **Mayor-Council Cities that Added CAO Position**

Source: ICMA, *Municipal Year Book*, 1988, 1993, and 1988.

(see Figure 4.2). In 1998, more than 50 percent of the mayor-council cities had a CAO while only 24 percent had a CAO in 1972. These results show that many mayor-council cities were accepting the notion that the mayor needed assistance in the executive function.

The fact that mayor-council cities are adding the position of CAO at an increasing rate each year can be seen in Figure 4.3. Between 1988 and 1998, the percentage of mayor-council cities that added a CAO increased each year.

Table 4.1

The Changing Characteristics of City Councils in Mayor-Council Cities, 1934–98

	1934	1950	1960	1968	1988
Mean size of council	15	7	7	–	6.88
Council elected by district	45%	40%	38%	32%	21.3%
Council elected at-large	16%	35.5%	37%	44%	49.1%
Council elected in mixed elections	39%	24.7%	25%	21%	29.7%
Council two-tear term	69%	42.1%	48%	46% (1965)	31.8% (1982)
Council four-year term	29%	45.2%	44%	43% (1965)	59.7% (1982)

Source: ICMA Surveys as reported in the *Municipal Year Book*, 1934, 1950, 1960, 1968, and 1988.

In 1998, about 8.5 percent of the responding mayor-council cities adopted a CAO. In 1988, only about 4 percent of mayor-council cities had added the position of CAO.

City Councils

The changing characteristics of the councils in mayor-council cities are as dramatic as the growth of CAOs. As Table 4.1 shows, councils in mayor-council cities have become much smaller, serve longer terms, and are more often elected by the whole city rather than by a single district.

As the work of Bledsoe (1993) and others indicates, the combination of these changes alters the political dynamics of cities in the definition of longer incumbency and a broader view of city issues. Such changes tend to increase the understanding of and support of the city administration. Such changes will also usually indicate a more pronounced "public regarding" or "public interest" stance on the part of councils (Kaufman 1991; Hirschman 1982). When the entire city council of a mayor-council city is elected on a citywide basis, it so softens the nature of the separation of powers that we categorize such cities as adapted political. Political cities may retain some of the elements of separation of powers, but the incremental adoption of the structural changes described here certainly inclines the functioning of these cities in the direction of greatly increased administrative capacity and power. These changes, taken together, enable us to make what we believe to be fundamental distinctions between political and adapted political cities. The aggregate effect of all the administrative adaptations, combined with at-large elections, causes these cities to look more like adapted administrative cities than like political cities. Based on ICMA data, only 181 cities in 1992 and 188 cities in 1996 with a directly elected mayor, no CAO, and a council elected by district could, therefore, be described as political cities. Conversely, using our definitions applied to the ICMA data, between three and four times these numbers would be categorized as adapted political cities, although on mayor-council platforms.

Because the ICMA data have several limitations, we took a 1998 sample survey with many more variables, described in detail in Chapter 7. Using these refined data and the definitions and categories set out in this chapter, we found about an equal number of political and adapted political cities, all on mayor-council platforms. In Chapter 1, we set out the details of these distinctions and their implications.

Descriptive numeric data can explain how cities have inherently adapted their political and administrative structures. To understand the actual effects of such changes, we turn to an example of a modern adapted political city.

Topeka

In 1854, President Franklin Pierce signed the Kansas–Nebraska Act, opening the Kansas Territory for settlement. Six months later, Pennsylvania business-man and politician Cyrus K. Holliday pinpointed a small piece of land on the Kaw River as a prime spot to start a municipality. Holliday helped establish a charter for his new city, which officially named it the Town Association of Topeka. On February 14, 1857, the Kansas legislature incorporated Topeka, and in 1858, Holliday was elected the first mayor of Topeka and unknowingly launched this municipality on a historic, sometimes turbulent journey through three different forms of government: mayor-council, commission, and now an adapted political city resting on a modified mayor-council charter.

Like virtually all American cities in the mid-1800s, Topeka was formed as a mayor-council city. The mayor was directly elected and held all executive powers. This system gave Holliday, the mayor of Topeka until the 1880s, great power, including the ability to disperse patronage, to veto council-passed legislation, and to be elected to an unlimited number of terms in office. All employees by district served at his behest. A council of eight was elected on a partisan ballot, with responsibility for city ordinances and approval of the budget. As was common in the nineteenth century, the council was primarily composed of local business leaders who in early accounts were Holliday's friends. Collectively, they were primarily concerned with economic devel-opment and growth.

A statewide ballot was held after Kansas was admitted to the Union in 1861, and Topeka became the capital. In the December 1954 issue of *Lykes*

Fleet Flashes, commending Topeka's centennial celebration, the city's early development was explained thus: "As might be expected, Topeka, its early economy based on such stable industries as railroading, government, and agriculture, developed as a quiet, conservative city, proud of its churches and schools."

Holliday and his friends designed the city with wide roads that still meet the transportation needs of the city. Holliday also used the development of the city to support his private business. "In 1869, business was going well for Holliday. He was elected for the second time as mayor, with his Excelsior Coke and Gas Co. he announced plans to light the city's avenues and the 'Cyrus K. Holliday' locomotive No. 1 entered service" ("Topeka Talks" 1999).

In the heyday of the reform movement, in the early 1900s, the city council of Topeka became interested in more administrative efficiency in government. By that time, many civic leaders were wary of the structural powers of the mayor and the privileged personal benefits that mayors took advantage of. Unfortunately, Topeka was also suffering from the nationwide economic depression in 1889. This economic crisis was exacerbated by overbuilding on the part of the Topeka business community in the halcyon years immediately after statehood. Then, in 1903, a great flood nearly devastated Topeka. The council began to consider a new structural form that was gaining currency nationally. At a public meeting of business and professional representatives held in the city council chamber in 1906, the Galveston Plan, or city commission form of government, modeled after the Texas cities of Galveston and Houston, was adopted.

Under the Topeka Plan of City Government, modeled on the Galveston Plan, four commissioners and one mayor were elected at large. The mayor was the chief executive and presided over council meetings. The mayor also signed all city ordinances. However, the mayor no longer had veto power over council-passed legislation. The mayor had an equal vote on the council and was the commissioner of the police and fire departments. "He is responsible for the enforcement of all municipal ordinances and police regulations in addition to the general supervision of the fire and police functions. For all practical purposes he is the head of government. He performs the ceremonial functions and presides at the weekly commission meetings" (McKenna 1962).

The other four commissioners held responsibilities for their own administrative branches of city government. The commissioner of finance and revenue managed the city's taxes, revenues, and expenditures. The city clerk, city treasurer, and the auditor served under him. Each of these three officers oversaw agencies such as the custodian of city documents, the city post office, and the accounting department. The lower departments reported to one of the three divisions of finance and revenue, who in turn reported to the overseeing commissioner. Another commissioner was responsible for the construction, maintenance, and operation of the city's waterworks, lighting plant, and streetlights. A third commissioner was in charge of streets and public improvements. The fourth commissioner headed all city services per-. taining to parks and city property, including forestry and public health. Collectively, the five commissioners served as the city legislative body. They enacted ordinances, adopted revenue measures, appropriated money, and made political appointments. The appointment of all department heads was made officially by a majority vote of the entire council.

Topeka operated under the commission form until 1984, one of the largest cities in America to do so, the commission form of government having generally gone out of fashion in the 1920s and 1930s. Six times between 1929 and 1983, the city manager form of government was proposed but not approved by the voters in Topeka. Mike Hall, a *Topeka Capitol Journal* reporter who has covered Topeka city politics since 1974, expressed the major perceived shortcomings of the commission form in Topeka. "The disadvantage of [commission] government was a lack of coordination among the city departments because each department was answerable administratively to a different commissioner. We had situations in which the street department would pave a street, then the next week the water department was digging a hole in the new street to lay a new water line" (Hall 2000).

Finally, after a citywide vote in 1984, Topeka had a directly elected mayor, a council elected by districts, and a chief administrative officer. A local newspaper article describes the current duties of the mayor as follows: "The charter lists 12 duties for the mayor, including specific duties such as preparing an annual budget for council consideration and setting the agenda for city council meetings. But it also charges the mayor to 'provide leadership in the communication and interpretation of city policy to the public'" (Hall 2000). The mayor is responsible for the operation of the city, but tends to leave the day-to-day details to the CAO. The mayor also has a strong booster role—campaigning for the city and its policies and projects.

The Topeka city council has nine members and is a purely legislative body. Council members are part-timers and therefore may not be as knowledgeable about technical matters as full-time council members might be. Meetings are monthly with the mayor presiding. The mayor is not allowed a vote in the city council, but does have veto power over council-passed legislation. The mayor, CAO, and council members all have fixed salaries.

Just four years after the mayor-council-CAO form of government was enacted, the mayor's power were compromised. Originally, the CAO was to be hired and fired by the mayor alone. In 1989, a charter change was introduced and passed by the city council. It required the mayor to consult with the council on the selection and/or dismissal of the CAO, giving council members considerable influence.

In recent years there has been a great deal of friction between the mayor and the council. "The council tends to often practice checks and balances against the mayor that they have modeled after state government. Because five of the nine council members work on the administrative side of the state government, they see how they manipulate the legislators on a state level and try to reverse it on the city level" (Arnold 2000). The contentiousness between the mayor and the council reached a critical point in early 2000. Topeka CAO John Arnold describes the issue as jealousy of power. Council members try to create outlets, like amending policies over budget, to establish greater commission controls; "To Dunn and Gardner and several others (Topeka city council members), it's not about finding ways to keep the city afloat; it's about dunking the mayor's head under water as often as possible. To them, the only problem is that mayor Joan Wagnon has more power than they do. It gnaws at them day and night") (Arnold 2000).

The Topeka city council in 2000 passed several city ordinances giving specific duties directly to the CAO, presuming to take those duties out of the hands of the mayor. Mayor Joan Wagnon vetoed the ordinances. In response, some council members supported changing the structure of Topeka's government to the orthodox council-manager or administrative city alternative, which would have made the mayor's role largely ceremonial. Mayor Wagnon said the attempt was "misguided . . . because a two-thirds majority wasn't there. There are four council members who would love to get rid of the strong mayor, but cannot" (Wagnon 2000).

The *Topeka Capitol Journal* favored the council-manager proposal:

> The council inexplicably stopped short of considering a complete overhaul of the mayor/council-manager form of government, despite years of creeping doubt about its efficacy since the city enacted it in the mid-1980's. Statistics seem to bear out that this form isn't serving the community well. . . . Topekans also know anecdotally that the city council is failing the city. While other communities are pulling together and making progress, Topeka is continually mired in discord. Some council members seem more intent on tripping up the mayor and her staff than on getting the city anywhere. . . . The council's attempt at reform was aimed not at itself, but at the mayor and her chief administrative officer. ("Only Where Needed," April 2000)

The "gang of four" on the Topeka city council successfully blocked initiatives by the mayor and other members of the council. Mayor Wagnon thinks this is the major problem with the council. "We can't identify what they

want. . . . They represent what some in Topeka call the CAVE people—
citizens against virtually everything. Until the council makeup changes, nothing can pass." If the council had not been so uncooperative, says Wagnon,
"we would have seen a lot more growth, industry, and innovation in Topeka"
(Wagnon 2000). A reporter covering the April council meeting described
some of the proceedings:

> "If you're going to bully us to push a vote on this, then this is wrong."
> —Jim Gardner to Mayor Joan Wagnon
>
> "You're out of order!"
> —Mayor Wagnon to several council members throughout the meeting
>
> "You're being extremely rude."
> —Fran Lee to John Alcala
>
> "I'm trying to be rude."
> —Alcala to Lee
>
> "Your question doesn't make sense to me."
> —Wagnon to Betty Dunn
>
> "Nothing makes sense to you unless things are going your way."
> —Dunn to Wagnon
> (Hall, April 23, 2000)

According to Wagnon, the "gang of four" phenomenon has its roots in
Topeka's political history. "There have always been neighborhoods in Topeka that believe they aren't getting their way and have a deep distrust for
government that goes back 100 years to the Kansas Populists." Wagnon originally campaigned on a platform that she said would "stop the bickering" on
the Topeka city council. By her own admission, she was unsuccessful in this
regard. Now, she sees only one solution for Topeka: "[O]nly elections can
solve the problems. What is flawed [about the city council] is the people
elected. If we have strong, civil leaders across the board, everything will
work well" (Wagnon 2000).

In November 2000, after just one term in office, Mayor Wagnon was de-
feated for reelection by a former mayor, Butch Felker. The open animosity
between the mayor and the council is now gone.

What went largely unnoticed throughout the stormy practices of checks
and balances in Topeka was the operations of the city administration. With a
CAO, merit-based civil service, and other administrative reform characteris-

tics, Topeka was reliable and effective in the routine, orderly conduct of city affairs. There was no scandal or corruption. Topeka has adapted in the direction of administrative effectiveness, softening the effect of the political separation of powers and checks and balances. With its CAO, Topeka is now an adapted political city.

Conclusion

In the past twenty years, the serious study of American local government has included considerable research describing changes or reforms in the council-manager form of cities—sometimes now known as the "reform of the reform." These changes have tended to be structural adoptions designed to increase political responsiveness, such as the direct election of mayors, the direct election of city council members, the provision of full-time and paid mayoral and council positions, and the provision of staff to mayors and council members. Much less well known and a generally well-kept secret are equally important structural changes in mayor-council cities designed to increase the efficiency of these cities, such as merit-based civil service systems, bid and purchase controls, auditing requirements, lengthened mayoral and council terms, and, most importantly, the rapid growth in the use and powers of the CAO.

It is increasingly evident that the council-manager and mayor-council categories are woefully inadequate as descriptors of modern reform in American cities. Certainly these two categories constitute the dominant legal or statutory platforms on which most American cities rest. But these categories mask very important reform distinctions within and between the categories. Our five-part scheme better explains the pattern of changes in American cities (Frederickson and Johnson 2001). In that scheme, pure mayor-council cities are called political cities, while mayor-council cities that have adapted the reforms described in this research are called adapted political cities. Many mayor-council cities now fall into the adapted political city category. Some of the largest and most important cities in America, such as Los Angeles, Houston, Salt Lake City, Atlanta, Buffalo, Minneapolis, and Tampa, fall into the adapted political category.

Council-manager cities have adapted in a similar way. Many pure council-manager administrative cities have reformed to become adapted administrative cities (Frederickson and Johnson 2001). While adapted administrative cities are still based on the logic of unity of powers, this logic is weakened by the separate direct election of the mayor and by the change from at-large council elections to some or all council elected by district.

The evidence presented here indicates that reformed mayor-council cities, the adapted political cities, have tended to come to resemble their adapted administrative cousins. This is particularly the case in adapted political cities with chief administrative officers. We return to this contention in our description of the evolution of many jurisdictions from administrative political to adapted administrative cities in the next chapter.

American cities are highly adaptive, malleable, and responsive institutions. They seldom change entirely from mayor-council to council-manager forms. But they change incrementally at a surprisingly rapid pace (Frederickson and Johnson 2001). When seen in the longer term, the aggregation of incremental structural adaptations in American cities tells a modern story of reform as important in its own way as the better-known story of municipal reform in the early twentieth century. These contemporary reforms are just as evident in cities with mayor-council platforms as they are in cities with council-manager platforms.

Note

1. Administrative officers in mayor-council cities go by a variety of titles, including chief administrative officer, chief executive officer, deputy mayor, or chief business officer.

The Evolution of Administrative Cities

The history of the council-manager form of government in the United States is well documented by both scholars and practitioners of local and municipal government. One city manager refers to the form as the "uniquely American contribution to local governance because of its unitary form" (Anderson 1989, 25).

From its inception, the council-manager form has proven to be extremely adaptable, changing to fit the needs of individual cities. "Changes in municipal governmental forms and structures reflect a continuing effort to develop organizational solutions to urban problems, with concern for the values of leadership, accountability, and efficiency" (Sanders 1979, 97).

Since the 1920s, the nomenclature or phrase "council-manager government" has remained relatively constant. Ordinarily this phrase has meant the classic structure of council-manager form of administrative cities with the essential elements of the unity of powers:

1. A small city council (five to nine members, who serve part-time) generally elected at large on a nonpartisan ballot, with legislative powers including control of revenues and expenditures. Perhaps most important among its responsibilities is the hiring and oversight and firing of the city manager.
2. A full-time, professionally trained city administrator who serves at the behest of the council but with full responsibility for the implementation of policy through day-to-day city operation, including hiring and firing of department heads and the preparation and administration of the city budget.
3. A council-selected mayor who serves primarily as a ceremonial official. (Rowe 1987)

Although the phrase "council-manager form" or "council-manager model" and the structural characteristics that this form is presumed to represent have remained constant, the actual structures of most council-manager cities have been significantly modified. In the past thirty years, many scholars have observed that the original council-manager form and its basic unity-of-powers characteristics have evolved:

> The ideal of apolitical management has withered over time, partly due to its basic prescription that it be a closed system. The managerial complexity of the modern city has forced changes, and the pure Child's model has been modified in many instances . . . over time, the original reform model has been altered due to changing societal forces and conditions that have been craved goals beyond efficiency in the operation of government. (Boynton and DeSantis 1990, 3)
>
> Beginning in the 1960s, council-manager cities started to face new challenges: The problems council-manager government was designed to solve— corruption, inefficiency, poor management . . . while still problems, are not as compelling as the problems of contemporary local government, economic development, political responsiveness, equity. Council-manager government, some argue, is a large and influential idea whose time has passed. (Frederickson 1996, 3–4)

A report by the International City/County Management Association (ICMA) task force on the council-manager plan concluded: "Emphasizing efficiency is not a strong selling point for the council-manager form today, in an era where choices among equally worthy services must be made. The system's ability to reduce conflict and create an environment conducive to problem solving is the element that needs to be promoted." (International City/County Management Association 1995, A-5).

Chester Newland, a long-time thoughtful observer of council-manager city government, recognized that the characteristics of the form have been changing. Nevertheless, he argues that council-manager and mayor-council cities are still distinct.

1. Council-manager government facilitates more collaborative civic authority, combined with coordinated institutionalized administration. Mayor-council government emphasizes separation of powers with the focus on mayoral leadership, and administration is more fragmented.
2. Transformational politics is the ideal of the council-manager form, searching for collaborative, communitywide orientation. Transactional politics is the ideal of the mayor-council form, facilitating brokerage among different interests.
3. Professionally expert administration is ideal in council-manager government, with neutrally equal access and responsiveness. Politically sensitive administration is ideal in mayor-council form, with nonroutinization to facilitate responsiveness. (Newland 1994, 278)

Newland's view may still be correct as regards the distinction between pure form political and administrative cities. However, over time, the majority of cities carrying council-manager or mayor-council labels have adapted their structures in ways that make them very nearly the same. Put another way, in most cities it is no longer the formal label of the city that reveals its actual structural characteristics.

To make the distinctions between council-manager cities that have retained a classic or pure structure and those that have significantly modified that structure, we use the concept of the adapted administrative city. In Chapter 1, we describe cities that have retained the pure manager-council structure as administrative cities. Council-manager cities that have significantly modified their structures, using the criteria we set out in Chapter 1, are described as adapted administrative cities. We use the adapted label because of our later argument that all three variants of adapted cities are more like one another than they are like either political or administrative cities, regardless of the characterization of most cities as either mayor-council or council-manager cities.

The two most important modifications of the classic council-manager structure of government have been the adoption of directly elected mayors and district-based elections of city council members. We consider first the effects of the direct election of mayors in council-manager cities.

Mayors in Administrative Cities

As Figure 5.1 shows, the pattern of change from ceremonial mayors who serve on the city council and are chosen by their city council colleagues to directly elected mayors is a relatively typical S-curve of innovation. By the early 1990s, 61.8 percent of mayors in council-manager cities were directly elected (Adrian 1988). Over time, directly elected mayors in administrative cities have tended to move from part-time to full-time and to be paid, particularly in larger cities. Gradually, staff reporting directly to the mayor were added in larger council-manager cities. Other increments of mayoral power have been added, including some influence over executive appointments and the preparation of the annual budget to be presented to the city council. By the early 1990s, as a result of these adaptions it was not uncommon for mayors and city managers to describe their relationship as an executive partnership.

The move to directly elected mayors has been prompted by the argument that American cities need more effective political leadership (Gurwitt 1993). The dynamic nature of urban politics, particularly regarding leadership, has prompted one scholar to observe that "over the past two decades local gov-

Figure 5.1   **Direct Election of the Mayor in Council-Manager Cities**

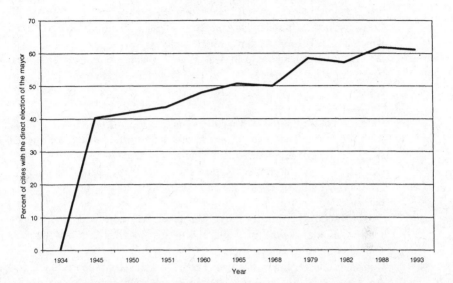

ernments have struggled to keep pace with rapid changes in society, the economy, technology, and intergovernmental relations" (Streib 1994, 239). The research on mayoral leadership in council-manager cities tends to focus on economic, political, and demographic changes and on increases in the level of citizen demands in the context of limited resources (Kemp 1988; Mercer 1991; Green and Fleischman 1989).

Studies of mayoral leadership in council-manager cities often focus on the role of the mayor as a policy leader (Adrian 1955). One of the first, based on three cities in Michigan with populations ranging from 50,000 to 80,000, found that mayors in two of the three cities did not play a leadership role, but the mayor in the third city was accorded respect due to his "high status" although "his leadership was rather inconspicuous . . . and he did not play the role of policy innovator, or of a chaperone of legislation through the council" (Adrian 1955, 210–11).

Bromage identified twelve roles designated as the "appropriate field of action" in which mayors can act in concert with the council to promote politics and policy:

1. Public relations with the citizens in explaining budget needs and tax policy.
2. Active leadership in selling a bond issue for capital improvements in any public referendum.

3. Explanation to the people of the need for regulatory ordinances, which involve public mores, moral issues, and civil rights.
4. Consideration of public reactions to matters of planning and zoning, which arouse response from property owners.
5. Objectivity and leadership in dealing with special issues, which arise from time to time, such as fluoridation of water.
6. Determination of proposed policy as to public ownership of utilities, subject to referendum.
7. Extension of municipal refuse collection to replace a private contractor.
8. Revision of city charter on issues of major political significance, such as the method of nominating and electing councilmen.
9. Leadership pertaining to semiautonomous agencies, boards, and commissions, which are outside the administrative hierarchy headed by the manager.
10. Establishment of policy for intergovernmental relations with other units such as counties, townships, villages, cities, school districts, and metropolitan authorities and districts.
11. Decisions concerning projects such as urban renewal which involve federal grants as well as local expenditures, or any program involving federal or state grants-in-aid.
12. Foresight in defining community goals as to social and economic development. (Bromage 1970, 24–25)

Based on the ideals of the council-manager plan and the logic of the unity of powers, the mayor in this view "relies upon informal aspects of leadership rather than formal powers" (Bromage 1970, 26).

Another early study surveyed city managers in forty-five cities with populations over 100,000 regarding the roles of mayors. In only three of the forty-five cities did mayors have veto power over council agendas, and very few exercised formal powers in policy recommendations to the council. However, two-thirds were able to appoint citizen advisory boards and commissions (Boynton and Wright 1971, 29). Mayors in the cities examined differed from the rest of the council members in their cities and were more likely to:

1. Have the most contact with political party leaders;
2. Be nominated as the major political leader in the city;
3. Be consulted by the manager about political issues; and,
4. Most frequently be involved in the administrative process in the city . . . with involvement measured as oversight of and contact with administrative officials. (Boynton and Wright 1971, 30)

Kotter and Lawrence analyzed how successful mayors accomplished their goals. They found that mayors attained their goals through agenda setting, a process by which mayors decide what they are going to do; network building, the mayor's accessibility to critical resources such as votes, money, laws, human skills, and task accomplishment capacity; and by accomplishing tasks (Kotter and Lawrence 1974, 49–87).

Kotter and Lawrence found that mayors in council-manager cities "tended to have smaller domains than mayors in cities with weak and strong mayor charters. No explanation is given, however, for the variation. The "larger the domain, the larger the mayor's job and that the size of the mayor's impact on policy is a function of the city charter, since it determines the mayor's responsibilities" (Kotter and Lawrence 1974, 61).

In 1979, Wikstrom studied the role of mayors as policy leaders in the council-manager form of government in forty-one cities in Virginia. He found that the majority of mayors viewed their role as "providing political leadership for a single or multiple array of purposes" while only a minority of those interviewed "restricted their role to that of presiding over council meetings and carrying out public representational duties" (Wikstrom 1979, 273).

Wheeland studied the preconditions necessary for mayoral leadership in four small cities in Pennsylvania. He found that all mayors perform mostly ceremonial roles, and only one performed additional leadership activities that reflected the facilitative model and in only one city "where the mayor is a regular voting member of the council, did the mayor emerge as 'facilitative leader'" (Wheeland 2002, 347). Having voting status on the council is an important precondition for facilitative leadership by the mayor.

In a more recent study of the leadership roles of mayors, Morgan and Watson found that mayoral leadership frequently relies on informal sources of power in addition to formal structural powers. "Council-manager mayors really do conform to the classic portrait; they hold very few formal powers" (Morgan and Watson 1992, 442).

Protasel found that the traditional council-manager roles, where the policy-making authority is vested in the council and the administrative functions are carried out by the manager, are now less visible in larger council-manager cities. In cities with a dominant manager, the manager acquired power outside the formal structure of the council-manager form and functioned as community leader and policy maker. Protasel concluded that the city manager had to go outside the formal structure to exercise leadership because the "traditional council-manager plan did not provide an institutional basis for the city manager to close the gap and exercise policy leadership" (Protasel 1995, 24). Fully half of the administrative cities Protasel studied had mayors and managers working together as an executive team or a directly elected mayor functioning as if in a political city context.

The method of mayoral selection has contributed to some changes of mayoral leadership roles. Protasel found that the governing team and strong mayor leadership patterns discovered in council-manager cities "have arisen from the changing role of the mayor in large communities with less stable political environments" (Protasel 1995, 25).

Protasel (1995) contends that the focal point of leadership is "absent or located elsewhere in small cities where fewer mayors are directly elected . . . that leadership is located in the hands of the manager if the mayor is not directly elected" (Protasel 1995, 205). Martin agrees: "Unless there is a directly elected mayor, or a council member with a vigorous personality to seize the policy initiative, the manager will guide the options considered and will deal with the question raised" (Martin 1990, 85).

Methods of mayoral selection were not the only factors affecting the roles of mayors. Efforts to change the leadership roles of mayors in council-manager cities have been debated along the lines of increasing the power and authority of the mayor. "Boosting the powers of the mayor through change to the strong mayor system can help larger communities to deal more effectively with their complex problems" (Gurwitt 1993).

The formal and informal powers of the mayor are changing (Wikstrom 1979; Morgan and Watson 1992; Svara 1990; Frederickson 1996). For example, Svara (1990a) classified the resources needed for the mayor to perform his or her role as formal or informal. He defined formal resources as the mayor's "control over budget formulation and the hiring of staff, appointment of members of boards, the veto power, and the right to issue executive orders to fill vacancies in elected office." The formal resources fit the roles of the executive mayor who usually has the power to formulate the city budget. Informal resources were those that determined the roles mayors could play, i.e., "independent of council, in policy formulation, policy implementation, or management" (Svara 1990a, 88).

Efforts to enhance the resources available to the mayor in council-manager government, such as the ability to appoint citizen boards and non-administration commissions and officials, are on the rise (Newland 1994). The formal factors that contribute to the effective performance of the mayor include access to information, strategic location for securing and channeling information and building relationships, the support of and interaction with the city or county manager, staff support necessary for filling the demands of the ceremonial role, and involvement in projects that enhance visibility.

Informal mayoral resources in administrative cities include the mayor's base of support in the community, the quality of the mayor's contacts and connections, the mayor's media attention and support, and whether the mayor has a clear conception of the office and sense of purpose. Personal factors, such as the amount of time the mayor can devote to the office and the quality of the

relationship between the mayor and the city manager are also important deter-
minants of mayoral leadership in administrative cities. Finally, mayoral skills
still matter. The mayor needs the ability to communicate (active listening and
effective speaking), to set goals and priorities and keep sight of broad goals
while making specific choices, and to resolve conflicts and differences.

It is the mix of formal and informal powers and resources that is essential
for effective mayoral leadership in council-manager cities. It is not just whether
the mayor is directly elected.

Most of the contemporary research on this subject finds that mayors are
becoming more visible and playing a significant role in policy making and
other activities (Newland 1994; Morgan and Watson 1992; Svara 1994;
Wheeland 1990; Wikstrom 1979; Frederickson 1996).

The direct election of the mayor in council-manager cities has been linked
to a decline in the power and longevity of city managers. Booth found that
elected mayors, in council-manager cities, contributed to the shortened tenure of the manager and curtailed the authority of the manager. Booth's findings match those of a 1962 study by Gladys Kammerer, which argued that
at-large election of the mayor posed "a political hazard to the manager"
(Kammerer, cited in Booth 1965, 575). Morgan and Watson (1991) found
that mayors in large council-manager cities provided strong leadership and
that managers in such settings are both less visible and less influential.

ICMA has identified four changes that affect leadership in council-
manager cities with directly elected full-time mayors: (1) changes in the
method of selection of the city manager; (2) control over the city council
agenda; (3) appointments to city boards and nonadministrative commissions;
and, (4) chairing the rules and finance committees. The systematic and often
gradual adoption of these changes has enhanced the power and leadership
roles of mayors in council-manager cities and thereby altered the unity-of-
powers logic. The addition of a full-time, directly elected mayor in a unity-
of-powers setting adds a powerful element of political leadership in a single
person. Even when such directly elected mayors continue to serve on the city
council and do not have veto authority over council actions, the research
literature indicates that such a change alters the role and functioning of the
city manager and the dynamics of the relationship between the city manager
and the city council. It is for that reason that council-manager cities with
directly elected mayors are placed in the adapted administrative category.
Based on ICMA data described in greater detail in Chapter 7, there are now
more adapted administrative cities than administrative cities. In Chapters 7,
8, and 9 we make the claim that adapted administrative cities resemble adapted
political cities more than they resemble administrative or political cities. The
fundamental reason is that adapted political cities and adapted administra-

Figure 5.2   **Council-Manager Cities with District and Mixed Elections**

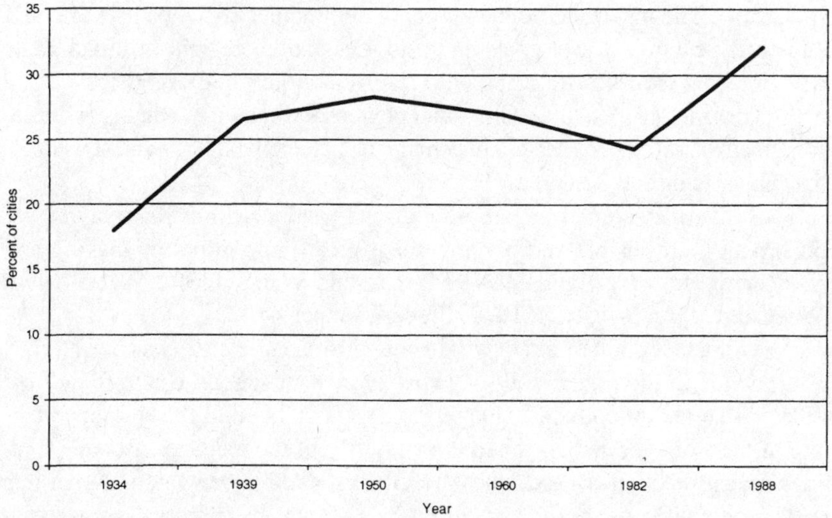

tive cities both have directly elected mayors *and* full-time professional city managers or chief executive officers.

The Shift from At-Large to District City Council Members

Although less dramatic, the number of council-manager cities that have changed the form of elections of some or all of the members of the city council from at-large to district also follows the S-curve of the diffusion of innovation. As Figure 5.2 shows, between 1934 and 1988, the percentage of council-manager cities changing at least some or all council members' elections from at-large to district increased from about 18 percent to about 32 percent. Although we have no more recent data on this trend, on the basis of our observations of the changing characteristics of city council electoral structures, we believe this trend to have continued.

The form of city council elections matters, as Susan Welch and Timothy Bledsoe (1988) claimed. They began their study with these questions:

Do district elections lead to parochialism and back-biting on the council? Do at-large systems promote more interest in the city as a whole? Which system provides for "better representation"—a system that forces representation from all parts of the community, or one that allows several, or even all, representatives to come from the same part of town? Just what are the consequences of one type of election system as opposed to another?

Controlling for median income, population, region, black population, council salary, and median education, Welch and Bledsoe found that at-large electoral systems are directly associated with higher income and education levels of the council members. Council members elected at large were found to be significantly better educated than district-elected council members. A member elected in a district is more than twice as likely as an at-large member to have an income of less than $15,000 and significantly less likely to earn more than $45,000. Those elected from districts are twice as likely to have only a high school education and considerably less likely to have postgraduate training. The smaller the district population, the lower the income and education of district elected council members, independent of the racial impact of these structures (Welch and Bledsoe 1988).

Welch and Bledsoe also found that at-large election systems have a Republican bias and that district elections eliminate that bias. Compared to at-large election systems, district-based elections minimize the financial resources necessary to run and win and enhance the power of neighborhood groups. The researchers also found that council members elected from districts allocate a higher proportion of their time to constituent services than do at-large council members. Council members elected by district spend about 45 percent more time doing personal services than do their at-large counterparts. At-large electoral systems elect members who tend to have a citywide focus of representation, and at-large members claim that their constituents are less interested in service than in issues even after the researchers controlled for income and race.

> The progressive reformers believed that, by altering the way members were elected to city councils, the relationship of members to their constituents would be changed. Those elected in at-large elections on nonpartisan ballots would, it was thought, be less likely to focus on the city as a whole. Those elected on "reform" ballots would be less interested in providing individual service to constituencies and more interested in broader legislative duties. To a modest extent these expectations have been fulfilled. Changing the way individuals are elected does change their view of their constituencies to some extent. This is especially true for those elected at-large compared to those elected by district. At-large members are more likely to see the city as a whole as their constituency, and those elected by districts to see the neighborhood as theirs. However, these differences should not be exaggerated. Most members elected by district also see the city as a whole as their focus, though few see it as their primary one. Many members elected at-large see the neighborhood as an important constituency, although almost none see it as their primary focus. (Welch and Bledsoe 1988, 77–78)

Like Welch and Bledsoe, Helig and Mundt found that council members in cities with district elections tend to see themselves more as ombudsmen than at-large members do (1984).

Welch and Bledsoe also found that at-large members favored raising taxes slightly more than those elected by district. Members elected by district are also more likely to acknowledge the presence of sharp factionalism on the council (49 percent compared to 40 percent) and less likely to respond that a high proportion of issues before the council were decided by unanimous or near unanimous votes. Conflict is more apparent in councils with district elections. Council members in district cities were also more likely to cite geographic rivalries as important. Welch and Bledsoe doubt that these differences are policy-based; instead, they are, conflicts over "allocative responsiveness," such as pork barrel issues resulting from geographic boundaries. It is conflict nevertheless.

The introduction of district-based council elections in council-manager cities importantly alters their political and policy-making characteristics (Banovetz 1994). Cities on council-manager platforms with district-based council elections are very likely to be more responsive to the interests of neighborhoods, to give more attention to allocative issues, and to see themselves more as ombudsmen for their constituents than their at-large elected counterparts. For these reasons, we categorize council-manager cities with more than half of their council elected by district as adapted administrative cities. Like the change to a directly elected mayor, the change from at-large to district city council elections will move a city into the adapted administrative category.

Kansas City, Missouri

To put life into the abstract consideration of changing American city structures, we turn to Kansas City, Missouri (KCMO). Although in its charter Kansas City is described as having a council-manger form of government, in its present situation Kansas City is now an adapted administrative city. Kansas City is a splendid example of structural dynamics because it has modified its structure on a regular basis.

In 1821, on the site that was to become (KCMO), the trading outpost of François Chouteau began drawing commerce and migration from the east along the Missouri River. In 1838, fourteen investors of the Town of Kansas Company bought some riverfront property from a French settler. Twelve years later, residents successfully petitioned the Jackson County court to be organized as the Town of Kansas. In 1853, the state of Missouri incorporated the City of Kansas and the first municipal elections were held.

KCMO began as a political city with most of the power in the hands of the mayor. By 1925 KCMO was a classic political machine city controlled by Tom Pendergast. Although he ran a corrupt city, boss Pendergast was quite popular with the citizenry. The municipal reformers in KCMO, made up mainly of Republicans and supported by the *Kansas City Star,* believed that the Pendergast machine stranglehold had to be broken. In the mid-1920s, these reformers worked on a new charter that would change the government from a partisan mayoral political city to an administrative city by the adoption of the council-manager form of government. Walter Matshceck, the director of the Kansas City Civic Research Institute at the time, summed up the logic of the reformers in KCMO: "The point is that the real business of government, particularly local government, is not governing in any strict sense. It's administering. It is doing work, carrying on operations like street cleaning, building sewers, putting out fires and so on. It's not a matter of political science, not of governing in the older sense. It's administrative science, and that's where democracy is working" (Matshceck 1925).

The Kansas City municipal reformers were successful, but from the beginning the council-manager model approved by the citizens was not the pure administrative city structure. The 1925 charter had nine members on the council, as opposed to the two-chambers model in the previous charter. Of the nine council members, four were to be elected by district, four elected at large but with district representation, and one, the mayor, elected at large as a mayoral candidate. The council, including the mayor, selected and approved the manager, and the manager appointed all department heads. So even at the outset, the Kansas City move to council-manager government included some district council elections and a visible mayor elected separately.

Although the 1925 charter created a council-manager form of government in Kansas City, in practice KCMO continued to be the classic political machine city. In the first postcharter election, Democrats and Republicans each formed caucuses and selected candidates. Pendergast now had to tell his voters to vote for specific names rather than simply looking for the Democratic party seal. His candidates easily captured five seats on the council and effectively retained control of the city. A Pendergast crony was appointed city manager and served the interests of the Pendergast machine.

Reformers were understandably dismayed. In their attempts to oust Pendergast, they had made him stronger. Pendergast began to expand his constituency to the middle-class residential wards of the city. The middle class did not need his patronage in the basic services of food, shelter, employment, and protection, so Pendergast recruited them to the social branch of his organization. His machine hosted parties and bridge games. He created baseball and bowling leagues. In the 1930s he owned speakeasies and underground saloons. He became a patron of the arts, supporting local jazz and blues clubs. The Pendergast machine began its decline when he was convicted of tax evasion in the mid-1930s and sent to Leavenworth.

Once Pendergast was gone, the Republicans formed the Citizens Association and set out to clear away all vestiges of corruption in KCMO. In the late 1930s, Mayor John Gage led a reform council in the cleanup of Kansas City. Gage was responsible for hiring one of the most influential city managers in America, L. Perry Cookingham (Knowl 2000). Cookingham simply began to enforce the 1925 charter. He introduced a formalized bidding process and modernized the city budget. He was responsible for annexing land north of the Missouri River, allowing the city to grow in a semicircle instead of a quadrant pattern that would have put the central downtown region on the outskirts of town. Along with city growth, Cookingham brought a major international airport to Kansas City (Gilbert 1978).

The city council wanted a "clean" government at any cost. Although Cookingham was charged with firing anyone who had held office under Pendergast, he regarded this as foolish: "Continuous pressure was put on me to terminate more employees and at a faster rate until at a meeting in late November . . . I informed the council that not all employees of the city government were bad, because, if all were, the government would have fallen of its own weight long before it did" (Gilbert 1978). When the council met on December 2, 1940, Cookingham presented a list of reasons why he would not fire all KCMO employees and a letter of resignation in case the council rejected his reasoning.

> I spent three hours reading and analyzing the report on the remaining employees and at the conclusion the councilman who had been most insistent on the rapid termination of the employees slapped his fist on the desk. I reached for my resignation, but much to my surprise, he said "That is a most commendable report." He said he had no idea of the personnel problems faced by the city manager and the tremendous responsibility which he has in keeping a qualified staff to operate the various utilities, institutions, and other functions performed by the city. He said as far as he was concerned he wanted no more turnover reports and was willing to leave personnel entirely in the hands of the city manager. (Gilbert 1978)

L.P. Cookingham managed KCMO for twenty years. Under his watch, Kansas City went from one of the worst-managed cities in the country to one of the best. Thirty-five of his protégées, interns, and assistants went on to become city managers in other cities.

In 1962, the citizens of Kansas City approved an ordinance to increase the number of districts in the city from four to six and to increase the city council from nine to thirteen members. This increase was instituted to address concerns about citizen representation.

Although the mayor is separately elected, the mayor continues to serve on the council and may vote. The mayor's term is four years, with a maximum of two terms. The mayor is a full-time employee earning $80,000 annually. The mayor may ask the council to reconsider any ordinance that the council has adopted or rejected.

KCMO has recently made several additional structural changes. In 1990, the charter was amended to include term limits for the mayor and city council members. In 1998, the charter was amended to give the mayor authority to veto acts of the council, review the proposed city budget before it is submitted to the council, and unilaterally appoint members to boards and commissions.

Council members in Kansas City are elected to four-year terms and limited to two terms. The council and the mayor are elected at the same time. Six of the thirteen council members are elected by district and six elected at large, although each must live in a separate district (described as at large with district representation). All council members receive an annual salary of $40,000 with a guaranteed 4 percent increase every year.

The city manager is nominated by the mayor and is hired with the support of the mayor and the approval of a majority of the city council. The city manager may be removed from office by the mayor and six city council members or by the vote of any nine council members. The city manager hires and supervises all the department heads. The manager also is responsible for submitting the annual budget to the mayor who in turn presents the budget to the council. KCMO has a merit-based civil service system and a formalized bidding process.

Mayor Kay Barnes, who took office in 1999, called for the adoption of a "strong mayor" model. She formed an advisory commission to investigate making further changes to the charter. She claimed that the mayor is held responsible for city affairs and must, therefore, have greater authority to manage city affairs. During nearly eleven months of deliberation, the charter review commission interviewed current and former appointed and elected city officials, as well as elected officials around the country, and it also held public forums around the city. The commission recommended the retention of the council-manager form of city government and that the mayor be authorized to terminate the city manager unless eight council members objected. The city council, however, voted unanimously against the recommendations of the charter review commission.

With a high-profile, full-time mayor with a staff and a professional city manager who reports to the council, and a city council elected primarily by the district, KCMO generally illustrates the characteristics of adapted administrative cities. Since the twenty-year reign of Perry Cookingham as city manager, all of the structural changes have been in the direction of enhancing mayoral power and council district representation. That having been said, it is also clear that the people of Kansas City wish to retain their version of the council-mayor form of government and have little interest in assuming a political city.

Conclusion

As the era of municipal reform passed, it was widely assumed that the dramatic structural adaptation of American cities had ceased. In fact, cities over the past thirty years have been busy regularly changing their structures. The majority of political cities incrementally adapted in the direction of greater administrative capacity, these adaptations generally following the S-curve of the diffusion of innovation. There are now more adapted political cities than political cities. A similar pattern was found over the past thirty years as the majority of administrative cities adapted incrementally to increase their political responsiveness through district-based council elections and to give more political power to directly elected mayors. Once again, the processes of adaptation followed the S-curve of the diffusion of innovation.

Despite the aggregation of incremental changes, the traditional language by which we presume to describe city political and administrative structures has persisted. It is increasingly evident that there is a wide variety of structural differences among cities that carry the council-manager label—that the label has become meaningless. This is a favorite topic among city managers, arguably the professionals who know the most about the subject and are most affected by structural details. In 1995, the International City/County Management Association appointed a task force on the council-manager plan. While the task force endorsed the so-called plan, it also recognized the range of variation now found among cities describing themselves as the council-manager form (ICMA 1995). The ICMA executive director, William Hansell (1999), describes the structural changes in the council-manager form of government over the past thirty years as the "reform of the reform." While he advocates the features of administrative cities as preferable for good government, he also suggests that many cities have "reformed the reform" in the ways described in this chapter. City managers should, he argues, learn how to be effective professionals in council-manager cities that are simply more political, as the KCMO case illustrates (Hansell 1999).

6

Model City Charters and Institutional Dynamics

"Dynamic" is hardly a word commonly associated with government. Neither is "changeable," "malleable," "adaptable," or "responsive." Yet properly understood, many American cities, particularly seen over the long term, are exactly that. Their structure and form change a bit here and a bit there and, when these changes are summed up, it is evident that cities are changeable things and that they change much more than is commonly understood.

One useful way to understand these changes is to trace the evolution of the Model City Charter. Studies of the diffusion of innovation show that professional and interest associations are often the carriers of change. The National Civic League (NCL), founded in 1894, is the oldest continuing association of those interested in cities and how they are governed. In its first sixty years, the NCL would have been categorized as a "good government" association, good government being understood to mean clean and well-managed government. One of the many ways the NCL went about achieving its purposes was to devise a Model City Charter and to press for the adoption, in as many cities as possible, of some or all of its features. First published in 1900 and revised six times since then, the charter provides a detailed history of the shifts from political to administrative cities. In recent years, the Model City Charter has struggled with the meaning of adapted cities. Because of its importance in the diffusion of innovation and its usefulness as a historical description of structural dynamics, we describe in detail the evolution of the National Civic League's Model City Charter.

The First Model City Charter

This examination of the evolution of the Model City Charter takes us back to Philadelphia, Pennsylvania, on January 25, 1894, when 147 citizens gathered in response to a call issued by the Municipal League of Philadelphia and the City Club of New York for the First National Conference for Good City Government. The impetus for this call was the perceived rampant graft, corruption, patronage, and spoils associated with city bosses and political machines. The reformers included Theodore Roosevelt, then a member of the U.S. Civil Service Commission; Charles W. Eliot, president of Harvard University; Marshall Field, a prominent Chicago business leader; and future cabinet members Charles Francis Adams and Charles J. Bonaparte. The purpose of this gathering was to consider ways to rid cities of corrupt political machines. But there was another side to the story.

> These primarily white, Anglo-Saxon, Protestant reformers had looked upon civil service reform as one way to wrench power away from ethnic political machines. Under the spoils system, political parties obtained workers and money via political patronage and assessments and patronage to obtain funds; however, the parties had to turn to businessmen and the wealthy for money. Political power was then transferred from the party members to the businessmen and other members of the elite who contributed to the party. (Moore 1985, 34–35)

Martin J. Schiesl describes the alternative as "the replacement of the ward system of public affairs with a centralized administration that would organize municipal services according to the business view of what was good for the community [thus reducing] the influence of lower-class groups in city government" (1977, 176). The group assembled in Philadelphia voted to create a national municipal league and to help local leagues.

The National Municipal League (now the National Civic League), founded in 1894, began producing and disseminating reports and papers. It was Edmund Janes James, a political scientist at the University of Pennsylvania, who first introduced the concept of a model charter. "A model city charter must be . . . adapted to local and temporal conditions. . . . That scheme of government is the ideal one . . . which under any given set of conditions makes the working of good influence easy and of bad influence hard" (Model City Charter 1989, xv). A committee of civic reformers and distinguished scholars was assembled in 1897 to develop "a municipal program." The committee reported its recommendations in 1899 and they were "published in 1900 as *A Municipal Program*" (Model City Charter 1989, xvi). The first Model City Charter recommended the mayor-council form of government, the mayor to be directly elected, to be paid, to have veto power, and to serve a two-year term: in other words, the political city. The members of the council would be elected on a general ticket from the city at large and would serve six-year staggered terms without pay. Because district-based and partisan elections were so much a part of early mayor-council government, the call for at-large elections in cities was an early signal of what was to come. The first Model City Charter recommended a city council of at least nine and not more than fifty members, the precise number being determined by the local conditions (Model City Charter 1900, 31). The charter called for an independent civil service commission whose "commissioners shall prescribe, amend and enforce regulations for appointment to, and promotion in, and for examinations in the administrative service of the city" (Model City Charter 1900, 23). Except for the at-large and nonpartisan components of this model, and because of the separately elected mayor with veto power, the first Model City Charter was similar to a unicameral version of the structures of the fifty states and the federal government. The separation of executive and legislative powers was key to the logic of mayor-council city government, the dominant form at that time.

The recommendation of a strengthened mayor-council was a departure from prevailing practice and gained little support. There was reluctance to give mayors such extensive powers and, as a result, there was a tendency to place boards and commissions (civil service, parks and recreation, etc.) between city departments and the elected chief executive. The desire was to prevent scandal, but the result was to diffuse responsibility (Model City Charter 1989, xv).

In the same year as the adoption of the first Model City Charter, a tidal wave hit Galveston, Texas. While it is argued that "the special commission used to deal with that emergency evolved into the commission form of government" (Model City Charter 1989, xvi), there is more to the story. A 1918 doctoral dissertation by a University of Iowa student suggests the following:

> The commission plan of city government, though popularly regarded as being created by the city of Galveston to meet a special emergency, is by no means in its essential principles an innovation of this century. . . . The old colonial system of borough government, the New England town government, the government of the national capital since 1878, the system of county government, and the plan of appointing commissioners to manage their municipal affairs in times of emergency adopted by various cities are all in some very important respect similar to the plan initiated sixteen years ago by the Texas city on the gulf. (Chang 1918, 49)

The author further contends that Galveston, "which was governed by a mayor and twelve aldermen elected by the people, had been characterized as 'one of the worst governed urban communities in the whole country'" (Chang 1918, 55). The commission form of government, which emerged in Galveston after the tidal wave, happened not only because of the emergency but also in response to a poorly managed city. And the commission plan was not a new entity but one that had been in existence for many years, particularly in American counties. In any case, for a brief period, the commission plan caught on, spreading to "over four hundred . . . cities" by 1915 (Chang 1918, 157). "Typically, this form [of government] has five commissioners elected at large. Collectively, they serve as the legislative body, but each commissioner heads one administrative department or more" (NCL 1993, 12). The National Municipal League found itself pressured to endorse the plan. "Then as now, however, the League rejected the commission plan because it fragmented the executive and permitted too little attention to policy development. The question was how to combine the 'short ballot' result that characterized the commission plan with the integrated, responsible executive provided in the League's first model" (Model City Charter 1989, xvi). It is important to note again that although the commission model is today a dominant form of county government in the United States, it has all but disappeared as a form of city government.

Revisions of the Model City Charter

1915 Model City Charter

In 1913, a League Committee on Municipal Reform was established to review the first model charter and to discuss other reform efforts. The man often credited with being the originator of the council-manager form of government, what we describe as the administrative city, appeared to strongly influence the drafting process of what would become the second Model City Charter. Richard S. Childs "promoted the ingenious combination of the experience in commission governed cities and the basic organizational feature of private business—the appointed chief executive officer. The committee's first report in 1914 endorsed what came to be known as the council-manager plan" (Model City Charter 1989, xvi–xvii). The words "came to be known as" were used here because, initially, the plan was referred to as the "commission-manager" plan. Beginning in 1908, Staunton, Virginia, had a general manager serving a two-house council and sharing the executive function with the mayor. In 1912, the city of Sumter, South Carolina, had a manager who was responsible to a single elected council. By the end of 1915, eighty-two cities had adopted the council-manager plan. It is interesting to note that "Richard Childs himself, however, acknowledged in the early 1970s that the council-manager plan may date back to 1904, when the Ukiah, California Board of Trustees appointed an 'Executive Officer' to serve at its pleasure" (NCL 1993, 16).

A description of the council-manager plan in the second Model City Charter includes the following details: a small council elected on nonpartisan at-large ballots and its selection of a professional executive to manage the administrative functions of the city. The council may choose a ceremonial mayor who would serve a one- to two-year term with no veto power. The council was to "elect one of its members as chairman, who shall be entitled mayor" (Model City Charter 1915, 13). The duties of the mayor in this first council-manager charter are as follows:

> The mayor shall preside at the meetings of the council and perform such other duties consistent with his office as may be imposed by the council. He shall be recognized as the official head of the city for all ceremonial purposes, by the courts for the purpose of serving civil processes, and by the governor for military purposes. In time of public danger or emergency he may, with the consent of the council, take command of the police and maintain order and enforce the laws. During his absence or disability his duties shall be performed by another member appointed by the council. (Model City Charter 1915, 14)

A merit-based personnel system would be in place along with routinized bid and purchasing, budgeting, and accounting procedures.

So between 1900 and 1915 there had been a dramatic shift of perspectives on the form and structure of American city government. By 1915, the logic of unity-of-powers, nonpartisan elections, and administrative city government was growing in popularity. The 1915 Model City Charter is an important early sign of what was, over the next fifty years, to be a dramatic S-curve of adoptions of administrative city government, particularly in smaller and suburban cities.

1927 Model City Charter

In 1925, the 1913 Committee on a New Municipal Program was reconstituted and charged with the further revision of the Model City Charter in light of ten years' experience with the council-manager plan (Model City Charter 1941, xi). While no important changes were adopted, the third edition of the Model City Charter does have a number of firsts. It includes, for example, the first mention of the council selecting a vice chairman or "mayor pro tem." This person would serve if a vacancy occurred in the office of the mayor or if the mayor was absent or disabled (Model City Charter 1927, 11–12). Also, in the third edition of the charter is the first mention of council staff: "The council shall choose a city clerk and such other officers and employees of its own body as it may deem necessary. The city clerk shall keep the records of the council and perform such other duties as may be required by this charter or the council. Officers and employees of the council shall not be chosen for a definite term but shall continue to serve during the pleasure of the council" (Model City Charter 1927, 12–13). Finally, the third Model City Charter was the first of three editions that did not specify the terms of the mayor or council. With regard to the civil service department, adjustments were made in terms of more centralized responsibility for the administration of city personnel systems.

1933 Model City Charter

By 1933 the effects of the Great Depression warranted some revisions to the Model City Charter. A committee appointed by National Civic League President Murray Seasongood produced a model calling for a department of personnel, the development of new provisions on slum clearance, new rules for counting ballots in a proportional representation election, and amplification of the sections on city planning and zoning (Model City Charter 1941, xi). This edition of the charter states that the clerk and other employees of the council are "in the classified service of the city, and shall be appointed, supervised and promoted, and may be reduced and removed by the city manager in accordance with the personnel section of this charter" (Model City Charter 1933, 24).

1941 Model City Charter

The fifth edition of the Model City Charter is referred to as the "completely revised fifth edition." The decision to further revise the charter was made in 1937 "in order that it might remain a modern document embodying the best that practical experience can offer" (Model City Charter 1941, vii). In light of the development and progress in the fields of finance, personnel, planning, zoning, housing, elections, public utilities, and special assessments, eminent specialists were called upon to review and revise the 1933 charter. As a result, the 1933 charter was completely rewritten.

The 1941 charter returns to the question of political separation of powers based on mayor-council government. The charter recommends the administrative council-manager plan, a ceremonial mayor and an assistant mayor to be elected by the council, and a city manager also selected by the council. But it also recommends that many of the advantages of professional administration are equally applicable to the mayor-council model of political city government with a few changes in the charter to provide for a professional administrator (Model City Charter 1941, xvi).

> The strong mayor form of government should be footnoted as "second best alternative" to the city manager plan. Motion by Fesler seconded by Bauer, carried unanimously. Amendment to resolution suggested by Upson that in appendix actual draft of strong mayor form should be incorporated. Some difference of opinion left to Drafting Committee. Footnote should make clear that there should be no departure from fundamentals and that strong mayor plan is merely suggested in cities where manager cannot be adopted. (Model City Charter Committee 1937, 1)

The drafting committee decided to include a description of the mayor-council form in the document, but relegated it to an appendix entitled "General note as to election of Mayor, under a 'strong-mayor' form of government" (Model City Charter Committee 1937, 139). While the previous four editions of the charter described civil service principles such as examinations and classification systems, the fifth edition is the first to use the word "merit."

Although the 1941 charter favors the council-manager form, it does provide guidelines for the election of a mayor. Many features of the mayor-council system offered in the first Model City Charter reappear in the fifth charter. For example, the directly elected mayor would have veto power and his or her election would be at-large. Department heads would report directly to the elected executive. However, the fifth charter mentions that the elected mayor may appoint an "assistant mayor" who would serve as the administrative officer of the city. In this case, depending upon the duties assigned to that position, department heads could report directly to the mayor or to the mayor through the assistant mayor. This is an early glimmer of the coming of adapted cities.

There are other differences between the first and fifth charters. The first charter, for example, specifies a two-year term for the elected mayor while the fifth charter did not specify term length. A number of changes were recommended regarding city councils. The first charter called for at-large elections but did not specify the Hare system (proportional representation) found in the fifth charter. The recommended size of the council decreased considerably from between nine and fifty in 1900 to between five and nine in 1941. The first charter did not address the issue of council pay, but the fifth edition of the charter indicated that some pay is acceptable. Finally, bid and purchasing procedures, along with routinized budgeting, accounting, and auditing procedures, were not outlined in the first Model City Charter but were set out in some detail in the 1941 version, further indications of the coming of adapted cities.

The 1941 Model City Charter is a very early glimpse of what would be, over the next forty years, another pattern of the S-curve of innovation. Political mayor-council cities would hire professional administrative officers, adopt elaborate civil service systems, establish solid bid and purchasing controls, set up independent auditing procedures, and make other changes to improve their administration. All these changes, as we show in Chapter 4 and describe in greater detail in Chapters 7 and 8, moved most of the formerly political cities into the adapted political category.

The 1941 Model City Charter was also an early clue as to what was to happen over the next fifty years to adapted administrative cities resting on unity-of-powers council-manager platforms. Directly elected mayors, as stated in the 1941 charter, became very popular in council-manager cities, and gradually many of these mayors were given greater powers, such as the veto, commission and board appointments, a staff, and so forth. As the 1941 model anticipated, and as we describe in Chapter 5 and in greater detail in Chapters 7 and 8, by the year 2000 most administrative cities would become adapted administrative cities.

1964 Model City Charter

The objective of the 1964 Model City Charter was to present a legal document in the form of a plan that was democratic but also capable of promoting efficiency and effectiveness (Model City Charter 1964, Introduction). Terrell Blodgett and William Cassella Jr. describe two streams of thought concerning the purpose of the Model City Charter: "One view insists that a *Model* present the 'ideal' structure of local government. The other view is to endorse a general principle of organization or process and present alternative means for achieving the basic end" (Model City Charter 1989, xi). For the first time, the Model City Charter presents, in addition to the preferred provisions, alternatives for the composition and election of the council and the selection of the mayor (Model City Charter 1964, xiv). As Luther Gulick, chairman of the revision committee, stated in the introduction to the sixth charter, "We recognize, of course, that there are cities, especially those in the largest population class, where the strong mayor plan is preferred. Provisions of the *Model* are appropriate for such a charter or can be readily adapted. This *Model* is not a text to be followed 'as is' but a guide and checklist, useful for all charters commissions and draftsmen. The charter for any city should be tailored to fit" (Model City Charter 1964, xiv).

The move toward flexibility and tailoring can be seen especially in the alternatives offered with regard to council elections in council-manager administrative cities. The alternatives are at-large elections, the combination of at-large elections with nomination by district, the combination of district and at-large elections, and proportional representation. In addition, the 1964 Model City Charter moves away from outlining rules, such as personnel rules, instead suggesting that such matters are better dealt with in a separate model administrative code. The 1964 charter once again addresses the issue of terms for council members. Seven council members are suggested, with the three candidates receiving the highest number of votes serving for four years and the candidate receiving the fourth highest number of votes serving for two years.

As has been the case since the second edition of the Model City Charter, the sixth edition endorses the council-manager form of administrative city government and describes other forms of government as options. For the first time, the charter describes the option in the council-manager form of government of a directly elected mayor who would serve a two-year term, an indication of what was to come.

A description of the mayor-council form of government, found in an appendix, recommends that the mayor serve a four-year term. There is also a description of how easily the word "mayor" could be substituted for the word "manager" in the language outlining provisions for the mayor-council form of government. Furthermore , the "assistant mayor" concept first described in the fifth edition is explained in more detail, particularly alternative titles for such a position, including city administrator, executive officer, or chief administrative officer.

1989 Model City Charter

James H. Svara describes two major concerns in the revision of the sixth edition of the Model City Charter. "First there was a perceived need to update the language and style of the charters, and it was feared that local groups considering charter revisions would give little credence to the documents because of their age. Second, there was a pervasive sense that the charters should confront issues regarding leadership and representation that had achieved greater salience since the previous editions were prepared" (Svara 1990b, 688). This second concern is especially evident in council-manager cities with larger populations. As previously mentioned, the two streams of thought regarding the purpose of the model charter—ideal structure or general principles with alternatives—were questions that this group of model drafters tried to resolve. What emerged was "A *Model* with Alternatives" that "will continue to endorse the council-manager plan, but will present alternatives for certain key provisions *without indicating an absolute preference*" (Model City Charter 1989, xii). The 1989 charter outlines provisions for a mayor to be elected and to serve a four-year term in a council-manager system. Alternatively, the council may select a mayor and deputy mayor who will serve at the pleasure of the council. In either case, the role of the mayor had been expanded well beyond ceremonial duties to include presiding at meetings of the council, representing the city in intergovernmental affairs, appointing, with the advice and consent of the council, members of citizen boards and commissions, presenting an annual state of the city address, and other duties specified by the council (Model City Charter 1989, 10). And, as in the sixth edition of the charter, the mayor-council form with a chief administrative officer is included in the appendix. However, for the first time, the assistant to the mayor is to be chosen based on professional management qualifications.

While merit principles were endorsed in all previous charters, the description of a full merit *system* first appears in the seventh edition. The city council shall "provide by ordinance for the establishment, regulation and maintenance of a merit system necessary to effective administration of the employees of city departments, including but not limited to classification and pay plans, examinations, force reduction, removals, working conditions, provisional and exempt appointments, in-service training, grievances and relationships with employee organizations" (Model City Charter 1989, 33).

The seventh Model City Charter describes the role of the mayor in council-manager government as follows:

> The mayor fills three facilitative roles that offer enormous leadership opportunities. First, the mayor can coordinate the activities of other officials by providing liaison between the manager and their council, fostering a sense of cohesion among council members and educating the public about the needs and prospects of the city. Second, the mayor provides policy guidance through setting goals for the council and advocating the adoption of policies that address the city's problems. Third, the mayor is an ambassador who promotes the city and represents it in dealing with other governments as well as the public. (Model City Charter 1989, 20)

While recognizing the coming importance of directly elected mayors in council-manager cities, the seventh charter retains the logic of unity of powers by arguing that "the mayor is preeminently a legislator, a member and leader of the council; the mayor is not an executive and not a full-time official" (Model City Charter 1989, 21). The charter, however, goes on to say that this nonexecutive needs staff support, which can be provided by the city manager. Working together to provide for this support, according to the seventh charter, "can often be arranged as part of a system whereby the mayor and the manager function as a team" (Model City Charter 1989, 21). The 1989 charter then backs away from this newly forged "team" by saying, "The mayor and council collectively, as a body, oversee the operations of the city by the manager" (Model City Charter 1989, 21).

Tying the Seven Model City Charters Together

At the time of this writing, the National Civic League has appointed a new Model City Charter Commission to write the eighth Model City Charter. The International City/County Management Association (ICMA), in a somewhat different form, is also considering generalized models of preferred forms of city government. ICMA does this in the form of "recognition." The present criteria provide for recognition of a position in the council-manager form of government and a position of general management that applies to a wide variety of governmental forms.

On January 7–8, 2000, a twenty-one-member task force, convened by the ICMA executive board and chaired by Northeast Vice President Phil Schenck (town manager of Avon, Connecticut), met to examine the ICMA's current council-manager recognition criteria and the process by which recognition should be determined in the future. The task force discussed how to simplify the process of determining who is a voting member of the ICMA and how to develop a separate process for determining whether or not a jurisdiction operates under the council-manager government.

The ICMA task force recommended that the ICMA define council-manager government in consultation with other relevant organizations, particularly the National Civic League, which develops and produces the Model City Charter. The ICMA does not want to be viewed as the "sole, self-serving supporter of council-manager government" (ICMA 2000a, 3). But the ICMA would like to work closely with the NCL to update and revise the 1989 Model City Charter. If there are "serious reservations either during the process or with the end product," then the task force recommends that ICMA decide on another course of action to define council-manager government (ICMA 2000b, 3). The ICMA executive board at its July 2000 meeting adopted these task force recommendations.

As both the NCL and the ICMA consider models and criteria for recognition, it is useful to review the changes in the Model City Charter. A fuller understanding of the changes in city government over the last century is important for the informed and reasonable development of future models. We tie things together in Table 6.1.

The Model City Charters has evolved from endorsing the mayor-council form to supporting only the council-manager form and, for the past sixty years, endorsing council-manager city government while at the same time setting out guidelines for preferred forms of mayor-council government that are acceptable if guidelines are followed.

The Model City Charter has evolved from recommending a directly elected mayor with executive powers to recommending a mayor chosen by the council with more limited powers and then, in 1964 and ever since, endorsing the ceremonial mayor in the council-manager form yet finding a directly elected mayor acceptable in both forms. Mayoral terms of office have generally moved from two-year to four-year terms.

For more than eighty-five years, the Model City Charter has endorsed the council-manager form of administrative government with a professional city manager chosen by the council on the basis of qualifications. Since 1989, the model charter has also recommended an appointed professional executive in the mayor form of cities selected on the basis of qualifications, chosen directly by the mayor. The charter recommends that city department heads report to the manager in council-manager cities and that the mayor retain executive control in mayor-council cities. Finally, all of the primary features of generally accepted good public management practices—a merit-based civil service; strict bid, contract, and purchase controls; an administratively developed budget, and so on—are found throughout the model charters for both forms of government.

With this picture in place, we turn to the present and to the challenges faced by those who will develop the eighth Model City Charter.

Easily the biggest challenge has to do with our findings that the majority of both mayor-council political cities and council-manager administrative cities increasingly resemble one-another and are now adapted cities. Over time, many mayor-council cities have changed structure in order to become more professional, efficient, honest, and accountable. Many council-manager cities have changed structure in order to provide for more political responsiveness in the form of directly elected political leadership and greater direct representation of districts and neighborhoods. These changes have been incremental. Many council-manager administrative cities have adopted important structural changes that place them in the adapted administrative city category, but few have abandoned their council-manager statutory or charter platform. Mayor-council political cities also have likewise adopted important structural modifications, putting them in the adapted political city category.

Evidence from recent research indicates the challenges faced by the NCL Charter Review Committee. Based on a 1996 ICMA survey, Tari Renner and Victor S. DeSantis (1998) examined structural changes in council-manager and mayor-council forms of government, as shown in Table 6.2. Ebdon and Brucato studied 193 cities over 100,000 population (1990 census number) between 1980 and 1994 and found there is evidence of convergence between the council-manager and mayor council form of government. Mayor-council cities still use district elections more than council-manager cities, but the gap is narrowing. Over one-half of larger council-manager cities use district elections. Eighty-seven percent of larger council-manager governments directly elected the mayor and only 10 percent still elected council on an at-large basis with the mayor being chosen from the council. "Both forms, then, are increasingly combining these two values in their structural design" (Ebdon and Brucato 2000, 2228).

Recently, even more profound adaptations are evident. Some large council-manager cities such as Cincinnati and Kansas City, Missouri, have enhanced the power of the mayor. In Cincinnati, the mayor is now directly elected at large, has veto authority, nominates and initiates termination of the city manager, appoints boards and committees, sets the council agenda, presents the budget, and hires assistants. In Kansas City, the mayor now has veto authority, nominates a city manager, appoints members to boards and commissions, and presents the budget to the council. At the same time, these cities have retained the council-manager form of government while significantly enhancing the power of the mayor. Oakland, California, has recently changed its charter from council-manager to mayor-council. The mayor can now terminate the services of the city manager without the consent of the council. Nevertheless, Oakland has retained the title of "city manager." These larger cities appear to have changed their charters in such a way as to be adapted cities.

It is important not to be preoccupied by the structural changes of a few large cities. The great majority of cities are still based on either the mayor-council platform, following the logic of separation of powers, or the council-manager platform, following the logic of unitary or parliamentary government. It is, however, also evident that the structures built on these platforms have changed and in some cases have significantly changed in the last fifty years.

To write the eighth Model City Charter, the National Civic League will be challenged to account for these changes. Because the differences and distinctions between the two dominant statutory platforms—council-manager and strong mayor—are now very blurred, some people feel a whole new approach is called for.

William Hansell, executive director of the International City/County Managers Association, in his article "Revisiting the Reform of the Reform," suggests that council-manager cities increasingly have "direct election of the mayor, district or part at-large and part district elections of council members, higher compensation for elected officials, partisan elections, veto power for the mayor, mayoral appointments of council committee and chairs, and mayoral appointments of citizens to serve on authorities, boards, and commissions"(Hansell 1999, 27). He proposes four variations, which he describes as (1) the mayor-council-manager form, in which the mayor is selected by his or her fellow council members; (2) the mayor (at large)-council-manager form, in which the

Table 6.1

The Evolution of the Model City Charter (MCC)

	1900	1916	1927	1933	1941	1964	1989
Mayor/council or council/manager	MC	CM	CM	CM	CM-endorsed MC-guidelines	CM-endorsed MC-guidelines	CM-endorsed MC-guidelines
Mayor							
Ceremonial, chosen by council	No	Yes	Yes	Yes	Yes	Yes	Yes
Directly elected	Yes	No	No	No	CM-No MC-Yes	CM-Yes MC-Yes	CM-Yes MC-Yes
Veto	Yes	No	No	No	CM-No MC-Yes	CM-No MC-Yes	CM-No MC-Yes
Term	2 years	½ year	Unspecified	Unspecified	Unspecified	CM-2 years if directly elected; MC-4 years	CM-4 years if directly elected; MC-4 years
Council							
Elections	At-large	At-large Hare system (proportional)	At-large Hare system (proportional)	At-large Hare system (proportional)	At-large Hare system (proportional)	4 alternatives	5 alternatives
Size	9–50	5–25	5–25	5–25	5–9	7	5–9
Paid	No	Yes	Yes	Yes	Yes	Yes	Yes

Term	6 years; staggered	4 years	Unspecified	Unspecified	Unspecified	3 council members/1-year term; 1 council member/2-year term; staggered	4 years staggered or concurrent with unspecified term
Administration							
Appointed based on qualifications	No	Yes	Yes	Yes	CM-Yes MC-No	CM-Yes MC-No	CM-Yes MC-No
Appointed by: Council / Mayor	No / Yes	Yes / No	Yes / No	Yes / No	CM-Yes MC-Yes	CM-Yes MC-Yes	CM-Yes MC-Yes
Departments report to executive	Yes	Yes	Yes	Yes	CM-Yes MC-Yes	CM-Yes MC-Yes	CM-Yes MC-Yes
Merit-based civil service	Merit principal	Merit principal	Merit principal	Merit principal	Merit principal	Merit principal	Merit principal/system
Bid and purchasing process	No	Yes	Yes	Yes	Yes	Yes	Yes
Routinized budget, accounting, inventory, auditing process	No	Yes	Yes	Yes	Yes	Yes	Yes

Table 6.2

1996 Survey of City Structural Change (percent)

1. Mayor-council cities with a CAO	50.8
2. Attempts to modify structure or form:	
Mayor-council	13.4
Council-manager	14.9
3. Council-manager cities with directly elected mayor	61.1 (1992)
4. Type of election system (all forms):	
At-large	60.9
District only	16.8
Mixed	22.3
5. Mayor not on council:	
In council-manager form	15.8
In mayor-council form	65.5
6. Mayor has voting power (council-manager form):	
On all issues	74.8
To break a tie only	22.9
Never	1.3
Other	1.1
7. Mayor's power to veto in council-manager form	11.1

Source: ICMA Municipal Form of Government Survey, 1996.

mayor is elected by the voters to the position of council leader with a council vote; (3) the mayor (empowered)-council-manager form, in which the mayor, who is separately elected by the people, has special veto power, authority to nominate a city manager, and the power to review the city manager's proposed budget before it is submitted to the council; and (4) the mayor (separation of powers)-council-manager form, in which the mayor does not serve on the council and does not vote. In this alternative, the mayor serves as the chief executive officer and a city manager is appointed by the mayor, subject to the approval by the council (Hansell 1999). Hansell's four-part schema captures many of the detailed structural variations now found in American cities.

Based on their research, Frederickson and Johnson write that "the formal legal description of a given city as either council-manager or mayor-council is less accurate than the particular structural variations that the citizens of a given community have chosen to adopt in order to make their government reflect citizens' preferences and values"(2001, 14). Research by Adrian (1988) and Frederickson and Johnson (2001, 13), suggests that "distinctions between cities on the basis of their legal platforms are less and less meaningful and have little explanatory power." The eighth Model City Charter will have to respond to these new realities.

For a century, the seven editions of the Model City Charter have served as guides and templates to anyone interested in how best to organize and manage cities. Looking back, the Model City Charters are splendid documents illuminating the changing values and beliefs of the leading city specialists of each era. In the sweep of history, these charters reflect the dynamics of structural adaptation. The evidence is clear: American cities are anything but static.

The challenges at hand are to somehow capture the range of beliefs and opinions as to how to best organize, govern, and manage the American city. The task before the National Civic League is nothing less than the development of the guide and template for the American city in the twenty-first century.

We now turn to a full description of adapted cities.

7

Adapted Cities

Earlier we pressed the claim that the structural differences between political and administrative cities have diminished and that, over time, the two types of cities have come to resemble each other. Political cities, usually resting on mayor-council platforms, resemble the presidential form of government with its emphasis on the separation of powers and checks and balances. Administrative cities, usually resting on council-manager platforms, resemble the parliamentary form of government, with its emphasis on the unity of powers. In describing the changing structural characteristics of American cities, our data indicate that the majority are a new type of category, the adapted city. The purpose of this chapter is to present survey-based evidence to support this claim and to describe the detailed characteristics associated with adapted cities.

The Big Picture

Over 92 percent of American cities are legally described as either council-manager or mayor-council form, as Table 7.1 indicates. Since there are over 7,500 American cities, most of which have a mayor-council or council-manager platform, there is an opportunity to test the following hypotheses. First, overall major changes from political mayor-council statutory platforms to administrative council-manager platforms are rare. When there are such changes, it is much more likely that mayor-council cities will become council-manager cities than vice versa. Second, cities make incremental structural changes to their existing form of government. The aggregation of incremental changes significantly alters the structural characteristics of cities. Third, over time, political cities adopt many of the features of administrative government to increase their management and productivity capabilities. Fourth, over time, administrative cities adopt many of the features of political cities to increase their political responsiveness, leadership, and accountability capabilities. Fifth, both political and administrative cities adapt to constitute a new category, the adapted city. Adapted cities include adapted political, adapted administrative, and conciliated cities. Adapted cities are more alike,

Table 7.1

Forms of City Government: All American Cities

Form of government	Number of cities
Mayor-council	3,263 (43%)
Council-manager	3,773 (49%)
Commission	151 (2%)
Town meeting	377 (5%)
Rep. town meeting	66 (1%)
Total	7,630 (100%)

Source: Municipal Year Book. 1999, xi. Washington, DC: ICMA.

although there are some important distinctions among them, than they are like either political or administrative cities.

We purposely use an entirely new nomenclature and new set of categories to describe the structure of American cities. This is done because the traditional categories no longer describe reality. There are, for example, extensive variations in structural details among cities that are technically categorized as mayor-council cities. As we describe in Chapter 4, many mayor-council cities now have professional chief administrative officers (CAOs) and highly developed civil service systems, bid and purchase controls, and auditing requirements. Others do not. As we describe in Chapter 5, many cities that are technically or legally categorized as council-manager cities have directly elected, full-time, paid mayors and council members elected by district. Others do not. The point is that the labels "mayor-council" and "council-manager" are legal categories, which utterly fail to describe very important similarities and differences in city structures. As we describe in Chapter 1, to more accurately describe these similarities and differences we had to create a new vocabulary and a new set of categories.

Findings

To test the hypotheses set out above and to further describe the differences in the structures of cities, we turn to our empirical research. To study all cities, we obtained data from the International City/County Management Association (ICMA) gathered through a series of surveys conducted by its Municipal Data Service. This database is updated at four-year intervals and continually modified to reflect changes during the interim years. Using the 1991 and 1996 ICMA survey data, we model longitudinal comparisons between the two bodies of data.

Since the bulk of Americans live in cities in the 10,000 to 1 million population range, all cities with populations above and below that range were deleted from the data sets. Thus, after culling the data set the following N values remain: 1992 = 3,028; 1996 = 3,924. Of these cities, in 1992, 57 percent reported having the council-manager form of government. In 1996, it was 66.2 percent. This finding is part of a general pattern. Each year from 1983 to 1999, an average of sixty-three cities adopted the formal council-manager form of government. From 1990 to 2000, an annual average of only 2.2 cities abandoned the council-manager form. Conversely, during that same period, an average of forty-three cities per year discontinued the mayor-council form of government. Four things are important to note here. First, these adoptions and abandonments are of the entire council-manager form of government and could not be considered incremental modifications or adjustments to that form of government. Second, in recent years, several large, visible council-manager cities have considered changing to the mayor-council form and some—Tampa, Spokane, and Oakland, California—have done so. Others, such as Cincinnati and Kansas City, Missouri, have so modified their council-manager legal platform as to set off debates in the ICMA about whether their claims to still be council-manager cities are accurate. Third, abandonment of a form of government requires a vote of city residents. In the case of council-manager cities, abandonment referenda are successful at a rate of about one in four. So the data indicate that overall change in the statutory or charter form of American city government is relatively rare. And when this change occurs it is much more often the discontinuation of the mayor-council platform in favor of the council-manager platform than the discontinuation of the council-manager platform in favor of the mayor-council platform, despite the few high-profile cities that have abandoned council-manager government.

The much bigger story is the less dramatic but much more widespread trend of smaller structural change in cities with either legal structural platform. The ICMA data all indicate that formal city government structures in the United States are surprisingly unstable. To demonstrate this, we turn to patterns of change *within* the formal statutory mayor-council and council-manager categories.

Respondents indicated whether, in the last twenty years, there were attempts to modify or adapt their government structures without abandoning them. Change in the form of government includes the following: a major change in the city charter from a mayor-council to a council manager form, or vice versa; a change in the election of council members from at-large to district elections; a change to a mixed system with some at-large and some ward or district elections; a change in the mix between the number of council members elected at large and the number elected by district; an increase, or

Table 7.2

Changes in Government Structure, 1987–92

Number of changes	Numbers of cities	Percent
0	2,828	93.4
1	148	4.9
2	39	1.3
3	10	0.3
4	1	0.0
5	1	0.0
6	1	0.0
Total	3,028	100.0

Source: ICMA Municipal Form of Government Survey, 1992.

Table 7.3

Changes in Government Structure, 1992–96

Number of changes	Number of cities	Percent
0	3,434	87.5
1	414	10.5
2	64	1.6
3	9	0.2
4	2	0.1
5	0	0.0
6	1	0.0
Total	3,934	100.0

Source: ICMA Municipal Form of Government Survey, 1996.

decrease, in the number of members who serve on the council; a change in the method of election of the mayor; a proposed change in having party affiliations appear on the ballot for council elections; and finally, the addition or deletion of the position of a chief administrative officer. The responses for the 1992 survey (which included attempts from 1987 to 1992) and the 1996 survey (attempts from 1992 to 1996) are presented in Tables 7.2 and 7.3.

This analysis suggests that the rate of structural adaptation in American cities is accelerating. In the period between 1987 and 1992, 6.4 percent of the cities surveyed reported at least one structural adaptation. From 1992 to 1996, 12.5 percent of American cities reported at least one structural adaptation. The results indicate that the mayor-council form is experiencing slightly more adaptation than the council-manager form of government. While 6.4 percent between 1987 and 1992 and 12.5 percent from 1992 to 1996 might seem slight, it is the long-range aggregation of change that matters if measured over, say, a twenty-five-year period.

Based on this analysis, we confirm the first two hypotheses set out earlier in this chapter. On one hand, change from one formal statutory form of city government structure to another is rare in American cities. On the other hand, incremental adaptation within the formal statutory categories is very common. It is clear that the structural details of American cities are malleable and unstable.

We now turn to the bigger question. How much structural adaptation in the form of diffusion based on borrowing features from other cities, often of the opposite legal type, is there in American cities? To answer these propositions, we unbundled the many structural features of cities this way.

First, political cities have the following characteristics:

- there is no chief administrative officer
- the council is paid and may have staff
- council members are usually elected by district
- the mayor is directly elected
- the mayor is full-time

Second, administrative cities have the following characteristics:

- the mayor is selected from among the council or has no executive powers
- there is a full-time professional administrator almost always called a city manager
- council elections are usually at large
- the mayor and council are part-time
- the mayor and council do not have staff

When the 1992 ICMA data are filtered for those cities with no chief administrative officer and with council elections by district, we discovered that of the original 3,028 cases, 181 cities remained. These were classified as political cities, based on the logic of the separation of powers. Conversely, when only those cities that had a professional chief administrative officer, a ceremonial mayor selected from among the council, and at-large elections were sorted out, there were only 507 pure administrative cities, based on the logic of the unity of powers. This left 2,340 cities or 77 percent of the cities that were neither pure political nor pure administrative cities. Using the same criteria for the 1996 ICMA survey data, there were 188 political cities, 537 administrative cities, and 1,759 cities, or 71 percent, open to classification.

Using the ICMA survey data, we determined that approximately three-quarters of American cities between 10,000 and 1 million population did not meet either political or administrative city structural criteria. But, because

the ICMA data do not have variables that could unbundle the structural characteristics of the remaining three-quarters of American cities, we did our
own sample survey. To unpack the characteristics of these cities, we wanted
to know in greater detail, for example, if the mayor is separately elected full-
time, is paid, has a staff, has veto power, has the power to appoint a chief
administrative officer independently from the city council, has the power to
appoint and terminate department heads or shares that power with a professional city administrator, or has the power to directly supervise city department heads. We wanted a similar level of detailed knowledge about the city
manager or CAO, city council, and city civil service staff.

Charles Adrian points out that the "organizational needs of one city are
much the same as those of another if one controls for size. It is to be expected, then, that cities might drift toward one another in structural pattern"
(Adrian 1988, 9).

Size is one factor that determines the structure of a municipality, but certainly not the only one. The structural changes we describe here appear to
verify the trend away from a preoccupation with efficiency and toward political problem solving in council-manager cities. At the same time, our findings indicate that mayor-council cities are adapting toward greater efficiency
and managerial capacity. Because the two forms look increasingly like each
other, the council-manager and mayor-council structural categories are less
distinct and therefore much less descriptive of reality. Our research indicates
that the formal legal description of a given city as either "council-manager"
or "mayor-council" is less accurate than the particular structural variations
that the citizens of a given community have chosen to adopt in order to make
their government reflect their preferences and values.

From our analysis of the 1992 and 1996 ICMA survey results, we found
that so many political and administrative cities have adopted the structural
characteristics of the other that the political and administrative city categories were much smaller than the adapted city category.

Further Refinement of the Logic of Adapted Cities

In 1998, we sampled 200 cities with populations between 10,000 and 1 million in order to gather a wide assortment of structural variables and to learn
more about the history and nature of structural change in American cities
over the last twenty years. One hundred ten surveys were returned, a response rate of 55 percent. In addition, we included six other cities that have
either undergone some institutional change since the survey was conducted
in 1998 or were considering such changes.

We then sorted these 116 cities using the survey variables to see if there were any clusters. Table 7.4 sets out the variables used to sort city structural characteristics by cluster. The political and administrative city clusters formed as expected based on our findings using ICMA data. Of the cities surveyed, 19 or 16.3 percent were found to be political cities and 17 or 14.7 percent were found to be administrative cities. Of the remaining 80 cities, 46 or 39.6 percent fell into the adapted administrative group; 19, or 16 percent, into the adapted political group, and 15, or 13 percent into the conciliated group. Although we sorted the survey cities into five structured categories, two are very distinct—political and administrative cities—the differences between adapted cities, however, are less distinct. There are some structured differences between adapted cities and we describe them here, although we believe they resemble one another more than they resemble either political or administrative cities. It is for this reason that we classified only these jurisdictions as adapted cities. All adapted cities have a directly elected mayor, a professional city administrator, some or all of the city council elected by district, an established merit-based civil service, and formalized bid and purchase contracts and an auditing requirement. Because two-thirds of American cities between 10,000 and 1 million in population have these common structural characteristics and because adapted city characteristics mingle the structural characteristics of political and administrative cities, it could be said that over the years American cities have created a new mixed form of local government.

Both the political city and the adapted political city are characterized by a separation of powers between the mayor and council. The elected executive has the sole authority to appoint and terminate the city manager, as well as to supervise department heads. But the similarity ends there, because important differences emerge between the political and the adapted political city. In the adapted political cities, there is a professional, full-time CAO and usually some council are elected at large. In addition, the council is part-time and does not have a separate staff.

Administrative cities have the features of classic council-manager government, with a council elected at large, together with an appointed professional city manager who directs the city officers on a day-to-day basis. Legislative and policy-making power resides with the council and is distinctly separate from the administrative powers of the city manager. The mayor is chosen by the council. The title of mayor is only symbolic in administrative cities, the mayor having no executive power. Adapted administrative cities retain elements of city council unification but significantly modify that unification by separately electing the mayor. Over time, particularly in larger cities, mayors in adapted administrative cities are increasingly full-time paid executives with growing executive powers. This, of course, introduces elements of a potential separation of power between the council and the mayor. Furthermore, in adapted administrative cities, some or all of the council are elected by district, emphasizing the needs and preferences of neighborhoods and reducing the prospects of city council concern for the whole city.

The conciliated city is a complete mix of the primary principles and logic of political and administrative cities. The conciliated city has the separation of political power between the mayor and the council found in political and adapted political cities. The mayor is a separately elected executive serving full-time with a city salary and staff. He or she does not serve on the city council and may veto its actions. But in the conciliated city the mayor and council have limited authority over the day-to-day management of city affairs because the CAO has executive authority over city departments. The CAO is appointed or terminated by the mayor and city council together. The CAO may report to the mayor, but conciliated cities vary in the precise details of how the mayor and the council share the power to appoint and terminate the CAO and city department heads.

The primary difference between an adapted political city and a conciliated city has to do with the limited executive authority of the mayor in the conciliated city. The mayor may not appoint or terminate the CAO without the consent of the council and the CAO has executive authority over city departments. The primary difference between an adapted administrative city and a conciliated city has to do with the separation of the mayor from any role in the city council other than possibly voting in the case of a tie.

Our 1998 survey included 19 political cities, 17 administrative cities, and 80 adapted cities. Table 7.5 shows that about 69 percent of the cities surveyed are adapted cities.

As seen in Figure 7.1, there are 19 (16.3%) political cities, 19 (16.3%) adapted political cities, 15 (13%) conciliated cities, 46 (39.6%) adapted administrative cities, and 17 (14.7%) administrative cities.

The association between city type and the legal or statutory charter platform as a council-manager or mayor-council city was about as expected. As Figure 7.2 shows, all political and adapted political cities rest on mayor council platforms and all but one administrative and adapted administrative cities are on council-manager platforms. Twelve conciliated cities are on council-manager platforms and three are on mayor-council platforms.

To understand these categories and how cities fit them, we turn to a detailed consideration of each of the five types, using our survey information. We now summarize the characteristics of the cities in each category and describe some of the cities included in our study. This description of the differences between political and adapted political cities follows the logic set out in Chapter 3, and this description of the differences between adminis-

Table 7.4

Types and Categories of American Cities

Political	Adapted political	Conciliated	Adapted administrative	Administrative
Mayor directly elected	Mayor directly elected	Mayor either directly elected or selected by council	Mayor directly elected	Mayor selected by council
Most council elected by district	Council elected by district, at large, or mixed	Council elected by district, at large, or mixed	Council elected by district, at large, or mixed	Most council elected at large
No CAO	Likely to have CAO	Has CAO	Has CAO	Has CAO
Mayor not on council	Mayor not on council	Mayor not on council	Mayor is on council	Mayor is on council
Mayor has veto power	Mayor has veto power	Mayor may have veto power	Mayor may have veto power	Mayor does not have veto power
Mayor full-time	Mayor full-time	Mayor may be full-time or part-time	Mayor is usually part-time	Mayor is part-time
Mayor has staff	Mayor has staff	Mayor may have staff	Mayor does not have staff	Mayor does not have staff
Council full-time	Council full- or part-time	Council may be full-time or part-time	Council is part-time	Council is part-time
Council has staff	Council may have staff	Council may have staff	Council does not have staff	Council does not have staff

Nonpartisan or partisan elections	Partisan or nonpartisan elections	Nonpartisan or partisan elections	Usually nonpartisan elections	Nonpartisan elections
Department heads report to mayor	Department heads report to mayor	Department heads report to CAO	Department heads report to CAO	Department heads report to CAO
Mayor serves as CAO	Mayor appoints or terminates CAO without consent of council	Mayor appoints and terminates CAO with consent of council	Council appoints and terminates city manage	Council appoints and terminates city manager
May have civil service	May have civil service	Usually has civil service	Usually has civil service	Usually has civil service
May have bidding system	Has bidding system	Has bidding system	Has bidding system	Has bidding system
Statutory charter form is mayor-council	Statutory charter form is likely to be mayor-council	Statutory charter form may be mayor-council or council-manager	Statutory charter form is likely to be council-manager	Statutory charter form is council-manager

Table 7.5

Distribution of American Cities by Type, 1998

Political	19	(16.3%)
Administrative	17	(14.7%)
Adapted	80	(69%)
Total	116	(100%)

Source: Frederickson and Johnson survey, 1998.

Figure 7.1 **Distribution of Cities by Category**

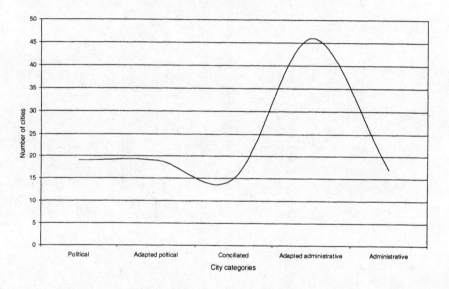

trative cities and adapted administrative cities follows the logic set out in Chapter 4.

There are nineteen political cities. Cities in this category conform to the criteria of a political city seen in Table 7.4. Green Bay, Wisconsin (with a population of 102,179 in 2000), is included in the 1998 survey. Green Bay is a classic mayor-council political city. The mayor serves as the chief executive officer, appoints and supervises department heads, and has the responsibility for preparing the city budget. Since 1978, the only structural change has been to reduce the number of council members. The mayor has veto power over council actions and votes only to break a tie. The mayor has a significant role in initiating policy and promoting cohesion among the council.

Figure 7.2 **Comparison of Legal Platform with City Category**

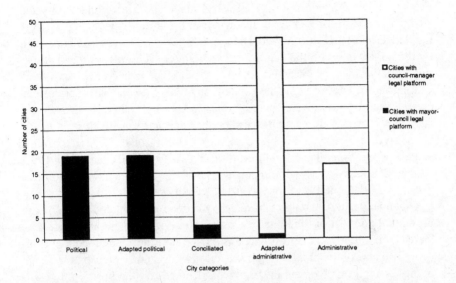

The voters directly elect the mayor and the mayor serves full-time and has a four-year term. All twelve council members are elected by district and serve two-year terms. Green Bay has developed nonpartisan elections, a professional merit civil service, purchasing and bidding standards, and a professional budgeting system. The municipal reform movement did not leave Green Bay untouched.

Green Bay retains virtually all of the key elements of the separation of powers and checks and balance between the mayor and the council.

In our survey there are also nineteen adapted political cities. All have retained the logic of a separation of political power between the mayor and council. In adapted political cities, the mayor has considerable executive authority and control over the city bureaucracy. However, almost all adapted political cities have a professional CAO appointed by the mayor. In cities with CAOs, the mayor still exercises executive authority to appoint and supervise the department heads, but tends to delegate the day-to-day operation of the city to the CAO.

In adapted political cities, there are a variety of ways by which council members are elected. Four (21 percent) of the adapted political cities elect all of the council members by district, six (32 percent) cities elect council members in a mixed fashion, and nine (47 percent) cities elect all council members at large.

Sixteen (84 percent) adapted political cities have full-time mayors.

The city of Atlanta, Georgia (population of 401,726 in 2000, is a splendid example of an adapted political city. The mayor is directly elected by the citizens, serves full-time, has a major role in initiating policy and preparing the budget, and has veto power. The city charter calls for a CAO appointed by the mayor but with the consent of the council. The mayor hires and dismisses department heads and supervises the CAO. The mayor serves a four-year term, does not serve on the council, and may not vote. There are fifteen council members, twelve elected by district. Council members also serve a four-year term but are part-time. Atlanta has nonpartisan elections, a merit-based civil service system, purchasing and bidding standards, and a professional budget. Since 1978, Atlanta has made two structural changes. In 1997, Atlanta decreased the total number of council members and changed three district-based council positions to at-large elections.

Green Bay and Atlanta both have a mayor-council legal platform and both have retained most of the logic of its separation of political power between the council and mayor. But Atlanta has moved into the adapted political category because of the charter requirement for a CAO and because of the level of city council involvement in the mayor's choice for that position. In addition, Atlanta has moved incrementally away from exclusively district-based city council elections toward some at-large seats.

In our survey, there are seventeen pure administrative cities in which the mayor is chosen by the city council, serves on the council, and has only the same voting powers as other council members. The city council together selects a professional city manager who serves as the chief executive officer. Beverly Hills, California (estimated 1998 population of 34,000), is a good example. The five-member Beverly Hills city council is elected at large and selects a ceremonial mayor to serve part-time for a one-year term. Together they appoint a professional manager who operates city affairs, including hiring and firing department heads. During the last twenty years, the city of Beverly Hills has not made any structural changes.

There are forty-six adapted administrative cities in the survey. The major differences between an administrative and an adapted administrative city is that in the adapted administrative city the mayor is directly elected and some of the council members are elected by district.

Again we use Kansas City, Missouri (population of 437,764 in 2000), as an example of an adapted administrative city. Resting on a council-manager platform, Kansas City has a separately elected mayor who serves on the city council. The mayor's powers have been expanded over the last few years to include the veto, review of the budget prior to the council, nomination of the city manager, and appointment of boards and committees. The city manager appoints, supervises, and terminates department heads, with the exception of the police chief and the director of the parks and recreation department. Members of boards and commissions appointed by the mayor are also approved by the council. City council members are elected in a mixed format, some at large with district residence and some by district.

If Atlanta is an example of an adapted political city and Kansas City is an example of an adapted administrative city, what are the similarities and differences? Are the differences so minor and the similarities so obvious that they justify the description of both Atlanta and Kansas City as adapted cities? The answer is yes.

Atlanta and Kansas City elect their city council members in essentially the same way. Both mayors are directly elected, full-time, paid, and have staff. The daily administrative operations of both cities are directed by professional administrators, a CAO in Atlanta, a city manager in Kansas City. Both cities have fully developed civil service systems, bid and purchase controls, and auditing requirements. The only consequential structural difference between Atlanta and Kansas City has to do with the powers of the mayors and administrative officers. The Atlanta mayor appoints the CAO with council approval, whereas Kansas City's council appoints and terminates the city manager, but only after the mayor's recommendation. Atlanta's mayor appoints department heads and has a direct line of supervision over them, whereas the Kansas City manager appoints and terminates most department heads and has a direct line of supervision over them. How consequential are these differences? In Chapter 8, we review research on this subject and conclude that the structural difference between Atlanta and Kansas City are inconsequential.

The Rates of Structural Changes

To achieve a somewhat more refined understanding of city structural dynamics, we used the 116 cities in our sample survey.

First, we examined the scope and nature of the structural changes. A structural change is defined as a change in how council is elected, the number of council members, how a mayor is elected, whether a chief administrative officer position is created or eliminated, and a change in platform. Of the 116 cities, thirty-seven cities made at least one structural change during the last twenty years. Of the thirty-seven cities, six cities made at least three structural changes, and ten cities made two structural changes. There was a total of fifty-six structural changes. The evidence in Table 7.6 shows that cities are malleable.

Next, we examined whether the structural change(s) in each city resulted in a change in government category or type, and whether the adaptations made by cities signaled a discernible trend toward a certain category or type

Table 7.6

Type of Structural Changes Made in 1998 Survey

Type of structural change	Structural changes made by cities
Change to a mixed system of elections	11
Change from all at-large to all district elections	10
Change the method of mayoral election to direct election	8
Change in the form of government	7
Decrease the number of council members	7
Add the position of CAO	5
Increase the number of council members	4
Increase the budget powers of the mayor	1
Give mayor power to nominate city manager	1
Give mayor the power to appoint boards and committees	1
Eliminate the CAO position	1
Total changes	56

Source: Frederickson and Johnson survey questionnaire, 1998.

of government. Seventeen of the thirty-seven cities with structural changes did not result in movement to another type or category.

Of the twenty cities that changed type or category, the structural changes in fifteen cities were enough to change the type of government. Eleven cities changed from administrative to adapted administrative, one changed from political to adapted political, one went from adapted administrative to political, one city went from a commission form to adapted administrative, and one city went from administrative to political. Of the cities that changed type, 87 percent changed to the adapted city category. The evidence shows that there is a pronounced movement toward adapted cities.

There were twenty cities, or 17 percent of our sample, that changed category as a result of structural changes during the last twenty years. Of these twenty cities, fifteen cities adopted more political structures and five cities adopted more administrative structures. Ten, or 50 percent, went from an administrative to an adapted administrative city, one city went from a political city to an adapted political city, three cities went from administrative or adapted administrative to conciliated, three cities went from adapted political to conciliated, one city went from administrative to political, one city went from the commission form to adapted political, and one city went from an adapted political to a political city. These modifications also show a movement toward adapted cities and that cities are coming to resemble one another.

Ten (27 percent) of the cities that made at least one structural change are now classified as conciliated cities. In four of the conciliated cities, the structural change(s) did not result in a change in city category.

Conclusion: A Diffusion of Change

Cities are not only adapting at a surprisingly rapid pace, but they are following previously discovered patterns of institutional dynamics (DiMaggio and Powell 1991). They appear to adapt or change following the S-curve of the diffusion of innovation, and institutional theory predicts that cities will gradually come to resemble one another and homogenize, to take on common characteristics. Other examples of the patterns of institutional isomorphism include all large-scale American research universities, pharmaceutical companies, and hospitals. Cities now fit this pattern. Our evidence indicates that the two statutory platforms of city government fail to account for their empirical structural characteristics. We have attempted to capture these characteristics under the adapted city label and demonstrate here that such cities are now the modal type. To provide further evidence for our claims, we now turn to our own survey.

Our research has confirmed that mayor-council and council-manager cities are adopting characteristics of the other. We have also devised a new model and a new language to describe and explain the criteria for the political, adapted political, conciliated, adapted administrative, and administrative city. Political cities adapt to enhance accountability, efficiency, and professionalism; administrative cities adapt to provide political leadership and increase political representation and responsiveness. In the middle is the conciliated city. The conciliated city is neither political nor administrative, but both.

Our research has shown that cities practice a form of structural dynamics, changing regularly, usually in ways that cause them to move toward the middle and increasingly resemble one another. Features of mayor-council government, such as a directly elected mayor and council members elected by districts, are increasingly being adopted in council-manager governments. In mayor-council governments, the reverse seems to be the case; that is to say, they are increasingly adopting structures resembling council-manager government, for example, a professional CAO, at-large elections, merit-based personnel systems, and professional accounting, budgeting, and procurement standards. The movement of political cities toward administrative cities seems to be less pronounced than the movement of administrative cities toward political cities. We speculate that the adoption of many administrative features in political cities occurred from the 1940s through the 1970s. It appears that the impact of the Progressive Era and the reform movement on political cities had already occurred by the late 1980s and 1990s.

Formal governmental institutions appear to be malleable and inclined to adapt. City government structures reflect citizen preferences and values, and because citizen values and preferences change, it should not be surprising that city structures also change. The evidence presented here indicates that there is much more structural change occurring in American cities than is commonly understood. The distinctions between the two traditional major forms of city government are blurring. The rate of structural change suggests that cities are more malleable than is commonly believed. The adapted American city is now more common than either the traditional political or the reformed administrative city.

Citizens and their local governments are engaged in a pattern of cocreation, where each produces and defines the other. Just as in nature, where the environment of an organism is composed of many other organisms, other governments importantly influence municipal governments. The theory of the diffusion of innovation aptly applies to the changing structures of the American city. In American cities, there is always the capability to move incrementally from one kind of political/administrative structure to another or to shift from a less effective structure to one more satisfying to the citizenry and elected officials. Cities seldom change entirely from political to administrative structures or vice versa (Protasel 1988). The notion of the adapted city suggests that local governments are innovative, flexible, dynamic, and results-oriented. American cities are much more subtly organized than the traditional legal forms imply. Indeed, the designation of mayor-council or council-manager to describe the institutional arrangements tells very little about the actual structure of a given city.

Council-manager government is frequently criticized, especially in larger cities, because its structure does not include a visible leader with power. Where municipal leaders face the difficulty of reconciling conflicting demands, strong political leadership, it is argued, can be particularly helpful. An elected mayor rather than an appointed manager is likely to have both public visibility and an orientation toward politics and coalition-building activities necessary for effective leadership. The revitalization of the mayor's role in many American cities is supported by numerous studies that emphasize the leadership potential of the mayor's office (Sparrow 1985; Protasel 1988; Pealy 1985, Wheeland 2002). In particular, Svara's research on leadership under the council-manager plan combines a concern for institutions and personality (Svara 1986). Svara suggests that institutional arrangements are important in establishing the preconditions necessary for mayoral leadership in council-manager jurisdictions. The direct election of the mayor, the mayor's power to appoint commission members, the presence of adequate mayoral staff, and an adequate salary are important variables. Going further, Svara argues that "cities cannot rely on an 'institutional fix' to assure effective mayoral leadership" (Svara 1986, 27).

This chapter has primarily focused on the different types and categories of American city government. Chapter 8 compares specific structural characteristics in political, adapted political, conciliated, adapted administrative, and administrative cities. A review of these important structural characteristics develops a more complete picture and a deeper appreciation of the complexity and diversity of the modern American city.

8

Probing the Complexity of
Adapted Cities

To further explain the adapted cities typology, we now turn to specific treatment of the key structural characteristics of American cities. As we review these characteristics and analyze our data, we will defend two claims: that through the diffusion of structural change, American cities are becoming more like each other; and that the dominant structural form of American cities is now adapted. As we describe in Chapter 7, about 70 percent of American cities are now classified as adapted political, conciliated, or adapted administrative: all forms of adapted cities. While there are several important structural distinctions that support the differences between political, administrative and adapted cities (see Table 7.5), in this chapter we will focus on the most critical: the powers of the mayor, the characteristics of the city council, the power of the city manager or the chief administrative officer (CAO), the reporting patterns for city department heads, and administrative procedures and processes.

Powers of the Mayor

The role of the mayor in American municipalities changes depending on whether the mayor is directly elected, is on the council and can vote, has veto authority, serves as the primary executive of the city, and serves full- or part-time. Using the data in our survey, Table 8.1 compares the powers of the mayor in the different city categories.

The traditional role of mayors in administrative cities could be best described as the figurehead. However, this role is changing. In some cities with council-manager statutory platforms, mayors are emerging as executives who rival the city manager for power and have transformed the council-manager system into a skewed version of a mayor-council system with a CAO. In some adapted administrative cities, the mayor and city manager work closely together in the formulation and implementation of public policy. In a study of forty-five large council-manager cities, Boynton and Wright found that a

Table 8.1

Structural Powers of the Mayor by City Category

	Political (%)		Adapted political (%)		Conciliated (%)		Adapted administrative (%)		Administrative (%)	
Frequency	19	(16.3)	19	(16.3)	15	(13)	46	(39.6)	17	(14.8)
Mayor is elected directly by people at large	19	(100)	19	(100)	15	(100)	45	(98)	0	(0)
Mayor has vote on council	1	(5)	0	(0)	0	(0)	46	(100)	17	(100)
Mayor can veto	19	(100)	17	(89)	10	(67)	4	(9)	0	(0)
Mayor also serves as CAO	19	(100)	3	(16)	0	(0)	0	(0)	0	(0)
Mayor is full-time	18	(95)	16	(89)	3	(20)	3	(7)	0	(0)

Source: Frederickson and Johnson survey questionnaire, 1998.

collaborative or team relationship involving the manager and the mayor in policy-making activities was the most frequently found leadership pattern (Boynton and Wright 1971). This finding was reinforced by Wikstrom's study of mayors in forty-one council-manager cities in Virginia where mayors were found to be exercising leadership as members of council-manager teams (Wikstrom 1979).

The direct election of the mayor in most council-manager platform cities gives the mayor an electoral base for exercising political leadership and puts such cities a step closer to the separation of political power between the mayor and the council. For this reason, we categorize such cities as adapted administrative cities. As Table 8.1 shows, mayors are directly elected in all the political, adapted political, and conciliated cities and in 98 percent of the adapted administrative cities. In all but two administrative cities, on the other hand, the mayor is chosen from among the council, and in those two administrative cities, the council member with the most votes becomes the mayor. In all the political and adapted political cities, the mayor is chosen at large directly by the people. Increasingly, the data show that the direct election of the mayor is becoming the norm for American cities.

In the traditional American separation-of-powers model, the elected executive is autonomous from the city council in that he or she does not serve on the council and cannot vote, unless to break a tie and, in this model, the mayor has veto power. As Table 8.1 indicates, in all but one of the political and adapted political cities the mayor does not serve on the council and cannot vote, and in all but two of these cities the mayor has veto authority. Conversely, in all administrative and adapted administrative cities, the mayor votes, and in only four, or 9 percent, of the adapted administrative cities the mayor has veto authority. In no conciliated cities does the mayor have the authority to vote, and in 10, or 67 percent, of the conciliated cities the mayor does have veto authority. In ten, or 67 percent, of the conciliated cites, the mayor cannot vote but can veto, and in five, or 33 percent, of the conciliated cities the mayor cannot vote and cannot veto.

A major distinction between political and administrative cities is that in political cities the mayor is the chief executive officer and in administrative cities a professional, appointed manager or administrator serves as the chief executive officer. Table 8.1 shows that in all political cities the mayor is the CAO. No mayors serve as the CAO in administrative, adapted administrative, or conciliated cities. A surprisingly high 84 percent of the adapted political cities have a CAO other than the mayor. In adapted political cities, however, the mayor still retains executive authority over the city bureaucracy. The CAO works for the mayor.

The obvious point is that adapted political cities retain key elements of the separation of powers because even with an appointed, professional CAO, the directly elected mayor is still the chief executive with administrative control over the day-to-day operations of the city. But our data indicate that in adapted political cities, the mayor delegates day-to-day management of the city to the CAO.

If an adapted political city has a CAO to whom much of the day-to-day management of the city is delegated, and if that city has a merit-based civil service, bid and purchase controls, and either internal or external oversight by auditors, is such a city very much different from an adapted administrative city with a directly elected full-time paid mayor and a professional city manager? Logic suggests that these two hypothetical cities are more structurally alike than different. It is for this reason that we call them both adapted cities.

The full- or part-time status of the mayor has an impact on the potential power and influence of the mayor vis-à-vis the manager and the council. If the mayor is part-time, then the power and influence of the mayor are likely to be approximately the same as the power and influence of the council members, and the mayor is unlikely to be importantly involved in administrative matters. However, if the position of mayor is full-time, the mayor is likely to have an office and possibly a staff and is likely to influence administrative matters, policy creation, and implementation. Table 8.1 shows that the mayor is a full-time position in 95 percent of the political cities and 89 percent of the adapted political cities (18 of the 19 adapted political cities reported on this question). However, the position of mayor is a full-time position in only 20 percent of the conciliated cities and 7 percent of the adapted administrative cities. All the mayors in administrative cities are part-time. The evidence is clear that in political and adapted political cities the mayor plays a more significant role in policy and administration than in conciliated, adapted administrative, and administrative cities. Based on these findings, we suggest that the direct election of the mayor in adapted administrative cities will move them somewhat in the direction of adapted political cities. But when the directly elected mayor in adapted administrative cities is full-time, and only a minor percentage are, then adapted administrative cities come to strongly resemble adapted political cities.

All conciliated cities have a CAO. In some conciliated cities, however, the mayor and city administrator may share executive power, but the final executive responsibility rests with the city administrator. In conciliated cities, the city administrator works for the mayor and the council. The data show that increasingly the norm in American cities is that the mayor does *not* serve as the CAO.

Research by DeHoog, Hoogland, and Whitaker (1990) found that in council-manager cities with directly elected mayors, those mayors were more likely to oppose incumbent city managers than were the mayors in cities whose mayors were chosen from among the council. This finding is especially important because the majority of council-manager cities now have directly elected mayors, thus falling into our definition of adapted cities. So the direct election of mayors, a feature borrowed from the logic of the separation of powers, is a direct challenge to city managers and to their career patterns. It is no wonder, then, that city managers tend, as a group, to be less than enthusiastic about the direct popular election of mayors. Some directly elected mayors form partnerships or teams with managers, as we indicated earlier. But some candidates for mayor, in direct election settings, essentially run against the city manager rather than against their mayoral opponent. When such candidates are elected, it can result in the exit of managers (Svara 1987; Booth 1965). DeSantis and Renner (1994) indicated a greater turnover among appointed executives in mayor-council cities than in council-manager cities. The expectation is that the presence of another full-time city executive with substantial formal authority will increase potential for conflict and create an environment that is less conducive to long-term policy management. The professional norms of managers may come into conflict with the interests of elected officials (Frederickson 1996). Cities with directly elected mayors, regardless of their statutory platform, are likely to have greater city manager or CAO turnover than cities with mayors chosen from among the city council. This is an obvious consequence of the logic of separation of powers (Feiock et al. 2000).

Svara (1987) contends that in mayor-council cities the mayor's leadership relies on the use of power, because such mayors have both executive and political authority. Conversely, the mayors in council-manager cities more often plays a facilitator role because, despite their direct election, their political power is equal to that of other council members and they have little executive control over the city manager. Svara argues that the mayor in council-manager cities seeks to empower others rather than seeking power as in mayor-council cities. Consequently, patterns of conflict result in mayor-council cities, and patterns of cooperation result in council-manager cities. Mayors can, of course, adopt leadership styles contrary to the formal rules of each form of government; doing so, however, may violate the "logic of appropriateness" and erode trust.

In "An Institutionalist Perspective on Mayoral Leadership: Linking Leadership to Formal Structure," Craig Wheeland (2002) expands upon and refines the leadership role of mayors in both mayor-council and council-manager cities. In the forty largest American cities, he found that the mayors in the twenty-six mayor-council cities generally favor an executive leadership style, while in the thirteen council-manager cities, the mayors generally display a

Table 8.2

City Council Characteristics by City Type

	Political (%)	Adapted political (%)	Conciliated (%)	Adapted administrative (%)	Administrative (%)
Frequency	19 (16.3)	19 (16.3)	15 (13)	46 (39.6)	17 (14.8)
Mixed council elections	7 (37)	7 (37)	3 (20)	6 (13)	3 (18)
Council—full-time	3 (16)	4 (21)	0 (0)	0 (0)	0 (0)

Source: Frederickson and Johnson survey questionnarire, 1998.

facilitative style of leadership. Wheeland found three types of facilitative mayors in council-manager cities—council leaders, community leaders, and partial executives. In two council-manager cities, the mayor had authority to prepare the budget and was a partial executive. In this category the city manager and the mayor would need to share executive authority and there would be the most potential for role conflict.

Wheeland found four types of executive mayors in mayor-council cities —strong leader, constrained leader, legislative leader, and weak leader. Classifications depend on whether the mayor can preside at council meetings, prepare the budget, veto, and appoint a CAO and department heads without the consent of the council. A strong leader can do all of these things.

According to Wheeland, Protasel contends that "Injecting the direct election of the mayor in a council-manager system would put the mayor on a collision course with both the council and the city manager. Policy-making deadlock—a continual threat in mayor-council systems—could be expected to occur periodically." Wheeland suggests that structural changes in council-manager cities that directly elect the mayor or that give the mayor the veto introduce institutional features that do not support executive or facilitative styles of leadership. If he is right, and we think he is, when cities move into the adapted category, mayoral powers and roles are often changed and made inconsistent, resulting in role ambiguity. Because adapted cities are neither entirely separation-of-powers nor unity-of-powers models, in such cities the role of the mayor can be fuzzy and left to interpretation and especially to political shifts.

The City Council

The city council is the legislative branch of the American city. City councils can vary in size, procedures, responsibilities, and traditions. But the individuals in these legislative bodies share one thing: all are directly elected by voters. The most common size for local legislatures is six, although they range in size from a low of two to a high of fifty. The average size of a city council is positively related to population size (Renner and DeSantis 1998).

District electoral systems emphasize political responsiveness, district representation, and constituent services. At-large electoral systems put the emphasis on citywide representation and a broadly defined public interest. Mixed electoral systems combine both sets of values. In our 1998 survey, 63 percent of the political and adapted political cities have district electoral systems, while 73 percent of the administrative and adapted administrative cities have at-large electoral systems. Eight or 53 percent of the conciliated cities have district elections.

As described in Table 8.2, of the twenty-six cities that have mixed electoral systems, sixteen, or 62 percent, are adapted cities. Political and adapted political cities have the highest proportion of mixed electoral systems with 37 percent, followed by conciliated cities with 20 percent. Although the evidence shows a diversity of electoral systems in American cities, a majority of political, adapted political, and conciliated cities have district city council elections, while a majority of administrative and adapted administrative cities have at-large council electoral systems.

Full-time council members are more likely than part-time council members to be involved in the formulation of policy and to influence the implementation of policy. Also, when council members are full-time, the political and perhaps administrative advantages of a full-time mayor may be diminished. We found, however, that city council members serve full-time in only about 6 percent of our 1998 survey. Political and adapted political cities are more likely to have full-time council members than conciliated, adapted administrative, and administrative cities. However, only 16 percent of the political cities and 21 percent of the adapted political cities have full-time council members. The norm in American cities is to have part-time councils.

In Chapter 5, The Evolution of Administrative Cities, we considered the research on the differences between at-large and district city council elections. As we described in Chapters 1 and 2, over the last thirty years elections by district have increased significantly in cities with council-manager statutory platforms. Should these changes have made a difference in the roles and behavior of city council members? The general answer is yes. When controlling for several other variables (e.g., income, race, education) Welch and Bledsoe (1988) found that at-large city council members are generally better educated and financially better off than district-elected council members. At-large council members spent much less time on constituent services and tend to have a broader, citywide perspective than their district-based colleagues. Welch and Bledsoe also found that conflict is more evident in district-based councils. All of these findings match a common sense understanding of the advantages and disadvantages of district versus at-large city council elections. On one hand, at-large elections produce better educated, better-off, less conflict-prone city council members who tend to think of themselves as representing the whole city. On the other hand, district elections do a better job of representing neighborhood and often underrepresented groups in the city.

District-based elections are a bedrock feature of political cities, all on mayor-council statutory platforms. As many of these cities have evolved into adapted political structures, many adapted at-large elections for some council seats. Conversely, as administrative cities evolved into adapted administrative cities, the adoption of district-based city council elections for some council seats has become more common. City managers who have experienced these changes or have worked in both at-large and district-based city council cities agree with both the commonsense view of the subject and the empirical research verifying that common sense. District-based city councils or cities with a mix of district and at-large seats are often contentious and tend to complicate the work of city managers. Because district-based council members represent their districts rather than the whole city, the common managerial assumption that services should be distributed on an equitable basis might not apply.

In a sophisticated treatment of this subject, James Svara (2001) asks, "Do council members relate to citizens as their trustees, acting in the best interests of the community, or as delegates who reflect the preferences of their constituents?" He also asks whether council members play an overall governance role or a representational role. Finally, he asks whether these different forms of council behavior relate to the structure of city government.

It was Svara's expectation that elected officials in mayor-council cities would emphasize constituent services and concern for specific issues or specific constituencies. Councils in council-manager cities would, he expected, emphasize overall governance roles, while councils in mayor-council cities would have higher self-ratings on representational roles. He also expected that councils in council-manager cities would have more positive assessments of relations between council members. Other institutional features, such as electoral methods, should create different council role expectations, with at-large elections emphasizing the governance function and district elections emphasizing representational roles.

Svara's research was based on a national survey in the spring of 2001 by the National League of Cities of 631 city council members in cities over 25,000 population. It is important here to note that Svara used a categorization of cities based on their statutory or charter platforms as either mayor-council or council-manager cities. Obviously, we regard these categories as overly simplified. Nevertheless, Svara's findings are very helpful.

He found that council member roles as constituent-serving or issue or district representative had more to do with the size of the city and the form of the government than with how the council was elected. In small or medium-size cities, there was little difference in council roles between councils elected by district or at large. But in cities over 100,000, council members elected by district were more apt to play a constituent-serving role than in cities with at-large elections. As city population increased he found that the amount and importance of constituency work went up, and this held for both mayor-council and council-manager statutory cities.

Svara also found that council members who played an activist role in council-manager cities had higher self-ratings on overall governance functions, but unexpectedly, council members in mayor-council cities did not have higher self-ratings on their handling of representational responsibilities than council members in council-manager cities. Council members in all cities were strongly oriented to their representational responsibilities regardless of form. However, council members in mayor-council cities expressed higher levels of agreement that their cities had representational characteristics.

As Svara hypothesized, council members in council-manager cities were more likely to report that relationships were more positive between the mayor and council than in mayor-council cities. Svara suggests that the separation of powers found in mayor-council cities allows greater conflict in the council and between the council and the mayor. We believe that his findings reflect the effects of both forms of government defined broadly as mayor-council and council-manager, as well as the influence of different forms of council elections embedded in the two forms.

Svara argues that although council members in mayor-council cities devoted more time and focused more attention to providing constituent services, particularly in cities over 100,000, the activist role (providing leadership for specific constituencies and concern for specific issues) of council members was equally prevalent with council members regardless of size or form of government. According to Svara,

> Elected officials in council-manager cities are approximating the governance ideals of the reform movement and at the same time they manifest a strong—and presumably growing—constituency orientation. . . . The choices for American council members can be summarized as follows: are they to be partners with the executive and administration . . . or do they represent citizens . . . and seek better services from administrative staff? It appears that council members in council-manager cities are becoming stronger representatives while reducing but not abandoning their traditional governance function. Council members in mayor-council cities may wish to shift in the opposite way: preserving their strong commitment to representation while becoming more active contributors to the policy-making process. (Svara 2001, 10–11)

We would interpret his conclusions as a description of council roles in adapted cities, cities that may have legal descriptions as council-manager or mayor-council but are, in fact, so adapted that the form of electing city council members matters more than the cities' statutory platform.

In political cities with district elections, an elected mayor, and the separation of powers, the role played by the council tends to emphasize constituent representation and constituent services. This can and often does result in competition for resources, logrolling, and pork barrel allocations. And it can result in highly dysfunctional council behavior. This is particularly so when one or more council members are positioning themselves to run for mayor. In administrative cities with at-large elections, an appointed professional manager, and unity of powers, council members play primarily trustee roles, representing the entire city. But, the majority of cities are now adapted, and in adapted cities the role of the mayor and council will likely move from delegate or trustee to "activist," using Svara's language. The activist elected official is a problem-solver, in part in response to constituent demands and concerns, but also in part reflecting his or her own sense of what should be done to improve the city. In short, the activist role is a blending of both the delegate and trustee style of representation and governance (Svara 2001). As cities have structurally become more like each other through the diffusion of innovation and as these cities have adopted district-based council election systems, there has been a convergence of the roles played by elected officials.

Chief Administrative Officer

Respondents in the 1998 survey were asked whether their municipalities have a chief administrative officer (CAO). Table 8.3 shows that there are no appointed CAOs in political cities. There are CAOs in 89 percent of the adapted political cities and in all of the conciliated cities, the adapted administrative cities, and the administrative cities. As we describe in Figures 4.2 and 4.3 in Chapter 4, there are now CAOs in over half of the cities that are on mayor-council statutory platforms, and the tendency of these cities to adopt this structural change appears to be continuing.

In adapted political cities, the role of the CAO may be limited to assisting the mayor with budget preparation and personnel management or conducting policy research and making policy recommendations. In these cities, the mayor is the chief executive officer and is able to hire, supervise, and terminate the CAO. In just under half of the adapted political cities, however, councils have a role to play in the hiring and termination of the CAO.

In its original conception, "the CAO should be appointed by the mayor and should perform, in general, such functions as the supervision of heads of various departments, preparation of the budget (or supervision of the budget director), and personnel direction" (Adrian 1955, 210). Over time, however, the role and responsibilities of the CAO appear to have expanded beyond the original conception.

There is a common assumption that in mayor-council cities the CAO is the mayor's handpicked assistant. Evidence shows, however, that the CAO is

Table 8.3

Jurisdictions with Chief Administrative Officer, 1998

	Political (%)	Adapted political (%)	Conciliated (%)	Adapted administrative (%)	Administrative (%)
Frequency	19 (16.3)	19 (16.3)	15 (13)	46 (39.6)	17 (14.8)
Have CAO	0 (0)	17 (89)	15 (100)	46 (100)	17 (100)
CAO accountable to mayor and council	0 (0)	8 (47)	15 (100)	46 (100)	17 (100)
CAO accountable to mayor only	0 (0)	9 (53)	0 (0)	0 (0)	0 (0)

Source: Frederickson and Johnson survey, 1998.

Figure 8.1   **Appointment Powers of Chief Administrative Officer in Mayor-Council Cities**

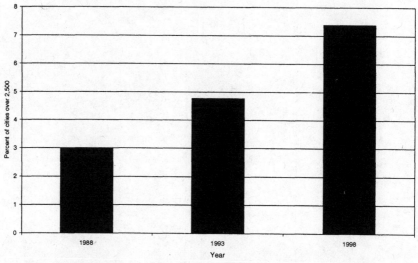

Source: ICMA, Municipal Year Book, 1989, 1993, and 1998.

usually selected either by the council and mayor together or by the council. According to 1996 and 1997 surveys by the International City/County Management Association (ICMA), the CAO is selected jointly by the mayor and council in 51 percent of the cities, by the council in 38 percent of the cities, and by the mayor alone in only 11 percent of the cities (Svara 1999).

It is also a common misconception that CAOs in mayor-council cities are personal friends of the mayor and have no experience in city administration. In fact, only 10 percent of all CAOs held a job in the private sector prior to their appointment, and more than half have served in another city prior to their current position. In larger mayor-council cities, 59 percent of the chief executive officers held a similar position in another city prior to their current job (Svara 1999).

As we take a closer look at the responsibilities of the CAO in mayor-council cities, we see that, over time, the CAO is gaining more responsibility in appointment and budgeting power—two staples of the city manager's position in a council-manager city. Figure 8.1 shows that between 1988 and 1998 about 4.5 percent of the mayor-council cities gave the CAO the authority to appoint department heads. Still, the CAO can appoint department heads only in about 7 percent of all mayor-council cities. Such appointing powers are still the exception. According to the 1996 ICMA survey, the mayor and CAO jointly appoint department heads in over 15 percent of the mayor-council cities (ICMA, *Municipal Year Book* 1998).

Figure 8.2 **Preparation of Budget in Mayor-Council Cities**

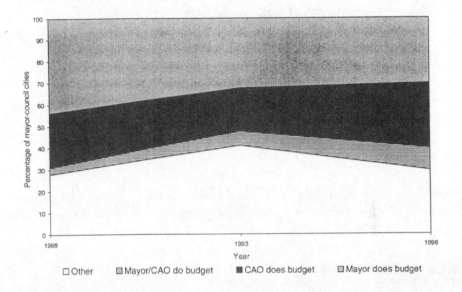

In council-manager cities, the city manager develops the budget. While not as common, increasingly the CAO is responsible for developing the budget in mayor-council cities. Figure 8.2 shows that between 1988 and 1998 the percentage of mayors who develop the budget, a traditional duty of the mayor in mayor-council cities, dropped from 40 percent to 30 percent. During that same time period, the percentage of CAOs in mayor-council cities who are responsible for the budget increased from 25 percent to 30 percent. Furthermore, the percentage of cities in which the mayor and CAO develop the budget together has risen from around 3 percent in 1988 to over 10 percent in 1998. In mayor-council cities, the budget may also be prepared by others, such as the budget director, finance committee (which can include or exclude the mayor and CAO), or some other official. The percentage of other officials with budgetary responsibility in mayor-council cities was about 28 percent in 1998.

The 1996 and 1997 surveys by the ICMA also gathered information regarding the responsibilities and authority of city managers and CAOs in U.S. cities. The respondents included 485 city managers from council-manager cities and 172 CAOs from mayor-council cities. Summarizing the survey results, Svara (1999) concludes that city managers and chief administrative officers are more

Table 8.4

Responsibilities of City Managers and CAOs, 1999 (percent)

Responsibilities or duties of chief executive	Mayor-council cities (%)	Council-manager cities (%)
Propose budget	82	95
Administer budget after approval	73	80
Supervise all or most department heads	73	98
Reorganize departments	57	87

Source: From Svara, 1999.

Table 8.5

Roles of City Managers and CAOs, 1999 (percent)

Dimension	Mayor-council cities (%)	Council-manager cities (%)
Policy innovator	71	74
Political adviser	57	56
Adviser without political advice	66	67
Classical manager	63	63
Organizational coordinator	70	72

Source: From Svara, 1999.

alike than is often presumed and that it is apparent that the council-manager form has been used as a model for the reform of mayor-council cities. Table 8.4 describes the percentage of mayor-council and council-manager cities that authorize the chief executive officer to perform budgetary and management duties. Although it is clear that city managers in council-manager cities have more administrative and budgetary authority and responsibility than the CAO in mayor-council cities, the difference in executive authority between the two positions is not as large as presumed.

To further illustrate these similarities, Table 8.5 describes the scores of city managers and city administrators in five different activity dimensions. Activities are measured on a 100-point scale, with 100 indicating the most importance, 50 indicating moderate importance, and zero indicating very little importance. It is clear from the results of the survey that there is little perceived difference in the roles played by the city manager and CAO.

Finally, city managers and chief administrative officers were asked to rate their influence in budgeting. On a 100-point scale, city managers gave themselves a rating of 92 and CAOs gave themselves a rating of 88 (Svara 1999).

Unlike the changing patterns of the adoption of civil service systems, bid and purchase controls, and independent postaudits in political cities, most of which occurred between 1920 and 1950, the widespread adoption of the position of chief administrative officer is more recent. The employment of CAOs in political cities and the evidence we have just presented regarding their increasing influence so changes the effects of the separation of powers, we believe, as to justify categorizing such cities as adapted political cities. The presence of a professional CAO, when coupled with the earlier merit and administrative adaptations, makes such cities more like adapted administrative cities (explained more fully in Chapter 7) than like their administrative city parents. It turns out that CAOs in cities with mayor-council statutory platforms are much like city managers in cities with council-manager platforms. In adapted political cities, the effects of the separation of powers appear to be softened, and even when there are serious political disagreements between the mayor and the council, the presence of a professional CAO and other administrative reforms greatly increases the probability that the city will continue to run smoothly.

Department Heads

At the core of the unity-of-powers and separation-of-powers models is this question: to whom do department heads report? In cities in which the mayor serves as the chief executive officer, department heads report to the mayor, which enhances executive powers. Ordinarily the mayor also appoints these department heads and they serve on the mayor's executive, administrative, or political team. Department head loyalty to the mayor may be valued as highly as professional experience or competence. Department heads that report to city managers or CAOs enhance the powers of the manager, even though these department heads are appointed on the basis of merit and qualifications. The city manager or CAO is the chief executive officer and serves at the pleasure of the city council (the mayor is a council member).

Department heads have the principal responsibility to manage the delivery of services. Presumably, they are experts in their respective fields: law enforcement, public works, park management, human services, personnel management, finance, and so forth. They serve as expert advisers to political leaders and the CAO.

Using our five categories, Table 8.6 compares the executive authority of the mayor, council, and CAO in American cities. The data show that in all but two of the political cities, the department heads report to the mayor, and in all administrative and adapted administrative cities, department heads report to the city manager or CAO. In all but three adapted political cities, department heads report to the mayor. In three other adapted political cities, the mayor and CAO share in the supervision of department heads. In all but two conciliated cities, the CAO supervises the department heads. In these two cities, the CAO and mayor share supervisory responsibility. The reporting patterns of city department heads are still primarily based on the logic of political and administrative cities. As we have described in much of this chapter, many structural features of political and administrative cities have been adapted to the point that we categorize them as adapted cities. The reporting lines of department heads are an exception to this generalization. Even with directly elected mayors and enhanced mayoral power in adapted administrative cities, the department heads still report to the city manager. And in adapted political cities, department heads report formally to the mayor. But we believe the presence of a professional CAO in adapted political cities interjects the CAO into this reporting line in the day-to-day work of the city.

Administrative Procedures and Processes

As we described in Chapter 4, merit-based civil service systems are now almost universal in American cities. Indeed, cities that are exceptions to this generalization, such as Utica, New York, are so unusual as to be described as extraordinary (Ehrenhalt 1996). As a foundation feature of the reform movement, civil service has been developed in most jurisdictions to the point of eliciting a strong countermovement. One of the key features of the "reinventing government" initiatives of the 1990s was to significantly modify civil service systems so as to give department heads and CAOs or city managers greater latitude in selecting their immediate subordinates (Osborn and Gaebler 1992). And, as part of the logic of "breaking through bureaucracy," the advocates of reinventing government thought that executives should be allowed to demote or fire subordinates who are not effective. None of the supporters of the movement for reinventing government suggested, however, that elected city officials be given greater influence in matters of civil service appointments or promotions. There is little evidence in the reinvention movement to suggest that the civil service firewall between city politics, especially partisan politics, and administration has been breeched. The near universality of civil service systems in American cities, regardless of their other possible distinguishing structural characteristics, renders them at best generally similar in their human resources policies and behavior.

Much the same can be said about city systems for letting contracts to private firms and nonprofit ongoing actions and the management of tender for services, materials, and supplies. The likelihood of contract kickbacks, skimming, and favoritism in American cities is now very low, in large part because of the layers of laws, regulations, and oversight governing jurisdictional relations with contractors. Exceptions to the norm tend to be news-

Table 8.6

To Whom Department Heads Report, 1998

	Political (%)	Adapted political (%)	Conciliated (%)	Adapted administrative (%)	Administrative (%)
Frequency	19 (16.3)	19 (16.3)	15 (13)	46 (39.6)	17 (14.8)
Mayor and council	2 (11)	0 (0)	0 (0)	0 (0)	0 (0)
CAO	0 (0)	0 (0)	13 (87)	46 (100)	17 (100)
Mayor and CAO	0 (0)	3 (16)	2 (13)	0 (0)	0 (0)
Mayor	17 (89)	16 (84)	0 (0)	0 (0)	0 (0)

Source: Frederickson and Johnson survey questionnaire, 1998.

worthy. Many of the exceptions have been associated with special district governments, particularly economic development authorities, which have been exempted from many city procedural controls so they could be more businesslike (Henriques 1986). Bid and purchase procedural controls tend to work equally as well in different forms of city government. When there is corruption, it tends to have less to do with the form of government and more to do with the presence or absence of procedural controls.

Auditing requirements are also now essentially universal in American local government.

Summary and Conclusion

Because no two cities are exactly alike, social scientists look for patterns, groups, categories, and clusters, recognizing that single cases are nevertheless unique and distinct. The term "adapted cities" describes a grouping or clustering of cities based on the details of their structures rather than their formal statutory labels. We believe that this description accurately describes American cities and we believe that the adapted city designation illuminates the similarities and differences of adapted cities.

The emergence of adapted cities is the culmination of a long series of structural adaptation. American cities, we learn, are surprisingly dynamic and changeable, and these changes tend to follow the S-curve of innovation or change. But these changes are incremental, step-by-step adjustments added to or subtracted from already established structures. In the case of cities on council-manager statutory or charter platforms, the most common of these adaptations is changing from at-large to district elections for city council members, changing the selection of the mayor from a choice among council members to a choice of the citizens, and gradually enhancing the powers of the mayor. These structural adaptations can significantly alter the orthodox logic of council-manager government, a logic that puts all lawmaking, fiscal, and policy power—a unity of those powers—in the hands of the city council, and vests all responsibility for the implementation of policy and day-to-day city administration in the hands of a city manager. Changing from at-large to district council elections can cause a city council to be considerably less unified, fragmented by the need of council members to serve the interests of their district, at least as much as the interests of the whole city. The direct election of the mayor and the gradual enhancement of the mayor's powers through the veto or through budget authority, or simply because the mayor moves to full-time, paid status or needs a staff, also importantly alter the logic of the unity of powers associated with the orthodox council-manager form of government. And this is especially true in cities in which the reporting lines of department heads shift from the city manager to the mayor, one of the subjects we deal with in our treatment of conciliated cities in Chapter 9.

What we have just described is now the largest single structural category of American cities, the adapted administrative city. These cities, usually on council-manager statutory platforms, retain elements of the logic of the unity of powers but have patched into that logic key features of the separation of powers. These incremental adaptations, all approved by the voters of each city, appear to be responses to a felt need for greater neighborhood, ethnic, or social representation and an identifiable elected political leader for the city. It is perhaps natural that the directly elected mayors, once in place, feel they need the power to accomplish what they believe their voters expect of them. When this happens, a key element of the separation of power is brought to a structure of city government designed to unify political powers and enhance administrative capabilities.

In cities on mayor-council platforms, incremental patterns of adaptation display a rather different pattern. First, in earlier periods, from the 1920s to the 1960s, many of the key elements of the reform movement, including merit civil service systems; contract, bid and purchase controls; and external auditing, were almost universally adapted. These steps significantly reduced patronage and corruption and greatly strengthened the administrative capacities of mayor-council cities. Then, beginning in the 1960s, many mayor-council cities adapted one form or another of what is generally described as a chief administrative officer. This person may be called deputy or vice mayor, chief executive officer, chief administrative officer, or even city manager. Our evidence indicates that the CAOs are mostly professional city executives with roles, skills, and professional instincts that are very much like those of city managers in council-manager cities. The continuing presence of an identifiable professional executive in mayor-council cities very likely strengthens the administrative capabilities, consideration, and general service effectiveness in such cities.

When the forces of merit civil service, bid and purchase controls, and a professional CAO are brought together, they shift the classic logic of separation of powers in the direction of unifying powers, and particularly the executive and administrative powers of such cities. These are the adapted political cities, the second largest category of American cities. To be sure, there are variations among cities so categorized because no two cities are alike. And adapted political cities still display many of the elements of the separation of powers, sometimes indicating factions, dysfunctional city councils, and checks and balances between the city council and the mayor.

Finally, what structural features do almost all adapted cities share? With few exceptions, all have merit-based civil service systems and bidding, and

Figure 8.3   **A Continuum of Political, Administrative, and Adapted Cities**

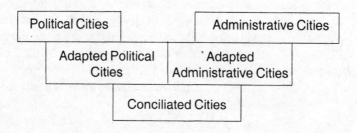

purchase, and audit control systems. Most have directly elected mayors, who increasingly are full-time with staff, and most have either city managers or CAOs. Because of these common structural characteristics they are adapted cities, but adapted administrative cities are still identifiably different from adapted political cities. Because there are differences between cities in each of these categories, some adapted administrative cities are essentially the same as some adapted political cities. But others, which still are adapted cities, are less alike. Consider the continuum in Figure 8.3. Some adapted administrative cities are near the center of the continuum and tend to re-semble adapted political cities, which are also near the center of the con-tinuum. Other administrative cities are nearer the outer pole of the continuum, while some adapted administrative cities are importantly different from some adapted political cities at the polar edge of that category. It is left to those most familiar with the structural details of each city to "place" their city along this continuum. It is also important to remember how dynamic the processes of structural adaptation are. Cities move along the continuum at a surprisingly rapid pace.

9

The Conciliated City

Our research uncovered a small but unique group of cities that so combine the statutory, structural, and theoretical elements of the two primary models of American city government as to defy classification. These cities are not the mayor-council form or the adaptation of that form nor the council-mayor form nor the adaptation of that form. We were therefore faced with a problem of classification. In the absence of generally accepted descriptive nomenclature for such cities, we found it necessary to invent one. After considering alternatives such as fused cities or mixed cities, we finally decided to label the new classification conciliated cities. "Conciliated" means to assemble or unite, to make compatible, or to appease. The conciliated city is a complete merging of the logic of political and administrative cities and is, therefore, the ultimate or completely adapted city.

This is not to suggest that the conciliated city is better or more effective than the other four city types. We are simply using the term empirically to describe cities that have adapted their structures so completely that they entirely mix the logic and the key structural characteristics of American city government.

Conciliated cities include critical elements of both the separation and the unity of powers. They have both an independently elected mayor with some executive authority and a professional city manager or chief administrative officer (CAO) who also has executive authority, particularly over city departments. Authority over the city manager or the CAO is shared between the mayor and the city council. Conciliated cities are neither administrative nor political cities—they are both. In their structural arrangements, conciliated cities provide for both high-profile political leadership in the office of the mayor and for professional management competence in the office of the city manager or the CAO. Conciliated cities combine the political values of direct responsiveness to particular citizen interests and a generalized administrative efficiency.

There are two ways to approach the classification of cities. The first way is by using the a priori criteria shown in Table 7.5 in Chapter 7. Most cities can be neatly classified into one of the five categories using these a priori criteria. No matter how comprehensive or general the criteria, however, some cities still defy classification because they are unique. In these cases, a more artistic approach to classification is called for. This method involves judgment, intuition, and experience to make a final classification, and we used this method to categorize as conciliated a few cities in the 1998 survey.

The easiest way to describe conciliated cities is to look in some detail at several of them. There are six particularly good examples of conciliated cities— Cincinnati, Ohio; Evanston, Illinois; Oakland, California; Hartford, Connecticut; Lenexa, Kansas; and the Unified Government of Wyandotte County and Kansas City, Kansas. The following descriptions of their structural adaptations put the subject of the conciliated city in context.

Cincinnati, Ohio

In 2000, the residents of Cincinnati voted in favor of a new charter. According to William Hansell, executive director of the International City/County Management Association (ICMA) at the time, "We have in Cincinnati yet one more experiment to empower the mayor while retaining council-manager government" (1999). The city's statutory form of government is council-manager. The new mayor has a four-year term, is limited to two terms, and serves full-time. In addition, the mayor may appoint a staff of his or her choosing. The new mayor does not have voting privileges on the council, but retains the power of the veto.

Under the new charter approved by the voters, there are nine council members elected at large on a nonpartisan basis, serving for two years. Members of the council are paid and may appoint assistants to be employed as unclassified legislative staff.

At first glance, Cincinnati would appear to be a typical political city based on the separation-of-powers model. But the new charter retains the title of city manager. The mayor, subject to council approval, appoints the city manager. The manager is responsible for the hiring and firing of all department heads, and all department heads report to the city manager, not the mayor. Neither the mayor nor members of the city council can interfere with the city manager in personnel matters. On executive matters the city manager reports to the mayor and on policy matters serves as an adviser to the city council. The city manager submits the budget first to the mayor for review and then to the city council with the mayor's recommendations.

Cincinnati has a civil service commission of three members appointed by the city manager. The new Cincinnati charter also includes a formal bidding process. After bids are received, the city manager and the commission jointly decide what bid will be awarded.

Cincinnati is a good example of structural changes in American cities. In 1802, when its first charter was passed, Cincinnati was set up as a typical political city with a boss mayor and the separation of powers. In 1924, as a response to corruption and scandal, the city manager form of government was adopted, its structural details typical of the administrative city. In 1976, the city charter was changed to provide more pay for the mayor and the council, consistent with the national trend (Renner and DeSantis 1993). The annual council salary jumped from $8,000 to $49,460. In 1987, the charter was changed to provide for the popular election of the mayor. This was an incremental step in the direction of administrative adaptation, while retaining the council-manager form of government.

In the 1980s and 1990s, Cincinnati experienced racial tension particularly associated with the use of deadly force by police officers. In the campaign for the possible adoption of the 2000 charter, those favoring the charter, including most of the leading business groups and associations, argued that in times of political turmoil it is important to identify political leadership and fix political responsibility. During the campaign there was a question as to whether the proposed new charter was a council-manager or a mayor-council platform. The executive director of the ICMA at the time, William Hansell, after consulting with ICMA leaders, concluded that although the proposed new charter significantly reduced the powers of the city manager, it would nevertheless still be a council-manager government. Following this pronouncement there were extensive and sometimes acrimonious debates among the members of the ICMA. One element, the Staunton Group, named after the first council-manager city, Staunton, Virginia, charged that by endorsing the new Cincinnati charter, the ICMA had abandoned its commitment to the council-manager form of government. Others argued that modifications of the pure council-manager form of government, what we call administrative cities, are now common.

Cincinnati is, thus, a conciliated city because it has essential elements of both the separation and unity of powers. The charter changes made in 2000 presented a challenge to the logic of classification. In the spring of 2002, Valerie Lemone, the well-known and respected city manager of Dayton, Ohio, was appointed as the first Cincinnati city manager under the new charter. Her appointment seemed symbolically to legitimate the conciliated city structure as acceptable to qualified city mangers.

Evanston, Illinois

The home of Northwestern University, Evanston, Illinois, is a very upscale suburb of Chicago, along the northwestern shores of Lake Michigan. In the

1950s, Evanston changed from a garden-variety mayor-council political city to a unique version of council-manager government. In the first place, the city council comprised of eighteen aldermen, all elected by district. Then in the early 1990s, by referendum, the number of aldermen was reduced to nine, still elected by district. Aldermen currently serve four-year terms, without term limits. Although they are clearly part-time, Evanston aldermen tend to serve multiple terms and tend to represent their districts somewhat in the fashion of Chicago precinct captains. Although they do not have physical office space in city hall, the aldermen's role tends to be a combination of ombudsman, conduit between district residents and city departments, and spokesperson for the interests of the district. One of the aldermen often refers to himself as the "little mayor" of his district.

The mayor of Evanston is separately elected for an unlimited number of four-year terms. The current mayor, Lorraine Morton, is in her third term. Mayoral pay is modest, $15,000, so the position is in a formal sense part-time. In an informal sense, however, Mayor Morton would probably be described as serving essentially full-time. The mayor has an office and a secretary, shared, on occasion, with members of the city council. The mayor presides at meetings of the city council but does not vote on council issues except to break a tie. In addition, the mayor may veto any act of the city council. In the traditions of Evanston politics, the mayor is clearly the elected leader of the city.

The structural arrangements between the Evanston mayor and city council show most of the characteristics associated with the political separation of powers and executive and legislative checks and balances. Evanston city politics has, therefore, many of the qualities one would associate with mayor-council cities, either of the political or the adapted political sort. But, in a formal sense, Evanston is a council-manager city. The city manager is appointed by a majority of six of the nine aldermen and the mayor and can be fired by the same majority. Obviously, the structure is designed so that the city manager is to serve the full city council. The city manager appoints, supervises, and dismisses all city department heads. Evanston has the full range of reform administration, including a merit-based civil service, bid and purchase controls, and independent auditing. In terms of formal structure, the administrative side of Evanston government looks like standard council-manager government, either of the administrative or adapted administrative sort. In terms of its history and reputation, Evanston would be perceived as a very well managed city, progressive and without corruption. The previous city manager, Eric Anderson, now the city manager of Des Moines, Iowa, is one of the acknowledged leaders in the profession. Serving now in his sixth year, Roger Crum is also a highly regarded city manager.

Evanston is an illustrative conciliated city because one sees in Evanston the combined logic of the political separation of powers associated with the mayor-council form of city government and the unity of administrative powers associated with the council-manager form of government. This combination of structural characteristics reveals patterns of behavior seen in other conciliated cities. The mayor and city manager of Evanston have tended to work well together. Although city administrative affairs are generally smoothly and efficiently run, aldermen sometimes intervene in administrative affairs seeking special services for their constituents or particular responses to constituents' complaints or suggestions. This pattern of behavior is not unusual, even in adapted administrative cities with district-elected council members.

Evanston city politics can be understood in terms of patterns of support for the mayor. At certain points and on certain issues, a majority of aldermen will support the mayor and at other points and on other issues will not support the mayor. Certain aldermen will, from time to time, appear to be positioning themselves for a possible challenge to the mayor for an upcoming term. City council meetings tend to be lively and interesting, usually civil, but sometimes rancorous. Much of Evanston politics has to do with the allocation of resources by district and neighborhood, and this political maneuvering is on display at the typical council meeting. Issues tend to be between particular factions on the council or between factions on the council and the mayor. Ordinarily, issues do not involve the city manager, although, on occasion, aldermanic criticism of city executive leadership will sometimes include the mayor and the city manager. Although direct public criticism of the mayor and the city manager are common, it takes a super-majority of the council to fire the manager because the council rather than the mayor appoints the manager. Therefore, unlike in adapted political cities in which city council members take on the mayor and the city manager together because the mayor appoints the city manager, in Evanston, although the mayor and the city manager could be regarded as a team, aldermen do not attempt to "get" the city manager through the mayor.

Evanston's mix of structural characteristics, personalities, and history appear to have resulted in good day-to-day city administration, lively city politics, and the clear identification of the directly elected mayor as the city's political leader. It could be said that Evanston has a professional leader for day-to-day administration, an identifiable political leader responsible for overall city political leadership, and identifiable political leaders for each district of the city.

Oakland, California

Oakland was established in 1852 and, in 1911, adopted the commission form of government as its first charter. In 1927, the charter was changed to an orthodox administrative city with a city manager and the classic features of the unity of powers. Over the years, Oakland has had twelve unsuccessful referendums to make changes to the city charter, changes generally in the direction of the adapted administrative city. Then, in November 1998, the residents of Oakland passed a new charter changing its statutory form of government from council-manager to mayor-council. In fact, however, Oakland became a conciliated city.

The mayor of Oakland is now elected at large on a nonpartisan ballot for a four-year term. The mayor may vote on the council only to break a tie and cannot veto council-passed legislation. The mayor of Oakland is a full-time city employee. According to the charter, the mayor submits the budget to the council, but in practice the city manager prepares and submits a budget to the mayor, who in turn submits a revised budget to the council. The mayor has a small staff and has access to the city manager's staff.

Council members in Oakland are elected on a nonpartisan basis for four-year terms, seven by district and one at large. Council members are paid $60,000 annually, but are allowed to have other jobs. All council members share a common office and just one staff member.

The mayor appoints and terminates the city manager with the council's approval, and the city manager reports directly to the mayor. But all department heads are appointed by and report to the city manager. Oakland has a merit-based civil service system and a formalized bidding process.

In February 1999, every city department head in Oakland received a letter from the city manager that stated, "This letter is to notify you that the city is contemplating possibly separating you from service in the near future. . . . Let me be brutally clear, the status quo . . . is unacceptable" (Gurwitt 2000). Three department heads, including the police chief, were asked to resign. A fourth department head was reassigned and sixty managers were given a final chance to "shape up." For these decisions, the city manager, Robert Bobb, received almost no criticism in the press. Under Oakland's new form of government, the political heat was directed toward the mayor, Jerry Brown, the very high-profile former governor of California. He was perfectly willing to take the heat.

When the citizens of Oakland voted to rewrite their city charter, critics warned that the city was being set up for a stalemate: a highly politicized mayor's office blocking the manager's good-government reforms. Since Brown took over as Oakland's mayor, the characteristics of Oakland city government have changed. The once-powerful council has lost much of its access to the mayor, who is no longer a council member. The mayor does not attend council meetings. Council member access to the city manager also sharply reduced. And the city mayor has retained de facto control over the

city administrator. Bobb, the city manager, describes the executive operations of Oakland as a team—the mayor and the manager.

Like Cincinnati, Oakland has merged the logic of separation and unity of
powers so completely that it can only be described as a conciliated city. One
of the most important points in the evolution of Oakland from an administrative city to a conciliated city is the obvious decline in the influence of the city
council. In the conciliated city, it appears that the powers of the mayor are
significant, as are the powers of the city manager or the CAO. But the power
of the city council and of individual council members appears to be diminished in the conciliated structure. By devising a structure by which the mayor
has enough power to be logically held responsible for the executive effectiveness of the city, and by leaving the basic element of the reform council-
manager model in place in the powers of the city manager or the CAO, the
new charter shows little concern for the diminished power of the city council. Over time, however, it is a safe prediction that there will be sharp political tension between the mayor and either significant elements of the city
council or individual council members, particularly as they position themselves to challenge the mayor in the next election.

Hartford, Connecticut

In 1947, the city of Hartford, Connecticut, changed from the mayor-council
form to the council-manager form of government. The only change in
Hartford's governmental structure since 1947 occurred in 1969, when the
mayor began to be directly elected instead of being chosen from among the
city council. Although the city has a council-manager legal platform, Hartford has been classified as a conciliated city because there is a separation of
political powers between the mayor and the city council, and the city manager serves as the chief executive officer. The mayor cannot vote, but has
veto power. The city manager is hired and terminated by the council and
appoints and supervises the department heads. City council members are
elected at large. Hartford is unique in that the mayor does not play a role in
the hiring or termination of the city manager. Political power is widely dis-
persed in Hartford, and the city manager is in the position of having to serve
as a facilitator and bridge between the mayor and council. Because the city
manager answers primarily to the city council rather than to the mayor, and
the mayor has veto authority over council legislative action, the mayor functions primarily as a policy advocate rather than a player in policy implementation. The power of the mayor rests solely on the ability to cobble together a
council coalition.

In the last decade, there have been three unsuccessful attempts to change the city charter in order to ameliorate the sense of citizen frustration with the Hartford government and the many problems facing the city. It was the commonly held opinion that the city was still not really run by anyone. The state had taken over the Hartford schools, the police department was beset by scandal, the fire department was vastly overstaffed and too expensive to run. The city government was struggling to deliver basic services, the city council went from one argument to another, and the mayor retained influence only through the strength of his personality. Hartford also ranked at or near the bottom of Connecticut cities on many economic indicators such as per capita income, market value of taxable property, housing permits, and unemployment (Gurwitt 2000). "Small surprise that the strong-mayor movement had support within the business community and among citizens looking for someone—anyone—to hold accountable" (Gurwitt 2000, 75). Eddie Perez, president of the Southeast Institutions Neighborhood Alliance, a community development organization, and the Hartford mayor since January 2002, said in 2000, "The question is, how do you make Hartford more livable" (Gurwitt 2000, 78).

Shortly after becoming mayor in January 2002, Perez formed a new fifteen-member charter review commission (CRC) to recommend changes in the form of Hartford's government. Mayor Perez is a supporter of the strong-mayor form of government. The CRC met with city residents in various locations to find out what they thought should be changed in Hartford government. In September 2002, the mayor and the city council approved the CRC recommendation that the government be changed from the council-manager to the mayor-council form. The goal of the CRC was to increase accountability without removing necessary checks and balances to ensure fiscal responsibility and prevent corruption. The CRC also recommended that the number of city council members be increased from nine to eleven and that, instead of all members being elected at large, as is currently the case, five members be elected at large and six members by district. However, the mayor and council did not accept this recommendation because they believed that district elections would further balkanize the city. Under the proposed charter, the mayor would have the following expanded powers:

• The mayor would be the chief executive officer of the city with the responsibility of the administration of the city and the power to appoint the chief operating officer (COO) and department heads subject to the consent of a majority of the city council. At the time, the city manager was appointed by the city council and the city manager appointed the department heads. However, to check the mayor's power, the new charter would create a three-member internal audit commission with the power to examine "all matters relating to the integrity, efficiency, and efficacy of the city."

- The COO and department heads would serve at the pleasure of the mayor, although the removal of the COO and department heads would be subject to the approval of six council members.
- The mayor would designate the COO to supervise and direct the department heads. The mayor or the COO would conduct an annual evaluation of each department head.
- The mayor would prepare and submit the annual budget to the council.
- The mayor's veto authority would be expanded to include all resolutions. At the time, the mayor had veto power for every ordinance (except emergency, budget appropriation, and tax levy ordinances). The mayor could also reduce or disapprove any expenditure line item(s) in an appropriation ordinance. The council could override the mayoral veto of ordinances and resolutions with six affirmative votes.

The Hartford Courant, the daily newspaper, came out in favor of the proposed strong-mayor form of government. While acknowledging that the mayor-council government would not be a panacea, the *Courant* contended that the mayor-council government worked well in Stamford and New Haven, Connecticut, and that

> it could help to pull Hartford out of its governance doldrums. . . . Power became so diffused between the manager, council, and mayor that there has been little accountability. . . . There has been no "go to" official in city hall with the clout to be an effective liaison to the state and federal government and to developers. During the past few years, city government has been almost a bystander as the state embarked on its downtown development program. The governor of Connecticut was only half jokingly called the "mayor" of Hartford (*Hartford Courant* Editorial, October 8, 2002).

On November 5, 2002, the voters of Hartford voted overwhelmingly to approve the new charter. Following the election, Mayor Perez said that Hartford will have a "results oriented government." The election results showed the charter revision passing by lopsided margins in every district. Allan Taylor, chair of the CRC, said that the absence of organized opposition showed how widespread was the perception that the council-manager form of government had not worked in Hartford.

Now that the Hartford will be a "strong-mayor" city, how should it be classified? Before the referendum, Hartford was a conciliated city because it featured both the separation of political power between the mayor and the council found in political systems and the separation of the executive and administrative function found in unity-of-powers (administrative) systems. The mayor could not vote on the council and had veto authority over ordinances approved by the council. The city manager served at the pleasure of the council and appointed and supervised the department heads. Under the new charter, the mayor will function as the chief executive officer with administrative authority to supervise the COO and department heads. There will no longer be a definitive demarcation between the executive and administrative function. In order to determine whether Hartford should be classified as a conciliated or adapted political city under the new charter, one must study the formal and informal relationships among the mayor, city council, COO, and department heads. If it can be said that the COO serves as the assistant to the mayor and is accountable only to the mayor, then Hartford would be an adapted political city. If it can be determined that the COO is still primarily accountable to the council and mayor and retains a measure of administrative authority and control over the supervision and management of the department heads, then Hartford would still be classified as a conciliated city. Under the new charter, a majority of the council confirms the mayor's appointment and six council members must ratify the mayor's removal of the COO; therefore it cannot be said that the COO is accountable exclusively to the mayor. Under such circumstances, the COO will most likely work to retain the support and confidence of the mayor and at least four council members. The role of the council in both the confirmation and removal of the COO serves as a check on mayoral powers and prerogatives. However, the new charter also gives formal executive and administrative powers to the mayor, and the COO will be accountable to the mayor on a day-to-day basis in the administration of the city. To the extent that the mayor exercises formal executive and administrative powers, Hartford will operate more like an adapted political city than a conciliated city. However, the new charter also permits the mayor to delegate the supervision, direction, and evaluation of the department heads to the COO. If the mayor chooses to delegate the administrative function to the COO, then Hartford will continue to function more like a conciliated than an adapted political city.

Only time will determine whether the new charter will have strengthened the mayor, retained a professional city manager, and thereby diminished the influence of the city council. The Oakland experience serves as an indication of this possibility.

Lenexa, Kansas

Lenexa, Kansas, is a wealthy suburb in the metropolitan Kansas City region, situated in Johnson County about twelve miles southwest of downtown Kansas City, Missouri. Lenexa was incorporated in 1907, with a standard mayor-council political city structure. Consistent with other political cities experiencing urbanization, the scope of government services expanded and the community and governing body recognized the increased need for professional government. Based on a reform referendum in 1975, Lenexa changed to an adapted political city. The mayor was given the power to hire and fire an assistant and also retained the authority to supervise and evaluate department heads. The mayor's decision to hire or fire department heads, however, required the consent of the city council.

To respond efficiently and professionally to the continued pressures and demands of rapid population growth, in 1984 the governing body changed the assistant to the mayor to a city administrator. David Watkins, the Lenexa city administrator who was hired shortly after the creation of the city administrator position, indicates that the transition was not seamless or smooth. Initially, the ordinance called for the city council rather than the mayor to evaluate the city administrator. The mayor, left out of the loop, lobbied for mayoral rather than council evaluation of the city administrator. As a compromise, the ordinance was amended to allow the council and the mayor to collectively evaluate the administrator.

Under the 1984 ordinance, the mayor and council hire and remove the city administrator and the administrator has the authority to hire, fire, supervise, and evaluate department heads; hiring and firing, however, are subject to the approval of the mayor and council. Watkins cannot remember a single instance when the governing body has rejected his recommendation to hire or remove a department head. Watkins contends that the Lenexa city administrator position is comparable to the city manager position in Overland Park, Kansas, a Lenexa neighbor and an adapted administrative city.

Lenexa meets the test of a conciliated city because there is a distinct separation of political powers between the mayor and city council. The mayor presides at city council meetings, but may vote only if there is a tie. The mayor has veto authority over city council decisions. As the only official elected at large, the mayor serves as the pivotal policy and political leader for the city. Watkins says that the direct election of the mayor has always worked well in Lenexa and that the community would not accept the process of choosing the mayor from among the city council, a practice used in all administrative cities and most adapted administrative cities.

In 1985, the charter ordinance was amended, this time to increase the mayor's term from two to four years. The four-year mayoral term coincides with the length of term of council members and enhances mayoral leadership and policy influence.

As we have found in other conciliated cites, the Lenexa mayor and the city administrator have a close working relationship. The mayor, unlike council members, has an office in city hall and meets with the administrator and/or his assistants daily. The mayor also receives an initial look at the city budget before the city council sees it.

Watkins says that the district method of electing the council has provided representation for all sectors of the community. If there were at-large elections, according to Watkins, the city council would be dominated by the old town (city core) coalition that tends to be conservative and not pro-growth.

Lenexa has shown political and administrative stability, teamwork, and cooperation. The city administrator has eighteen years' tenure, and Lenexa's professional staff and elected officials are perceived as innovators, leaders, and network brokers in the Kansas City metropolitan area. Lenexa has successfully overcome the challenge of unifying the values of both the political and administrative city. Much of this success has to do with both professional and political leadership and competence. But, like the councils in other conciliated cities, the Lenexa city council does not appear to be especially influential.

Unified Government of Wyandotte County and Kansas City, Kansas

In 1995, a citizen's task force in Kansas City and Wyandotte County, Kansas, concerned with high taxes, corruption, and the increasing costs of service delivery, pressed the state legislature to adopt a bill calling for a public vote on the issue of consolidating the two jurisdictions. The Chamber of Commerce, the League of Women Voters, and the city council also endorsed the task force. In 1996, the state legislature authorized the governor to appoint a commission to advise the legislature on the matter of the possible consolidation of Kansas City and Wyandotte County. After ten months of deliberations and thirty-two public hearings, the Consolidation Study Commission (CSC) recommended full consolidation.

The proposed Unified Government of Wyandotte County and Kansas City, Kansas, could have taken any of the structural forms described in this book. The CSC recommended a structure combining characteristics of both the mayor-council and council-manager forms of government. As in all other conciliated cities, the proposed structure included the separation of political powers between the mayor and council and a county administrator who served as the chief executive officer. The mayor was to serve full-time, be elected at large, vote only to break a tie, and have veto power over council actions. The county administrator was to be hired and terminated by the mayor and council. The county administrator was to supervise the department heads. There were to be two council members elected at large and eight elected by district.

On April 1, 1997, over 60 percent of the voters of Kansas City, Kansas, voted to consolidate both governments, using the structure recommended by the CSC. There were many reasons that consolidation was approved, such as the desire to reduce fiscal stress, reduce property taxes, reverse population loss, combat the flight to the suburbs, improve service delivery, and enhance efficiency and effectiveness (Leland and Thurmaier 2000; Johnson and Leland 2000). However, the driving force behind consolidation was the overwhelming desire to improve accountability through the development of a unified, professional civil service system and a professional budgeting system. Although a reformed Kansas City government created in 1982 had adopted a modernized professional personnel system and budgetary system, the county had not. Also, unlike the city, the county had no central administrator or centralized purchasing system. The reformers in Wyandotte County advocated merging the city and county governments to modernize and professionalize the county government, which was run at the time by three full-time partisan commissioners dominated by the local Democratic Party. The reformers hoped that modernization of the county, through consolidation, would improve the image of both governments, reverse urban decline and fiscal stress, and enable the jurisdiction to effectively compete with other local governments in the region.

What can be said about the performance of the unified government since the 1997 consolidation? First, the unified government has kept the promise to professionalize local government, reduce the number of employees, and reduce the tax rate (Frederickson and Wood 2001). Second, the Wyandotte County population has stabilized. Third, the unified government has made significant strides in economic development initiatives. For example, the selection of Wyandotte County as the site for a new National Association of Stock Car Automobile Racing (NASCAR) track and its surrounding commercial development has been an enormous boost to both the economy and the image of the unified government. Had it not been for the existence of the unified government, many believe that this project would not have been built in Wyandotte County. Fourth, many socioeconomic measures such as per capita income, median household income, retail sales, and the employment rate in Wyandotte County have improved. While some of this improvement can be attributed to a strong regional economy, it is interesting to note that the average annual rate of improvement in median family income and retail sales was greater in Wyandotte County than in Johnson County (a wealthy neighboring county), suggesting that the improvement in Wyandotte County can be attributed to factors other than economy (Frederickson and Wood 2001). Fifth, a survey of citizens in the Kansas City metropolitan area showed that Wyandotte County residents were as satisfied with the performance of the unified government and as trusting of their governmental leaders as were the citizens in other jurisdictions in the metro area. Given the history of political corruption and citizen frustration and disappointment in Wyandotte County, the results of the analysis are encouraging. Sixth, the mayor and the county administrator have formed an effective partnership that has provided the necessary leadership to fulfill the promise of consolidation. In 2002, Mayor Carol Marinovich was honored with the Excellence in Local Government Award from the League of Kansas Municipalities. Mayor Marinovich was also one of eleven public officials in the United States to receive the Public Official of the Year Award from *Governing* magazine for "stepping forward to deal with problems others considered too difficult to solve."

While not causing a renaissance, the unified government has begun to achieve results. It is difficult to determine how much of this success can be attributed to the consolidation of city and county services and how much to the creation of a conciliated city.

The conciliated cities described in this chapter range in population from 40,000 (Lenexa, Kansas) to 365,000 (Oakland, California) and are located across the United States. Similar to political and adapted political cities, the conciliated cities we have identified from our survey are characterized by the political separation of powers between the mayor and council. The mayor does not serve on the council and cannot vote except perhaps when there is a tie. But, like administrative and adapted administrative cities, in conciliated cities the mayor and council exercise limited executive authority and control over the city bureaucracy. The city manager or CAO holds that power. The mayor cannot unilaterally appoint and remove the city manager or the CAO nor does the mayor exercise executive power over the CAO.

All the conciliated cities have a CAO, who is hired and terminated by and accountable to both the mayor and council. In all these cities, the city manager or CAO appoints, removes, and supervises the department heads. In three conciliated cities in our survey, the mayor and council appoint the department heads upon the recommendation of the city manager, and the city manager supervises them. In two conciliated cities, the department heads report to both the mayor and CAO. However, we still classified these five cities as conciliated because the CAO has executive authority over the department heads and manages the city on a day-to-day basis. It is clear, however, that in a few conciliated cities the mayor and CAO work closely together as an executive and administrative team.

The council serves part-time in all of the conciliated cities. Only three of the conciliated cities elect council members in a mixed electoral system. Eight of the conciliated cities elect the council by district, and four of the conciliated cities elect the council at large.

Table 9.1 shows the structural characteristics of the six conciliated cities included in the 1998 survey that have been described at length in this chapter, using a priori criteria from our typology.

Artistic Method of Classification

One way to understand the structural qualities of conciliated cities is to consider the cases of cities that were not included in this category. Some cities in the 1998 survey, such as Topeka, Kansas, and Minneapolis, Minnesota, were classified as adapted political cities but, depending on an interpretation of their structural characteristics, could have been classified as conciliated cities. Likewise, the cities of Ann Arbor, Michigan; Arlington, Texas; and Kansas City, Missouri, were classified as adapted administrative cities but could also have been classified as conciliated cities. Table 9.2 summarizes the structural characteristics of these five cities and the narrative that follows explains why these cities are not conciliated.

Topeka and Minneapolis provide for shared executive powers between the mayor and the CAO. The mayor and council in both cities jointly select the CAO as is typical of conciliated cities. Unlike conciliated cities, however, the Topeka and Minneapolis mayors play a role in the supervision of department heads. In Topeka, all formal executive authority resides with the mayor, although the CAO has been delegated day-to-day management responsibility. In Minneapolis, the mayor has formal supervisory authority of department heads. In both cities, the mayor also has considerable influence over the budget and budget process. The decision to classify Topeka and Minneapolis as adapted political cities rather than conciliated came down to the judgment call that in both cases executive authority, including the details of day-to-day administration, rested ultimately with the mayor, even though in practice the mayors have tended to delegate that authority to their CAOs. Because the delegated power of the CAO is not in the charter or statutory platform, that delegation can always be overridden or withdrawn by the mayor.

The difficulty in classifying Ann Arbor, Arlington, and Kansas City lay in our interpretation of the details of separation of powers and unity of powers between the mayor and council. The mayors in Ann Arbor, Arlington, and Kansas City are members of their respective city councils and can vote on all issues. This structural characteristic is typical of the unity-of-powers model found in adapted administrative cities. These mayors, however, have veto authority, associated with the logic of separation of powers found in conciliated cities. The decision to classify Ann Arbor, Arlington, and Kansas City as adapted administrative cities rather than conciliated cities came down to the judgment call that the veto power alone was not a sufficiently powerful

Table 9.1

Sample of Conciliated Cities in 1998 Survey, Using Criteria from Table 7.5 in Chapter 7

	Cincinnati, Ohio	Evanston, Illinois	Hartford, Connecticut	Lenexa, Kansas	Oakland, California	Unified government of Wyandotte
Statutory charter	Council-manager	Council-manager	Council-manager	Mayor-council	Mayor-council	Council-manager
How is mayor elected?	At large	At large	At large	At large	At large	At large
Can mayor vote?	No	Only to break a tie	No	Only to break a tie	Only to break a tie	Only to break a tie
Does mayor have veto power?	Yes	Yes	Yes	Yes	No	Yes
Term of mayor	4 years	4 years	2 years	4 years	4 years	4 years
Does mayor serve as CAO?	No	No	No	No	No	No
Salary of mayor	2 times council pay	$12,000	$30,000	$850 per month	70–90% of average pay of mayors	$62,080 (1998)
Mayor's status	—	Part-time	—	Part-time	Full-time	Full-time
How is council elected?	At large	District	At large	District	Mixed	Mixed

Term of council	2 years	4 years	2 years	4 years	4 years	4 years
Salary of council	¾ salary of county commissioners	$6,500	$15,000	$450 per month	$60,000	District—$12,000 At large—$14,400
Council's status	—	Part-time	Part-time	Part-time	At discretion of council	Part-time
Is there a professional administrator?	Yes, city manager	Yes, city manager	Yes, city manager	Yes, CAO	Yes, city manager	Yes, county manager
How is administrator appointed?	Mayor nominates and council approves	—	Council only	Mayor and council	Mayor nominates and council approves	Mayor and council
To whom do department heads report?	City manager	City manager	City manager	City manager	City manager	County manager
Is there a merit based civil service system?	Yes	Yes	Yes	Yes	Yes	Yes
Are there bid and purchasing procedures?	Yes	Yes	Yes	Yes	Yes	Yes

Source: Frederickson and Johnson survey questionnaire, 1998.

Table 9.2

Cities Not Classified as Conciliated Cities, Using the Artistic Method, 1998

	Minneapolis, Minnesota	Topeka, Kansas	Ann Arbor, Michigan	Arlington, Texas	Kansas City, Missouri
Statutory charter	Mayor-council	Mayor-council	Council-manager	Council-manager	Mayor-council
How mayor elected?	At large	At large	At large	At large	At large
Can mayor vote?	No	No	Yes	Yes	Yes
Does mayor have veto power?	Yes	Yes	Yes	Yes	Yes
Term of mayor	4 years	4 years	2 years	2 years	4 years
Does mayor serve as CAO?	No	No	No	No	No
Salary of mayor	$72,000	$55,000	$17,250	$3,000	$61,476
Mayor's status	Full-time	Full-time	Part-time	Part-time	Part-time
How is council elected?	District	District	District	At large	Mixed
Term of council	4 years	4 years	2 years	4 years	4 years
Salary of council	$59,000	$8,000	$8,500	$500 per month	$27,324

Council's status	Full-time	Part-time	Part-time	Part-time	Part-time
Is there a professional administrator?	Yes, CAO	Yes, CAO	Yes, CAO	Yes, city manager	Yes, city manager
How is administrator appointed?	Mayor and city council	Mayor nominates, council approves	Mayor and council	Mayor and council	Mayor nominates, council approves
To whom do department heads report?	CAO and mayor	CAO and mayor	CAO	City manager	City manager
Is there a merit-based civil service system?	Yes	Yes	Yes	Yes	Yes
Are there bid and purchasing procedures?	Yes	Yes	Yes	Yes	Yes
Classified category	Adapted political	Adapted political	Adapted administrative	Adapted administrative	Adapted administrative

Source: Frederickson and Johnson survey questionnaire, 1998.

feature of the separation of powers between the mayor and council to negate the more important aspects of unity of powers associated with the mayor being part of the city council.

San Jose, California (population 918,800), was not included in our 1998 survey but is an interesting case. San Jose has a directly elected mayor and ten council members elected by district. The mayor and council are full-time, although some of the council members also have separate jobs. The mayor has a large staff, including a chief of staff, a public information officer, a budget director, five policy analysts, a schedule coordinator, and an administrative assistant. Each council member has a chief of staff, two policy analysts, an administrative assistant, and an intern. The mayor serves on the council, can vote on all issues, and does not have a veto. In addition, the city charter gives the mayor the authority to recommend increases in the proposed budget and, with the consent of the council, to redirect resources after budget approval.

The mayor nominates the city manager, who is confirmed by the council. The city manager hires department directors, again with the consent of the council. Once confirmed by the council, department heads are supervised by the city manager. The city manager has the authority to terminate department heads, as well as hire and terminate all other city employees. San Jose has a civil service system and bid and purchasing procedures and standards.

Relations between council members and between the council and mayor are usually harmonious and cooperative, although the propensity for conflict increases with large, controversial public issues. Although San Jose has non-partisan elections, the party identifications of elected officials are well known.

We consider San Jose an adapted administrative city because the mayor serves on the council and can only nominate the city manager. In the end, the manager is appointed by and terminated by the full council. It is evident, however, that the mayor has significant powers of oversight regarding the city manager and the city staff. Even though the mayor and the city council approve the appointment of department heads, it is our judgment that the city manager still serves as the chief executive officer of the city. If the mayor had not been on the council and had veto authority (separation of powers) or if the mayor had been given executive authority over the city bureaucracy, then San Jose would have been categorized as a conciliated city.

Conclusion

In our 1998 sample survey of 116 cities, fifteen cities, or just about 13 percent, are best categorized as conciliated. We hesitate to argue that 13 percent of the universe of American cities are now conciliated, given the nature of our sample. Nevertheless, our findings suggest that there are more conciliated cities than we had assumed and certainly more than is generally thought among students of local government. It is clear that larger cities have tended toward conciliation. Only time will tell whether the conciliated city blend of separation and unity of powers will catch on in a diffusion of change in the same way that many political and administrative cities became adapted cities. We consider this and other similar questions in Chapter 10.

Although there are variations among conciliated cities in the smaller details of structure, it appears that the key characteristics of the conciliated form can be seen in broad outline. Although many cities have only recently taken on conciliated characteristics, based on our research we have observed that, increasingly, American cities have (1) a directly elected mayor to provide centralized political leadership, accountability, and citywide representation, (2) city councils all or most of whose members are elected by district, thereby facilitating neighborhood responsiveness, (3) city councils that tend toward an activist form of constituent and district representation, (4) city councils and individual city council members that are less powerful in conciliated cities than they are in political and adapted political cities, (5) an appointed, professional, full-time city manager or CAO who provides centralized administrative leadership, (6) a mayor and CAO share executive duties, the mayors playing primarily a political role while the city managers or CAOs play primarily an administrative role, and (7) mayors who play a strong leadership role with council but have a facilitative relationship with the CAO.

10

Conclusion

We began this study of the changing structure of American cities with both simplistic assumptions and an even more simplistic nomenclature. Like virtually everyone else studying American cities, we understood that there were reformed cities, usually called council-manager cities, but sometimes called the city-manager form. And we understood that so-called unreformed cities were generally the mayor-council form. But, on the basis of simple observation and experience, we knew that these categories were overly simplistic and failed to account for patterns of structural change we knew were happening in many cities.

We began with a bimodal assumption that to this point all American cities had been grouped into two statutory or charter categories, as illustrated in Figure 1.1 in Chapter 1. Each modality, it was assumed, had characteristics unique to it and distinct from the characteristics found in the other modality. This bimodal distribution was assumed to broadly represent the standard garden-variety understanding of the two structural forms of American cities.

Based on observation and experience, we knew that this bimodal assumption was inaccurate as an empirical representation of city structures. We also knew of a growing literature describing how cities were incrementally changing their structures (Renner and DeSantis 1998; Svara 1999). Based on our reading of this literature and our direct observations, we then made the opposite assumption, that American cities, regardless of their legal descriptions, were coming increasingly to resemble each other structurally and that the normal curve, as shown in Figure 1.2 in Chapter 1, is a more accurate representation of that assumption. In this assumption, central tendency describes the majority of American cities having approximately the same structural characteristics. At the standard deviation of each tail of the curve we would find fewer cities that could be accurately described as having the distinct characteristics of mayor-council or council-manager cities. This study tests the assumption represented by the normal curve shown in Figure 1.2.

To test the normal curve assumption, we unbundled all of the distinct structural characteristics of cities. This unbundling is described in Chapter 1, is elaborated in much greater detail in Chapter 7, and, in simplified form, is repeated here in Table 10.1. In the course of this unbundling, we learned that the language we were using, such as reformed or unreformed city, council-manager or mayor-council city, seriously limited our ability to describe empirically how American cities have designed and redesigned their governments. So we developed a new language to describe the nuances and variations in city structures. This language is set out in Chapter 1 and is used throughout the book. Although this language is often awkward and complicated, without it we could not have tested the assumption that American cities tend to redesign their structures to increasingly resemble one another.

From Political Cities to Adapted Political Cities

We started with a description of the common form of American cities before the reform movement. Structurally, these cities were copies of state governments and the federal government, designed on the basis of a separation of powers between an elected mayor functioning as the executive and a city council elected by districts. There are designed checks and balances in this model. We describe these cities as political cities. The power granted the mayor in this form determines whether there is a "strong mayor" or a "weak mayor." The strong mayor has the authority to prepare the budget and to control the administration of that budget, to appoint and remove department heads, and to direct the activities of city departments. The mayor may also have the power to appoint a chief administrative officer (CAO) to assist in managing the city. The weak-mayor form is characterized by limited powers of appointment, a number of principal city offices being filled by direct election or by the council. In addition, the weak mayor may lack the authority to develop the budget and have little or no administrative control over operations. Although it is difficult to draw a distinct line between the strong-mayor and weak-mayor plans, the latter is more common. In the typology used here, strong-mayor forms are likely to be political cities while weak-mayor forms tend to be adapted political cities or conciliated cities.

This is the form of city that prompted the municipal reform era, because it was pathologically prone to corruption and influence peddling. As we describe in Chapters 3 and 4, political cities are now relatively rare—less than 10 percent of American cities. Even the few remaining political cities have all been profoundly affected by the reform movement, as we describe in Chapter 4. Much of this reform is the result of state government requirements that all cities have merit-based civil service systems, bidding and purchasing controls, and independent auditing procedures. Because of these changes, even political cities would be structurally unrecognizable to prereform mayors or city council members. It could be argued, therefore,

Table 10.1

A Five-Part Breakdown of the Structural Characteristics of American Cities

The political city	The Adapted City			The administrative city
	The adapted political city	The conciliated city	The adapted administrative city	
No CAO	Likely to have a CAO	Has CAO	Has CAO	Has CAO
Mayor directly elected;	Mayor directly elected;	Mayor directly elected or selected by council	Mayor directly elected	Mayor selected by council
At least one member of city council elected by district	Most council elected by district	Council elections approximately an even mixture of at large and district elections	Majority of council elected at large	Council not paid; no staff
Mayor does not serve on council	Mayor does not serve on council	Mayor serves on council	Mayor serves on council	Mayor serves on council
Mayor serves full-time	Mayor serves full-time	Mayor serves either full- or part-time	Mayor serves either full- or part-time	Mayors serves part-time
Statutory or charter form of government is mayor-council	Statutory or charter form of government is likely to be mayor-council	Statutory form of government is either mayor-council or council-manager	Statutory of charter form of government is council-manager	Statutory or charter form of government is council-manager

that even political cities are adapted. Certainly a twenty-first-century Boston or Chicago is very different structurally and therefore politically from an early twentieth century Boston or Chicago. Quietly, over the decades, these cities professionalized their operations and reduced corruption, while retaining most of the salient features of political separation of powers and checks and balances. Although American municipal reform has been under way for a century, in the research literature the study of municipal reform has been mostly associated with the emergence and popularity of the council-manager form of city government. Our findings indicate that the most important features of municipal reform also profoundly changed the way mayor-council cities are structured and function. Large-scale patronage, graft, and corruption, even in political cities, are now relatively rare. The important influence of municipal reform on non–council-manager cities has been little understood and seldom studied.

Over the past fifty years, most political cities have changed, to become what we describe as adapted political cities. In Chapter 4, we describe in detail how the municipal reform movement influenced the structures of American cities. In recent decades, many cities on mayor-council charter platforms have provided for the appointment of a full-time professional administrator known variously as chief administrative officer, chief executive officer, deputy mayor, or vice mayor for administration. The method of CAO appointment varies. When a CAO is appointed exclusively by the mayor, we regard that city as an adapted political jurisdiction. Most of these CAOs function very much like city managers, and many of them have previously served as managers in cities with council-manager charters. We believe that the increase in the adoption of the CAO position in political cities, when added to their other administrative and managerial adaptations, alters the functioning of political cities in the direction of increased efficiency and managerial effectiveness to a degree that warrants the description of such jurisdictions as adapted political cities.

In the adapted political city with a professional CAO, that CAO ordinarily influences policy. In the day-to-day operations of the adapted political city, the mayor still has a great deal of structural power to enforce his or her policy preferences, but tends to delegate to the CAO supervision of the functioning of the city administration. In such settings, the mayor and the CAO are often described as a team. In adapted political cities, there is still clear separation of power between mayoral and CAO executive prerogatives on the one hand and the legislative and budgetary powers held by the city council on the other hand. Checks and balances are commonplace. City council representation of district interests is routine. It is not uncommon for city council members to anticipate running for mayor and, when in mayoral campaign mode, to use their council position to oppose not only the policies and programs of the mayor, but also the CAO.

Based on our findings, we conclude that there continue to be distinct elements of the separation of political power, and checks and balances, in adapted political cities. But we also find much less political influence over day-to-day city administrative matters in adapted political cities than we find in political cities. Therefore, in adapted political cities, the separation of powers is not two-way, between mayoral/executive power and council/ legislative power, but three-way, between mayoral/executive and council/ legislative power on one hand *and,* on the other hand, between political power generally and the exercise of administrative power in the conduct of the day-to-day operations of the city. We return to this separation-of-powers issue later in these conclusions. In the adapted political city, there is also a separation between the processes and much of the substance of city administration on one hand and both mayoral/executive and council/legislative powers on the other.

From Administrative Cities to Adapted Administrative Cities

The council-manager plan grew out of the reform movement at the turn of the century with the explicit goal of cleansing municipal government of graft, corruption, and inefficiency. This form, which has been recommended by the National Civic League's Model City Charter for over seventy-five years, vests all city political powers in a council elected at large, which appoints a professional manager who functions as the city executive and is continuously responsible to and removable by the council. In classic administrative cities, the council does not share policy-making authority with a separately elected mayor. Therefore, political power is unified; hence, the council-mayor form of city government is often referred to as a unity-of-powers structural model. The mayor tends to be ceremonial and weak, merely the presiding member of the council. City councils are small. The mayor in a classic administrative city is a member of the council, is selected by the council, is not paid, and serves part-time, usually for a single year. Such mayors have little structural power over policy and almost none over implementation. Council members are elected at large, greatly reducing the influence of neighborhoods and ethnic or racial areas of the city. There are few political checks and balances. Once the council majority has spoken and the manager is appointed, there is a unity of powers. Because of their distinct emphasis on efficiency and professional management, such jurisdictions are best described as administrative cities.

In administrative cities, the city manager tends to have a very wide scope of influence, including control of virtually all policy implementation, a good bit of city policy making, and even some influence over the city mission, although always in a nonpolitical way (Nalbandian 1991). Politics in administrative cities tends to cluster around elections and then to recede sharply after the election. The emphasis is on effectiveness, efficiency, and professional management. It is no wonder that administrative cities flourished in homogeneous American suburbs and in the midwest, southwest, and west. These are the crown jewels of municipal reform. But the municipal reform movement is over and administrative cities are increasingly rare, by our estimate only about 20 percent of American cities.

We hypothesized in Chapter 1 and described in detail in Chapter 5 the trajectory of cities as distinctly in the direction of structural adaptations that are characteristic of adapted cities. These adaptations were almost always advanced to enhance political responsiveness and political accountability.

Responsiveness to neighborhoods was to be enhanced by changing from city council members elected at large to city council members elected by district. Most American cities now elect all or at least some of their council members by district. In addition, over time more and more cities with district-elected city council members have arranged some monthly pay and certain forms of support, such as offices, cellular telephones, home computers, cars, and access to staff help, for council members. Adaptations in this direction are almost always associated with size, larger cities being more inclined to these changes.

In the classic administrative city, the council tends to be made up of business leaders who meet one evening a week to make city policy and engage in oversight of city administrative affairs. Seldom do city council members of this type anticipate long-term political careers. Political representativeness and responsiveness in such a model is thought to be general, to apply to everyone in the city. In broad policy terms, it is likely that at-large city councils in administrative cities are primarily concerned with representing the whole city. It is wordplay, therefore, to claim that at-large councils are not representative or responsive, because they are. The question of representation changes from the quality of generalized representation of the whole city to a question of the quality of specific representation, or, to put it another way, representativeness on whose behalf. Obviously not all residents of the city are alike. There is no question that at-large elected council members in administrative cities are primarily white, male business leaders who live in middle- and upper-class neighborhoods (Bledsoe 1993; Welch and Bledsoe 1988). Therefore, specific responsiveness to minorities, ethnic groups, and the poor has been the issue over the past thirty years. As a result, the vast majority of at-large council election formats in administrative cities have

been changed to the election of all or at least a majority of council members
on the basis of districts—all in the name of political representativeness and
responsiveness. Cities with all or part district-elected council are adapted
administrative cities. Council policy processes in adapted administrative cities tend to reflect neighborhood and group patterns of representation and, in
larger cities, patterns of political careerism and some of the elements of political checks and balances, depending on how the mayor is elected and how
extensive the mayor's powers are (Ehrenhalt 1991). Professional career city
mangers and administrators as well as most of those who study city management agree that, when compared with administrative cities, generalized administrative efficiency is often diminished in adapted administrative cities
because of district-elected council (Newland 1994).

Probably more important in patterns of structural adaptation from administrative cities to adapted administrative cities is the changed role of the mayor.
The distinct majority of cities with council-manager statutory or charter legal platforms have altered those platforms to provide for the direct election
of a mayor. In most of these adaptations, the directly elected mayor is still a
member of the city council, serving as the presiding city officer, but with few
powers not held by other city council members. It could be said that such
cities have the symbols of a mayor without the substance, but those symbols
are not unimportant. There is still an essential unity of political powers in a
council that includes a directly elected mayor with only symbolic powers.
And when the entire city council selects the city manager, with no special
role played by the mayor in that selection, and the appointed city manager
has full administrative powers over day-to-day city affairs, it could be said
that there is a unity of political powers in the council and a distinct separation between council-exercised political powers and management-exercised
administrative powers.

The trends, as we describe in Chapters 5, 7, and 8, are all in the direction
of enhanced mayoral powers. As cities grow and become more heterogeneous, mayors tend to move from voluntary to part-time and then to full-
time. In the process of this adaptation these mayors require offices, salaries,
and staff. It is not unusual, as the Kansas City, Oakland, and Cincinnati cases
illustrate, for full-time mayors to seek the full range of mayoral powers, to be
strong mayors. When these trends are observed, it is almost always the case
that they are accompanied by patterns of political separation of powers and
checks and balances between the mayor and the council.

At the crux of the distinctions in the adaptation processes between administrative and adapted administrative cities is the issue of who selects the city
manager or administrator. Beyond the question of the selection of the city
manager or administrator is the issue of administrative reporting patterns. In

adapted political cities, the administrator tends to be appointed by the mayor and to report to that mayor. In adapted administrative cities, the manager tends to be appointed by the council. But mayors in adapted administrative cities tend to expect managers to report to them. In either setting, the relationship between the mayor and the manager is often described as a partnership (Svara 1987). The background and day-to-day work of professional managers in either setting have been found to be more similar than different. Nevertheless, to those in the city management profession, the manner of managerial appointment, the reporting pattern of the manager (to the council or to the mayor), and the formal power of the manager to appoint and supervise department heads are the marking distinctions between the council-manager and mayor-council forms of city government and between unity-of-powers and separation-of-powers structures (Hansell 1999). From the professional manager's perspective, these distinctions are understandable. Our findings indicate that these distinctions have blurred and, over time, are blurring even further. This structural blurring has, we believe, resulted in what is essentially the most common form of American city—the adapted city, although we readily recognize a range of variation within the adapted city description.

What Is an Adapted City?

To defend this assertion, we turn to the answer to this question: what, exactly, is an adapted city?

First, all or most of the city council members are elected by district. As cities get larger, city council members tend to receive salaries, serve full-time, and may have offices and staff support.

Second, the mayor is separately elected. In large cities, mayors receive salaries, serve full time, and have offices and staff support. In the adapted political variant, the mayor is not a member of the city council and exercises many city executive powers, whereas in the adapted administrative variant the mayor is a member of the city council and has fewer formal executive powers.

Third, there is a professional city manager or CAO. In the adapted political variant of cities, the administrator is appointed by and reports to the mayor, whereas in the adapted administrative variant the administrator is appointed by the council and reports to it. In the adapted political variant, the city administrator exercises such executive powers as are delegated to him or her, whereas in the adapted administrative variant the city administrator has formal executive powers over the city administration.

Fourth, all or virtually all city employees are appointed and promoted on the basis of merit and are part of the city civil service.

Fifth, city accounts are required to be independently audited.

Sixth, bidding on city purchases and contracts is handled by selecting the most responsible or qualified low bid, and there are controls over the possibility of bid rigging or purchasing favoritism.

Within the generalized adapted city architecture there are many small variations, such as whether the civil service is unionized and has bargaining rights, whether the mayor prepares or presents the budget, and whether the mayor has a veto. Under particular circumstances or on particular issues, each of these variations may be important. But the importance of each variation is played out within the broader common architecture of the adapted city.

Is the adapted city a unity-of-powers or a separation-of-powers government structure? It is neither and both. Adapted cities are not pure unity-of-powers models and do not replicate American corporate structures or the structures of parliamentary national governments. The standard arguments for the unity-of-powers format have to do with the majoritarian democratic capacity to make policy with dispatch and the executive capacity to implement that policy efficiently. Because administrative cities are unity-of-powers models and because many adapted administrative cities were previously administrative cities, there is little question that adapted administrative cities have traded some city council-based majoritarian democratic capacity to decide and some administrative capacity to efficiently implement policy in return for greater representation and greater direct involvement of elected officials in city executive and administrative functioning.

The standard arguments for the separation of powers are based on the logic of limited government. Those who designed the separation-of-powers model were determined to stamp out hereditary and despotic governments and believed that this could be accomplished by pitting democratic ambition against ambition, structurally achieved by bicameral legislative bodies and a separately elected executive (president, governor, or mayor) able to check legislative excesses. For several reasons, adapted political cities cannot be properly described as a separation-of-powers model. First, there is an established merit-based civil service and a professional administrator who directs its day-to-day work either by delegated mayoral authority or by direct statutory or charter-based executive power. Second, there is now a wide range of administrative policies, processes, and procedures that mitigate against direct meddling in city administrative affairs by city council members and even by mayors. Because most adapted political cities evolved from political cities, they have traded many of the classic features of the separation of powers and the politics of checks and balances in return for greater administrative efficiency.

If neither a unity-of-powers nor a separation-of-powers democratic polity, what is an adapted city? Adapted cities are a blend of two logically opposite models of democracy. It appears that the citizens who have, over the years, voted for the incremental steps that have brought us adapted cities were evidently less interested in the contrasting logic of these two models and much more interested in attempting to somehow reconcile competing notions of democracy. City voters appear to want both the advantages of direct neighborhood representation and the assignment of overall political accountability to a mayor. But they also want professional leadership and a merit-based city administration functioning without political mischief.

Several questions remain: are these two forces compatible? can they be effectively blended? and if the great municipal reform movement is over, is this blended administrative city the synthesis? Empirically, the answer to each of these questions appears to be yes. City residents want the blending of the contrasting logic of unity of powers and separation of powers and believe this blending to be compatible. Or they take logical purity less seriously than they take wanting the best from both forms of logic and can find no reason why the best of each form of logic cannot be combined. Through the processes of incremental structural adaptation, city residents have essentially invented the adapted city.

In the short run, it appears that adapted cities are functioning about as their residents want. They may be less efficient than the advocates of unity of powers want and they may be less politically manipulable than separation-of-powers advocates may want, but adapted cities appear to be what the people want. At least in the eyes of the people, thus far, adapted cities have successfully combined the two types of contrasting democratic logic.

It is very important, however, to remember how malleable and dynamic American city structures are. The present dominance of the adapted city structure will no doubt adapt, the direction of that adaptation open to the forces of changing circumstances and the changing salience of winning ideas.

The patterns of structural adaptation in American cities match in a general way the research scholarship on the changing structures of nation-states. We will briefly review the work of Arend Lijphart (1984) to illustrate this point.

Lijphart describes and examines the two models of democracy: the parliamentary or the Westminster model, which is a unity-of-powers structure very similar to that of administrative cities, and the presidential model, which is very similar to the structure of political cities. The logic of the parliamentary model is a system of majoritarian rule in which executive power is concentrated and there is a fusion of executive and legislative powers. The parliamentary model is best suited to homogeneous societies in which no group is consistently left out of the political process or consistently opposed to those in power. Lijphart characterizes these systems as "majoritarian," able to make policy relatively quickly and to carry it out relatively efficiently. Majoritarian systems tend to be well developed and to have respected civil service systems. Although he was describing New Zealand, Ireland, Norway, the United Kingdom, and other countries with parliamentary governments, Lijphart could have been describing American suburban cities with administrative unity-of-powers structures in 1970.

The logic of presidential systems is a system of consensual rule based on a separation of powers, checks and balances, and a structure accommodating the clash of interests. Generally speaking, heterogeneous countries such as the United States, Switzerland, and Belgium are examples of countries with consensual structures. "In pluralist communities . . . , the flexibility necessary for majoritarian democracy is absent. . . . Minorities that are continually denied access to power will feel excluded and discriminated against and will lose their allegiance to the regime. In plural societies, majority rule spells majority dictatorship and civil strife rather than democracy" (Lijphart 1984, 22–23). Plural societies, according to Lijphart, govern better with consensus instead of opposition, inclusion rather than exclusion, maximizing the size of the ruling majority, and refusing to be satisfied with a bare majority. "Whenever problems of deep differences and tensions between groups in society form a challenge to stable and effective democracy, consensual solutions are to be recommended" (209). Consensus democracy aims to restrain majority rule by encouraging or requiring the sharing of power between the majority and the minority through coalitions, the dispersal of power between the executive and legislature (separation of powers), and a formal limit of power by veto. The consensual model is essentially the same as the structure of American political cities, which are modeled on the federal and the state constitutions. These systems are often slow, inefficient, highly political, and liable to favoritism and corruption, particularly in the absence of an established and respected civil service.

A country's level of pluralism, size of population, and cultural influences are linked to the type of regime it is most likely to have. Non-Anglo-American, plural societies with large populations tend to have consensus regimes, while Anglo-American, homogeneous societies with smaller populations tend to have majoritarian systems.

Lijphart describes patterns of structural adaptation between 1945 and 1980 not unlike the patterns described in our findings. It appears, however, that American cities are somewhat more adaptable, or change their structures incrementally at a more rapid pace, than nation-states. In general terms, Lijphart finds trends of adataption that approximate our findings. As majoritarian countries grow and become more heterogeneous, they modify and adopt features of consensual government, and vice versa. Several countries, including the United States, are not described by Lijphart as "intermediate," blending features of the logic of both unity of powers (majoritarian) and separation of powers (consensual). Lijphart characterizes the results as follows: "The fact that several countries have successfully combined majoritarian and consensual-federal features demonstrates that the two opposite sets of characteristics are not incompatible" (219). His conclusions approximately match ours. Like many nation-states, American adapted cities have combined the logic of unity of powers and separation of powers. Only time can tell whether, over the long-term, this fusion will be successful.

That American cities regularly modify their democratic and administrative structures is one of our most important findings. In Chapter 2, we developed a theory of institutional dynamics designed to account for and explain these patterns of city structural modification. Institutional dynamics blends theories of the diffusion of innovation and theories of epochs. Studies of hundreds of policy changes, technological adaptations, and organizational modification patterns all show an S-curve of institutional change. First, one or just a few institutions will develop a new technology, or change their policy, or change their institutional structures. If the innovation catches on, it will then migrate to other similar institutions, first in a gradual slope, then in a steep slope, and finally leveling off in another gradual slope—thus forming the S-curve of the diffusion of innovation. In the theory of diffusion of innovation, the forces of change are explained by institutional proximity (nearer institutions adapting first), the influences of consultants, professional associations, media influence, the drive for institutional legitimacy or status, or simply changing tastes or fads.

Using the definitions of political, administrative, and the three variants of adapted cities, our findings exhibit several distinct S-curves of institutional change. The administrative city S-curve is shown at the bottom of Figure 10.1, beginning between 1880 and 1900 and growing steadily to the 1960s, one of the primary innovations of the municipal reform movement. Most of the cities categorized as administrative cities by 1960 had previously been political cities, but many were new suburban cities.

Beginning in the 1920s, administrative cities themselves began to adapt, reflecting an upward S-curve to the 1960s, and then, as classic administrative cities began to disappear, there was a reverse S-curve, shown as the downward sloping line between administrative and administrative adapted cities, beginning in the 1960s. Now, at the turn of the twenty-first century, there are many more adapted administrative cities than there are administrative cities. This could be described as one aspect of an "adapted city reform" process, or what some have called "the reform of the reform" (Hansell 1999). By the 1970s, these two S-curves accounted for more than half of American cities.

Figure 10.1 **City Structural Adaption and the Forces of Reform**

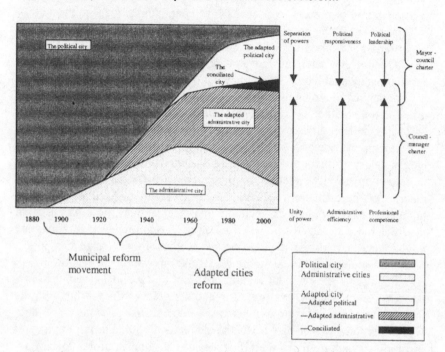

Equally important but much less generally understood as part of the adapted cities reform is the pattern of adaptation of political cities to adapted political cities, beginning in the 1950s, shown as an S-curve in the upper right-hand quadrant of Figure 10.1. Now, at the turn of the twenty-first century, there are very few pure political cities and many more adapted political cities.

Finally, beginning in the 1980s, a few adapted cities so completely amalgamated the features of adapted political and adapted administrative cities as to defy categorization. These are the conciliated cities we describe in detail in Chapter 9.

On the far right-hand side of Figure 10.1, we use two arrows to illustrate the forces driving these structural changes—the drive for administrative efficiency and professional competence coming from one direction and the drive for political responsiveness and leadership coming from the other. These arrows empirically represent competing theories of democratic government. Our findings can be interpreted as a test of Herbert Kaufman's theories (1971) that over time American democratic politics swings in a wide arc between the search for neutral administrative competence at one pole and for political representativeness at the other. Based on the 120 years represented in Figure

10.1, the structural adaptation arc of city democratic structures does not appear to go from one pole to the other. Instead, the arc of change appears to be pulled from one pole to the other, usually settling somewhere in between.

The rhetoric of change is a polar language, but the actual incremental, democratic, structural adaptation of cities appears to be more cautious and intermediate. This rhetoric is captured by Albert Hirschman's "disappointment" thesis (1982). Like Kaufman, Hirschman observes a wide arc of change over time between efficiency and political responsiveness. The magnetic forces pulling structural adaptation through that arc in one direction or the other have to do with the power of contemporary winning arguments, based on democratic expressions of disappointment. For example, a typical political city could be easily described, particularly after a scandal, as riddled with patronage and corruption and, therefore, a disappointment. Such a disappointment suggests the need for structural adaptations favoring a merit-based civil service and tight bid and purchase controls. This is exactly the rhetoric of the municipal reform movement, and vestiges of that movement are still found in the processes of adaptation of political cities to adapted political cities.

Much more obvious in the past twenty years has been the rhetoric of disappointment with the cold, efficient, neutral administration of administrative cities. When things go wrong, and they always do, there is a logical instinct to fix responsibility, and in democratic political systems responsibility ultimately rests with elected officials. If they are to be held responsible for city affairs, they argue, should they not have greater political power to influence those affairs? While our findings generally support the disappointment thesis, we suggest that the processes of change, at least as those processes are represented by the incremental adaptation of city structures, are less sweeping and more tentative than the disappointment thesis suggests.

Our findings fit comfortably in the so-called new institutionalism perspective. Large-scale synthesis of many studies of comprehensive institutional reform in complex public systems concludes that reform and reorganization "within a simple scheme [are] unlikely to be politically digestible" (March and Olsen 1989, 7). Actual change is almost always incremental because existing structures usually reflect long historical processes as well as repeated consideration of competing interests and preferences and a good bit of compromise. Patterns of adaptation respond to the issues that are winning the battle for limited public attention (March and Olsen 1983). Shifting attention is a function of scandal, crisis, disappointment, and the skills of leaders. Initial proposals for city structural adaptation, such as a proposal that an administrative city change to a directly elected mayor or give that mayor more power, or that a political city change to provide for a

CAO, are usually not successful. Instead, they are ideas, preferences, and perspectives competing with other ideas, preferences, and perspectives. Ideas for structural change can be understood as solutions waiting for problems or answers waiting for questions. At some point—a crisis, a consultants' report, the advent of a dynamic and popular leader—a change proposal will "find" the problem to which it is the solution (March and Olsen 1983; Kingdon 1984). Under such circumstances, the prospects for democratic approval increase. But such change are seldom the wholesale abandonment of a particular comprehensive democratic logic in favor of its opposite.

The three forces driving contemporary patterns of city structural diffusion are the drive for political leadership, the drive for political responsiveness, and the drive for administrative effectiveness. These forces lead to fewer and fewer structural distinctions between American cities. Other studies of diffusion (DiMaggio and Powell 1991) find growing isomorphism among companies and institutions as a result of adaptation. Put another way, American cities are increasingly like one another structurally and there are fewer and fewer outliers. Put in the terms of this study, there are more and more adapted cities and fewer and fewer political and administrative cities.

References

ACIR (U.S. Advisory Commission on Intergovernmental Relations). 1993. "State Laws Governing Local Government Structure and Administration." Compiled by Melvin B. Hill Jr., Washington, DC.

Adrian, Charles R. 1955. *Governing Urban America.* New York: McGraw-Hill.

———. 1961. "Recent Concepts in Large City Administrations." In *Urban Government: A Reader in Politics and Administration*, ed. Edward C. Banfield. New York: Free Press.

———. 1967. *State and Local Governments.* New York: McGraw-Hill.

———. 1988. "Forms of City Government in American History." In *Municipal Year Book.* Washington, DC: International City/County Management Association.

Alford, Rovert R., and Harry M. Scoble. 1965. "Political and Socioeconomic Characteristics of American Cities." In *Municipal Year Book.* Chicago, IL: International City/County Management Association.

Ammons, David N., and Chardlean Newell. 1984. *City Executives: Leadership Roles, Work Characteristics, and Time Management.* Albany: State University of New York Press.

Anderson, Eric. 1989. "Two Major Forms of Government: Two Types of Professional Management." In *Municipal Year Book.* Washington, DC: International City/County Management Association, 25–32.

Arnold, John. 2000. Personal interview. October 24.

Bailey, Mary Timney, and Richard T. Mayer, eds. 1992. *Public Management in an Interconnected World.* New York: Greenwood.

Banfield, Edward C., and James Q. Wilson. 1963. *City Politics.* Cambridge, MA: Harvard University Press.

Banovetz, J.M. 1994. "Council-Manager Government's Response to Economic Development." In *Ideal and Practice in Council-Manager Government.* Washington, DC: International City/County Management Association, pp. 203–15.

Behrman, Jere R., and Steven G. Craig. 1993. "The Distribution of Public Services: An Explanation of Local Government Preferences." *American Economic Review* 77 (March).

Belsley, Lyle. 1938. "Personnel Administration." In *Municipal Year Book.* Washington, DC: International City/County Management Association, 18–27.

———. 1939. "Personnel Administration." In *Municipal Year Book.* Washington, DC: International City/County Management Association, 10–15.

———. 1943. "Personnel Administration." In *Municipal Year Book.* Washington, DC: International City/County Management Association, 29–36.

Berry, Francis Stokes, and William D. Berry. 1990. "State Lottery Adoptions as Policy Innovations: An Event Historical Analysis." *American Political Science Review* 84: 395–415.

175

Bledsoe, Timothy. 1993. *Careers in City Politics: The Case for Urban Democracy.* Pittsburgh, PA: University of Pittsburgh Press.

Bollens, John C. 1952. *Appointed Executive Local Government: The California Experience.* Los Angeles, CA: Hayes Foundation.

Booth, David A. 1965. *Council-Manager Government, 1940–1964: An Annotated Bibliography.* Compiled by David A Booth. Chicago: International City Manager's Association.

Boyne, George A. 1992. "Local Government Structure and Performance: Lessons from America?" *Public Administration* 70 (Autumn): 333–57.

Boynton, Robert P., and Victor S. DeSantis. 1990. "Form and Adaptation: A Study of the Formal and Informal Functions of Mayors, Managers, and Chief Administrative Officers." *Baseline Data Report*, Vol. 22. Washington, DC: International City/County Management Association.

Boynton, Robert P., and D.S. Wright. 1971. "Mayor-Manager Relationships in Large Council-Manager Cities: A Reinterpretation." *Public Administration Review* 31: 28–36.

Bozeman, Barry, and Jeffrey D. Straussman. 1990. *Public Management Strategies.* San Francisco, CA: Jossey-Bass.

Bridges, Amy. 1997. *Morning Glories: Municipal Reform in the Southwest.* Princeton, NJ: Princeton University Press.

Brock, William Ranulf. 1970. *The Evolution of American Democracy.* New York: Dial Press.

Bromage, Arthur W. 1957. *Introduction to Municipal Government and Administration.* New York: Appleton-Century-Crofts.

———. 1970. *Urban Policy Making: The Council-Mayor Partnership.* Chicago: Public Administration Service.

Chang, Tso-Shuen. 1918. *History and Analysis of the Commission and City-Manager Plans of Municipal Government in the United States.* Ph.D. diss., Iowa City: University of Iowa.

Childs, R.S. 1965. *The First 50 Years of the Council-Manager Plan of Municipal Government.* New York: American Book–Stratford Press.

Clark, Terry N. 1968. "Community Structure, Decision Making, Budget Expenditures and Urban Renewal in 51 Cities." *American Sociological Review* 33: 576–93.

Clingermayer, James C., and Richard C. Feiock. 1990. "Constituencies, Campaign Support, and Council Member Intervention in City Development Policy." *American Politics Quarterly* (March) 16: 55–67.

Cohen, Steven, and William Eimicke. 1995. *The New Effective Public Manager: Achieving Success in a Changing Government.* San Francisco, CA: Jossey-Bass.

Consolidated Study Commission (CSC). 1996. Transcripts from public hearing held on September 6. Kansas City, KS.

———. 1997. "Final Recommendations for the Consolidation of the Governments of Wyandotte County and Kansas City, Kansas," submitted to the State of Kansas Legislature and the governor on January 13, 1997.

Cooper, Phillip J. 2003. *Governing by Contract: Challenges and Opportunities for Public Managers.* Washington, DC: CQ Press.

Coulter, Philip B. 1988. *Political Voice: Citizen Demand for Urban Public Services.* Tuscaloosa: University of Alabama Press.

Cox, Kevin R. 1973. *Conflict, Power, and Politics in the City: A Geographic View.* New York: McGraw-Hill.

Cremer, Helmouth. 1990. "Residential Choice and the Supply of Public Goods." *Journal of Urban Economics* 27: 168–87.

Davis, Charles R. 1996. *Organization Theories and Public Administration.* Westport, CT: Praeger.

Davis, Michael L., and Kathy Hayes. 1993. "The Demand for Good Government." *Review of Economics and Statistics* 75 (February): 147–52.

DeHoog, Ruth Hoogland, and Gordon P. Whitaker. 1990. "Political Conflict or Professional Advancement: Alternative Explanations of City Manager Turnover." *Journal of Urban Affairs* 12, no. 4: 361–77.

Deller, Steven C. 1990. "An Application of a Test for Allocate Efficiency in the Local Public Sector." *Regional Science and Urban Economics* 20: 395–406.

Deno, Kevin T., and Stephen Mehay. 1987. "Municipal Management Structure and Fiscal Performance: Do City Managers Make a Difference?" *Southern Economic Journal* 57 (January): 627–42.

DeSantis, Victor. 1996. "Local Government Managers' Career Paths." In *Municipal Year Book.* Washington, DC: International City/County Management Association.

DeSantis, Victor, and Tari Renner. 1993. "Contemporary Patterns and Trends in Municipal Government Structures." In *Municipal Year Book.* Washington, DC: International City/County Management Association.

———. 1994. "The Impact of Political Structures on Public Policies in American Countries." *Public Administration Review.* Washington, DC: American Society for Public Administration 54, no. 3: 291–95.

DiMaggio, Paul J., and Walter B. Powell, eds. 1991. *The New Institutionalism in Organizational Analysis.* Chicago, IL: University of Chicago Press.

Dye, Thomas R. 1973. *Politics in States and Communities.* Englewood Cliffs, NJ: Prentice-Hall.

———. 1990. *American Federalism: Competition Among Governments.* Lexington, MA: Lexington Books.

Ebdon, Carol, and Peter F. Brucato. 2000. "Government Structure in Large U.S. Cities: Are Forms Converging?" *International Journal of Public Administration* 23, no. 12: 2209–35.

Ehrenhalt, Alan. 1996. *The Lost City: The Forgotten Virtues of Community in America.* New York: HarperCollins.

Eisinger, Peter. 1988. *The Rise of the Entrepreneurial State: State and Local Economic Development Policy in the United States.* Madison: University of Wisconsin Press.

Elazar, Daniel J. 1994. *The American Mosaic: The Impact of Space, Time, and Culture on American Politics.* Boulder, CO: Westview Press.

Elkin, Stephen L. 1987. *City and Regime in the American Republic.* Chicago, IL: University of Chicago Press.

Etzioni, A. 1988. *The Moral Dimension.* New York: Free Press.

Fairlie, John. 1908. *Essays in Municipal Administration.* New York: Macmillan.

Feiock, Richard C. 1989. "The Adoption of Economic Development Policies by State and Local Governments: A Review." *Economic Development Quarterly* 3: 266–70.

Feiock, R., S. Ahmed, C. Stream, J. Clingermayer, B. McCabe. 2001. "Politics, Administration, and Manager Turnover." *State and Local Government Review.* Athens, GA: Carl Vinson Institute of Government.

Feiock, Richard C., and James C. Clingermayer. 2001. *Institutional Constraints and Policy Choice: An Exploration of Local Governance.* Albany: State University of New York Press.

Fiorina, Morris. 1992. *Divided Government*. New York: Macmillan.

———. 1996. *Divided Government*. 2d ed. Boston, MA: Allyn and Bacon.

Flentje, H. Edward, Jr., ed. 1993. *Selected Solely on the Basis of Administrative Ability*. Wichita, KS: Wichita State University.

Frederickson, H. George. 1997. "The Architecture of Democratic Government: The Type III City." In *Future Challenges of Local Autonomy in Japan, Korea, and the United States,* eds. Fukashi Horie and Masaru Nisho. Tokyo: National Institute for Research Advancement, pp. 152–65.

———. 1997. *The Spirit of Public Administration*. San Francisco, CA: Jossey-Bass.

Frederickson, H. George, and Gary A. Johnson. 2001. "The Adapted American City: A Research Note." *Urban Affairs Review* (July): 872–84.

Frederickson, H. George, and Jocelyn M. Johnston. 1999. *Public Management Reform and Innovation: Research, Theory, and Application*. Tuscaloosa: University of Alabama Press.

Frederickson, H. George, and Curtis Wood. 2001. "Unified Government: Promises Kept." Unpublished paper.

Gilbert, B. 1978. *This City, This Man: The Cookingham Era in Kansas City*. Washington, DC: International City/County Management Association.

Glaab, Charles N., and A. Theodore Brown. 1967. *A History of Urban America*. New York: Macmillan.

Goodnow, Frank. 1910. *City Government in the United States*. New York: Century.

Gottfried, Frances. 1988. *Merit System and Municipal Civil Service: A Fostering of Social Inequality*. Westport, CT: Greenwood Press.

Government Finance Officers Association (GFOA). 2001. Available at www.gfoa.org. (January 28, 2003)

Gray, Virginia. 1973. "Innovation in the States: A Diffusion Study." *American Political Science Review* 67: 1174–85.

———. 1988. "Competition, Emulation, and Policy Innovation." In *New Perspectives on American Politics*, ed. Lawrence C. Dodd and Calvin Jillson. Washington, DC: CQ Press.

Gray, Virginia, and David Lowery. 1996. *The Population Ecology of Interest Representation*. Ann Arbor: University of Michigan Press.

Green, Gary P., and Arnold Fleischman. 1989. "Analyzing Local Strategies for Promoting Economic Development." *Policy Studies Journal* 17, no. 3: 557–73.

Griffith, Ernest S. 1974. *A History of American City Government: The Progressive Years and Their Aftermath: 1900–1920*. New York: National Municipal League.

Gurwitt, Rob. 1993. "The Lure of the Strong Mayor." *Governing*, July: 36–41.

———. 2000. "Mayor Brown and Mr. Bobb: Can a Strong Mayor and a Strong Manager Find Happiness Together in a City with Big Problems?" *Governing,* January: 16–22.

———. 2000. "Rudderless in Hartford." *Governing*, September: 75–80.

Hall, Mike. 2000. "City Form of Government Still Up in the Air." *Topeka Capitol Journal* (April 23).

Hannan, Michael T., and Glenn R. Carroll. 1992. *Dynamics of Organizational Populations*. New York: Oxford University Press.

Hannan, Michael T., and John Freeman. 1977. "The Population Ecology of Organizations." *American Journal of Sociology* 82: 929–64.

Hansell, William. 1995. "Foreword." In *Ideal and Practice in Council-Manager Government*, ed. H. George Frederickson. Washington, DC: International City/County Management Association.

———. 1999. "Revisiting the Reform of the Reform." *Public Management Magazine* (January): 27–28.

Hays, Dennis. 1988. "A Study of Potential Areas for Governmental Consolidation in Wyandotte County, Kansas," Master's thesis, Department of Public Administration, University of Kansas.

Hayes, Kathy, and Semoon Chang. 1990. "The Relative Efficiency of City-Manager and Mayor-Council Forms of Government." *Southern Economic Journal* 57 (July).

Heilig, Peggy, and Robert J. Mundt. 1984. *Your Voice at City Hall: The Politics, Procedures, and Policies of District Representation*. Albany: State University of New York Press.

Henriques, Diana. 1986. *The Machinery of Greed: Public Authority and What to Do About It*. Lexington, MA: Lexington Press.

Hirschman, Albert O. 1982. *Shifting Involvements: Private Interest and Public Action*. Princeton, NJ: Princeton University Press.

Hofstadter, Richard. 1955. *The Age of Reform; from Bryan to F.D.R.* New York: Knopf.

Holtz-Eakin, Douglas, Tilly Schuyler, and Harvey S. Rosen. 1994. "Intertemporal Analysis of State and Local Government Spending: Theory and Tests." *Journal of Urban Economics* 35: 159–74.

Hood, Christopher, and Michael Jackson. 1991. *Administrative Argument*. Brookfield, VT: Dartmouth.

Horton, Raymond D. 1987. "Expenditures, Services, and Public Management." *Public Administration Review* 47, no. 5(September/October): 378–85.

Hughes, Owen E. 1994. *Public Management and Administration*. New York: St. Martin's.

Inman, Robert P. 1989. "The Local Decision to Tax: Evidence from Large U.S. Cities." *Regional Science and Urban Economics* 19.

International City/County Management Association (ICMA). *Municipal Year Book*. Washington, DC: various years, 1934–1999.

———. 1994. *Managing Small Cities and Counties: A Practical Guide.*

———. 1995. *Task Force Recommendations on Council-Manager Plan.*

———. 2000a. *Task Force Recommendations, ICMA Newsletter* 81 (no. 7, Supplement no. 1, March 27).

———. 2000b. *Council-Manager Recognition Task Force Recommendations Implementation Issues.* June 14. Handout.

Isabell, David T. 1993. "Local Government in Transition: A Case Study of City Government in Kansas City, Kansas, During Its Transition From the Commission Form of Government to a Mayor-Council Administrator Form of Government," Master's thesis, Department of Public Administration, University of Kansas.

Jacob, Herbert. 1988. *Silent Revolution: The Transformation of Divorce Law in the United States*. Chicago, IL: University of Chicago Press.

Jacobson, Gary. 1990. *The Electoral Origins of Divided Government: Competition in U.S. House Elections, 1946–1988*. Boulder, CO: Westview Press.

Jreisat, Jamil E. 1997. *Public Organization Management: The Development of Theory and Process*. Westport, CT: Quorum Books.

Judd, Dennis, and Paul Kantor, ed. 1992. *Enduring Tensions in Urban Politics*. New York: Macmillan.

Kammerer, Gladys M. 1962. *City Managers in Politics: An Analysis of Manager Tenure and Termination.* Gainsville: University of Florida Press.

Kantor, Paul. 1988. *The Dependent City: The Changing Political Economy of Urban America.* New York: Scott, Foresman/Little, Brown.

———. 1995. *The Dependent City Revisited.* Boulder, CO: Westview Press.

Katznelson, Ira. 1981. *City Trenches: Urban Politics and the Patterning of Class in the United States.* New York: Pantheon Books.

Kaufman, Herbert. 1963. *Politics and Policies in State and Local Governments.* Englewood Cliffs, NJ: Prentice-Hall.

———. 1971. *The Limits of Organizational Change.* Tuscaloosa: University of Alabama Press.

———. 1991. *Time, Chance, and Organizations: Natural Selection in a Perilous Environment.* London: Chatham House.

Kemp, R.L. 1988. *America's Cities: Strategic Planning for Public Managers.* New York: Quorum Books.

Kettl, Donald F., and H. Brinton Milward. 1996. *The State of Public Management.* Baltimore, MD: Johns Hopkins University Press.

King, Paula. 1989. *Policy Entrepreneurs: Catalysts in the Policy Innovation Process.* Ph.D. diss., University of Minnesota.

Kingdon, John W. 1984. *Agendas, Alternatives, and Public Places.* Boston: Little, Brown.

Kipp, Robert. 2000. Former city manager of Kansas City, Missouri. Phone interview. October 19.

Knowl, Richard. 2000. Assistant to the city manager of Kansas City, Missouri. Phone interview.

Kotter, John P., and Paul R. Lawrence. 1974. *Mayors in Action: Approaches to Urban Governance.* New York: John Wiley.

Krane, Dale, Platon N. Rigos, and Melvin B. Hill Jr. 2001. *Home Rule in America.* Washington, DC: CQ Press.

Leland, Suzanne, and Kurt M. Thurmaier. 2000. "Metropolitan Consolidation Success: Returning to the Roots of Local Government Reform." *Public Administration Quarterly* 24, no. 2: 202–21. London: Royal Institute of Public Administration.

Lewin, Kurt. 1936. *Principles of Topological Psychology.* McGraw-Hill.

Lijphart, Arend. 1984. *Democracies: Patterns of Majoritarian and Consensus Government in Twenty-One Countries.* New Haven, CT: Yale University Press.

———. 1992. *Parliamentary Versus Presidential Government.* Oxford, England: Oxford University Press.

Lineberry, Robert L. 1977. *Equality and Urban Policy: The Distribution of Municipal Public Services.* Beverly Hills, CA: Sage.

Lineberry, Robert L., and Edmund P. Fowler. 1967. "Reformism and Public Policies in American Cities." *American Political Science Review* 61: 701–16.

Linz, Juan J. 1990. "The Perils of Presidentialism." *Journal of Democracy* 1: 51–69.

Lockard, Duane. 1969. *Big City Mayors: The Crisis in Urban Politics.* Bloomington, IN: Indiana University Press.

Longoria, Thomas. 1994. "Empirical Analysis of the City Limits Typology." *Urban Affairs Quarterly* 30 (September): 102–13.

Loveridge, Ronald O. 1971. *City Managers in Legislative Politics.* New York: Bobbs-Merrill.

Lowi, Theodore. 1964. *At the Pleasure of the Mayor: Patronage and Power in New York City 1898–1958.* New York: Free Press.
———. July 1964. "American Business, Public Policy, Case Studies, and Political Theory." *World Politics* 16: 677–715.
Lynn, Laurence E. 1993. "Policy Achievement as a Collective Good: A Strategic Perspective on Managing Social Programs." In *Public Management Theory*, ed. Barry Bozeman. San Francisco, CA: Jossey-Bass.
———. 1996. *Public Management as Art, Science, and Profession.* London: Chatham House.
MacReynold, Merlin. 1998. "Is It Time to Reform the Reform?" *Public Management* (December).
Madison, James. 1788 [1961]. "The Federalist # 51." In *The Federalist*, ed. Jacob E. Cooke. Middletown, CT: Wesleyan University.
March, James G. 1978. "Bounded Rationality, Ambiguity, and the Engineering of Choice." *Bell Journal of Economics* 9: 587–608.
March, James G., and Johan P. Olsen. 1983. "Organizing Political Life: What Administrative Reorganization Tells Us About Government." *American Political Science Review* 77: 281–96.
March, James, and Johan Olsen. 1989. *Rediscovering Institutions: The Organizational Basis of Politics.* New York: Free Press.
Martin, David L. 1990. *Running City Hall: Municipal Administration in America.* Tuscaloosa: University of Alabama Press.
Matscheck, Walter. 1925. "Charter-making and Campaigns." English Book: Thesis/dissertation. Paper for presentation to the Governmental Research Conference, November 17, 1926.
Mayhew, David. 1991. *Divided We Govern: Party Control, Lawmaking, and Investigations, 1946–1990.* New Haven, CT: Yale University Press.
McComb, David B. 1986. *Galveston: A History.* Austin: University of Texas Press.
McCoy, Edgar C. 1940. "Patterns of Diffusion in the United States." *American Sociological Review* 5 (April): 219–27.
McKenna, Joseph. 1962. *The Topeka Metropolitan Area: Its Political Units and Characteristics.* Lawrence, KS: University of Kansas Governmental Research Center.
McManus, Susan. 1978. *Revenue Patterns in U.S. Cities and Suburbs: A Comparative Analysis.* New York: Praeger.
Menzel, Donald C., and Irwin Feller. 1977. "Leadership and Interaction Patterns in the Diffusion of Innovation Among the American States." *Western Political Quarterly* 30: 528–36.
Mercer, James L. 1991. *Strategic Planning for Public Managers.* New York: Quorum Books.
Miller, William Lee. 1973. *The Fifteenth Ward and the Great Society: An Encounter with a Modern City.* Boston: Houghton Mifflin.
Model City Charter. 1900. 1st. ed. New York: National Civic League.
———. 1915. 2d. ed. New York: National Civic League.
———. 1927. 3d. ed. New York: National Civic League.
———. 1933. 4th ed. New York: National Civic League.
———. 1941. 5th ed. New York: National Civic League.
———. 1964. 6th ed. New York: National Civic League.
———. 1989. 7th ed. New York: National Civic League.

Model City Charter Committee. 1937. "Memorandum as to Decisions Reached at Meeting of Model City Charter Committee," June 4–6, Chicago.

Moore, Perry. 1985. *Public Personnel Management: A Contingency Approach.* Lexington, MA: Lexington Books.

Morgan, David R. 1989. *Managing Urban America.* Stamford, CT: Brooks/Cole.

Morgan, David R., and Jeffrey Brudney. 1985. "Urban Policy and City Government Structure: Testing the Mediating Effects of Reform." Paper presented at the annual meeting of the American Political Science Association, New Orleans: August 1.

Morgan, David R., and Michael W. Hirlinger. 1991. "Intergovernmental Service Contracts: A Multivariate Explanation." *Urban Affairs Quarterly* 27 (September): 128–44.

Morgan, David R., and John Pelissero. 1980. "Urban Policy: Does Political Structure Matter?" *American Political Science Review* 74: 999–1006.

Morgan, David R., and Sheilah S. Watson. 1991. "Political Culture, Political System Characteristics and Public Policies Among the American States," *Publius* 21: 31–48.

———. 1992. "Policy Leadership in Council Manager Cities: Comparing Mayor and Manager," *Public Administration Review* 52 (September/October 1992): 438–45.

Nalbandian, John. 1991. *Professionalism in Local Government: Transformations in Roles, Responsibilities, and Values in City Managers.* San Francisco, CA: Jossey-Bass.

Nathan, Richard P. 1993. *Turning Promises into Performance: The Management Challenge of Implementing Workforce.* New York: Columbia University Press.

National Civic League (NCL). 1993. "Forms of Local Government: Meaningful Reform for a New Century." Denver, CO: National Civic League Press.

Neustadt, Richard. 1990. *Presidential Power and the Modern Presidents: The Politics of Leadership from Roosevelt to Reagan.* New York: Free Press.

Newland, Chester A. 1994. "Managing from the Future in Council-Manager Government." In *Ideal and Practice in Council-Manager Government,* ed. H. George Frederickson. Washington DC: International City/County Management Association, pp. 263–83.

"Only Where Needed." 2000. *Topeka Capitol Journal* Web site (April 20).

Osborne, David, and Ted Gaebler. 1992. *Reinventing Government: How the Entrepreneurial Spirit Is Transforming the Public Sector.* Reading, MA: Addison-Wesley.

O'Sullivan, Elizabeth Ann, and Gary R. Rassel. 1989. *Research Methods for Public Administrators.* New York: Longman.

Pealy, Dorothy. 1985. "Charter Commissioners at Work: Ann Arbor, 1953–55." English Book: Thesis/dissertation, University of Michigan.

"Perez Charter Drive Confident, Cautious." 2002. *Hartford Courant.* October 2.

Peters, B. Guy, and Donald J. Savoie, eds. 1995. *Governance in a Changing Environment.* Montreal and Kingston: McGill–Queen's University Press.

Peterson, Paul E. 1981. *City Limits.* Chicago, IL: University of Chicago Press.

Peterson, Paul E., and Mark C. Rom. 1990. *Welfare Magnets.* Washington, DC: Brookings Institution.

Pohlman, Marcus D. 1992. *Governing the Postindustrial City.* New York: Longman.

Poulson, Barry W. 1981. *Economic History of the United States.* New York: Macmillan.

Pressman, Jeffrey L. 1972. "Preconditions of Mayoral Leadership." *American Political Science Review* 66: 511–24.

Protasel, Greg J. 1988. "Abandonments of the Council-Manager Plan: A New Institutional Perspective." In *Ideal and Practice in Council-Manager Government*, ed. H. George Frederickson, pp. 199–212. Washington, DC: International City/Council Management Association.

———. 1995. "Leadership in Council Manager Cities." In *Ideal and Practice in Council Manager Government*, ed. H. George Frederickson, pp. 20–28. Washington, DC: International City/County Management Association.

Rainey, Hal G. 1997. *Understanding and Managing Public Organizations*. San Francisco, CA: Jossey-Bass.

———. 2000. *Advancing Public Management: New Development in Theory, Methods, and Practice*. Washington, DC: Georgetown University Press.

Ranney, Austin. 1954. *The Doctrine of Responsible Party Government, Its Origins and Present State*. Urbana: University of Illinois Press.

Reich, Robert. 1983. *The Next American Frontier*. New York: Times Books.

Renner, Tari. 1988a. "Municipal Election Processes: The Impact on Minority Representation." In *Municipal Year Book*. Washington, DC: International City/Council Management Association.

———. 1988b. "Elected Executives: Authority and Responsibility." *Baseline Data Report*. Vol. 20. Washington, DC: International City/County Management Association.

Renner, Tari, and Victor S. DeSantis. 1993. "Contemporary Patterns and Trends in Municipal Government Structures." In *Municipal Year Book*, pp. 57–69. Washington, DC: International City/County Management Association.

———. 1998. "Municipal Form of Government: Issues and Trends." In *Municipal Year Book*. Washington, DC: International City/County Management Association.

Riggs, Fred W. 1988. "The Survival of Presidentialism in America: Paraconstitutional Practices." *International Political Science Review* 9: 247–78.

Rogers, Everett M. 1995. *Diffusion of Innovations*. New York: Free Press.

Rowe, B.J.D. 1987. "Theory and Myth vs. Practice: What Research Reveals About Council-Manager Government and the Principles of Public Administration." *Public Management* (February): 11–16.

Rusk, David. 1993. *Cities Without Suburbs*. Baltimore, MD: Johns Hopkins University Press.

Sanders, H.T. 1979. "Governmental Structure in American Cities." In *Municipal Year Book*. Washington, DC: International City/County Management Association.

Schiesl, Martin J. 1977. *The Politics of Efficiency: Municipal Administration and Reform in America*. Berkeley: University of California Press.

Schultz, Ernst B. 1949. *American City Government: Its Machinery and Processes*. New York: Stackpole & Heck.

Sharp, Elaine B. 1986. *Citizen Demand Making in the Urban Context*. Tuscaloosa: University of Alabama Press.

Shaw, Albert. 1883. *Local Government in Illinois*. Baltimore, MD: Johns Hopkins University Press.

Sonenblum, Sidney, John C. Ries, and John J. Kirlin. 1977. *How Cities Provide Services: An Evaluation of Alternative Delivery Structures*. Cambridge, MA: Ballinger.

Sparrow, Glen. 1985. "The Emerging Chief Executive: The San Diego Experience." *National Civic Review* (December): 114–28.

———. 1994. "The Emerging Chief Executive 1971–1991: A San Diego Update." In *Facilitative Leadership in Local Government: Lessons from Successful Mayors and Chairpersons*, ed. James Svara. San Francisco, CA: Jossey-Bass.

Steffens, Lincoln. 1931. *The Autobiography of Lincoln Steffens.* New York: Harcourt, Brace.

Stein, Robert M. 1990. *Urban Alternatives: Public and Private Markets in the Provision of Local Services.* Pittsburgh, PA: University of Pittsburgh Press.

Steinmo, Sven, Kathleen Thelen, and Frank Longstretch. 1992. *Structuring Politics: Historical Institutionalism in Comparative Analysis.* Cambridge, England: Cambridge University Press.

Stephens, G. Ross, and Nelson Wikstrom. 2000. *Metropolitan Government and Governance: Theoretical Perspectives, Empirical Analysis, and the Future.* London: Oxford University Press.

Stillman, Richard. 1974. *The Rise of the City Manager: A Public Professional in Local Government.* Albuquerque: University of New Mexico Press.

Stone, Alice B., and Donald C. Stone. 1975. "Early Development of Education in Public Administration." In *American Public Administration: Past, Present, Future,* ed. Frederick C. Mosher. Tuscaloosa: University of Alabama Press.

Stone, Clarence N. 1987. "Competing Paradigms: A Rejoinder to Peterson." *Urban Affairs Quarterly* 22: 598.

Stone, Clarence N., ed. 1987. *The Politics of Urban Development.* Lawrence: University of Kansas Press.

Stone, Harold, Don K. Price, and Kathryn Stone. 1940. *City Manager Government in the United States.* Chicago, IL: Public Administration Service.

Strang, David, and P.M. Chang. 1993. "The International Labor Organization and the Welfare State Institutional Effects on National Welfare Spending, 1960–1980." *International Organizations* 47: 235–62.

Strang, David, and Sarah A. Soule. 1998. "Diffusion in Organizations and Social Movements: From Hybrid Corn to Power Pills." *Annual Review of Sociology* 24: 265–90.

Strate, John J., Harold Wolman, and Alan Melchior. 1993. "Are There Election-Driven Tax and Expenditure Cycles for Urban Governments?" *Urban Affairs Quarterly* 28.

Streib, Gregory. 1994. "Strategic Capacity in Council-Manager Municipalities: Exploring Limits and Horizons." *Ideal and Practice in Council-Manager Government.* ed. H. George Frederickson. Washington, DC: International City/County Management Association.

Svara, James. 1986. "The Responsible Administrator." *Popular Government* 51: 18–27.

———. 1987. "Mayoral Leadership in Council-Manager Cities: Preconditions versus Preconceptions." *Journal of Politics* 49, no. 1: 207–27. Oxford: Blackwell.

———. 1989. "Dichotomy and Duality: Reconceptualizing the Relationship Between Policy and Administration in Council-Manager Cities." In *Ideal and Practice in Council-Manager Government,* ed. H. George Fredrickson. Washington, DC: International City/County Management Association.

———. 1990a. *Official Leadership in the City.* New York: Oxford University Press.

———. 1990b. "The Model City and County Charters: Innovation and Tradition in Reform Movement." *Public Administration Review* 50: 688–92.

———. 1994. *Facilitative Leadership in Local Government: Lessons from Successful Mayors and Chairpersons.* San Francisco, CA: Jossey-Bass.

———. 1996. "The Politics-Administration Dichotomy Model as Aberration, or, Why an Idea Without Heritage or Legacy Should Be Removed from a Place of Honor in

Public Administration Thinking About Local Government." Paper presented at Public Administration Theory Network National Symposium, Savannah, Georgia, February.

————. 1999. "U.S. City Managers and Administrators in a Global Perspective." In *Municipal Year Book*. Washington, DC: International City/County Management Association.

————. 2001. "Council, Roles, Performance, and Form of Government." Paper presented at the 2001 American Political Science Association Conference.

————. 2001. "Council, Roles, Performance, and Form of Government." Paper presented at the 2001 American Political Science Association Conference.

Taebel, Delbert A. 1977. *Political Economy of Urban Transportation*. Port Washington, NY: Kennikat Press.

Teske, Paul, Mark Schneider, Michael Mintrom, and Samuel Best. 1993. "Establishing the Micro Foundations of a Macro Theory: Information, Movers, and the Competitive Market for Public Goods." *American Political Science Review* 87: 702–16.

Tiebout, Charles M. 1956. "A Pure Theory of Local Expenditures." *Journal of Political Economy* 64: 416–24.

Tolbert, Pamela S., and Lynne G. Zucker. 1983. "Institutional Sources of Change in the Formal Structure of Organization: The Diffusion of Civil Service Reform, 1880–1935." *Administrative Science Quarterly* 28: 23–39.

"Topeka Talks Community Participants." 1999. *Topeka Capital Journal*. October 19.

U.S. Advisory Commission on Intergovernmental Relations. 1993. "State Laws Governing Local Government Structure and Administration." Compiled by Melvin B. Hill Jr., Washington, DC.

U.S. Department of Commerce. 1998. *Statistical Abstract of the United States*.

Wagnon, Joan. 2000. Mayor of Topeka, Kansas. Interview. December 4.

Walker, Jack L. 1969. "The Diffusion of Innovations Among American States." *American Political Science Review* 63: 880–99.

Wallis, J.J. 1993. "Form and Function in the Public Sector: State and Local Government in the United States, 1902–1982." Paper presented at the Development of the American Economy Program Meeting at the National Bureau of Economic Research, Cambridge University. March.

Weaver, R. Kent, and Bert A. Rockman. 1993. *Do Institutions Matter? Government Capabilities in the United States and Abroad*. Washington, DC: Brookings Institution.

Welch, Susan, and Timothy Bledsoe. 1988. *Urban Reform and Its Consequences: A Study in Representation*. Chicago, IL: University of Chicago Press.

Wheeland, Craig M. 2002. "An Institutionalist Perspective on Mayoral Leadership: Linking Leadership to Formal Structure." *National Civic Review* 21, no. 1: 25–39.

Whicker, Marcia Lynn, and Todd W. Areson, eds. 1990. *Public Sector Management*. New York: Praeger.

Wikstrom, Nelson. 1979. "The Mayor as Policy Leader in the Council-Manager Form of Government: A View from the Field." *Public Administration Review* 39: 270–76.

Wilson, Edward. 1992. *The Diversity of Life*. Cambridge, MA: Harvard University Press.

Wilson, James Q. 1973. *Political Organizations*. New York: Basic Books.

Wolfinger, Raymond E. 1984. "Why Political Machines Have Not Withered Away and Other Revolutionist Thoughts." In *Readings in Urban Politics: Past,*

Present, and Future, ed. Harlin Hahn and Charles H. Levine. New York: Longman Press.

Wolman, Harold L. 1994. "Evaluating the Success of Urban Success Stories." *Urban Studies* 31.

Wood, Curtis H. 2001. "Consolidated Versus Fragmented Government: A Study of the Metropolitan Kansas City Region." Paper presented at the 33rd Annual Conference of the Mid-Continent Regional Science Association, Kansas City, MO, May 30–June 1, 2002.

Wood, Robert. 1958. *Suburbia, Its People and Their Politics.* Boston, MA: Houghton Mifflin.

Zinc, Harold. 1939. *Government of Cities in the United States.* New York: Macmillan.

Index

About the Authors

H. George Frederickson is the Edwin O. Stene Distinguished Professor of Public Administration at the University of Kansas, a position he has held for fifteen years. Earlier he was for ten years the president of Eastern Washington University at Cheney and Spokane. He is editor in chief of the *Journal of Public Administration Research and Theory,* author of *The Spirit of Public Administration*, and the coauthor of *The Public Administration Primer.* He has received the Gaus, Waldo, Levine, and Distinguished Research awards and is an honorary member of the International City/County Management Association.

Gary A. Johnson is an assistant professor of political science at the University of North Carolina in Charlotte, where he teaches in the Master's of Public Administration and the Ph.D. in Public Policy programs. He has published in *Urban Affairs Review, Journal of Public Administration Research and Theory*.

Curtis H. Wood is a Ph.D. student in public administration and political science at the University of Kansas. He received an MPA degree from Kansas University in 1980. He has twenty years' experience in city government in Kansas. He has also been an adjunct professor in public administration and public budgeting at Kansas State University in Manhattan, Kansas.